THE DOMESTIC VIOLENCE SOURCEBOOK

EVERYTHING YOU NEED TO KNOW

by
Dawn Bradley Berry

LOWELL HOUSE

LOS ANGELES

CONTEMPORARY BOOKS

CHICAGO

Library of Congress Cataloging-in-Publication Data

Berry, Dawn Bradley.
  The domestic violence sourcebook : everything you need to know /
by Dawn Bradley Berry.
      p.   cm.
  Includes bibliographical references and index.
  ISBN 1-56565-873-6
  1. Family violence. 2. Family violence—United States—Prevention.
3. Victims of family violence—Services for—United States. 4. Abused
children—Psychology. 5. Abused women—Psychology. I. Title.
HQ809.B47 1995
362.82 ' 92—dc20   95-7548
                                                                        CIP

Published by Lowell House, Los Angeles
Distributed by Contemporary Books, Chicago
Publisher: Jack Artenstein
Associate Publisher, Lowell House Adult: Bud Sperry
Text design: Laurie Young

Manufactured in the United States of America
10 9 8 7 6 5 4 3 2

*For all the good people working to prevent and
put an end to the plague of domestic violence;
and in memory of Patricia White.*

Also by Dawn Bradley Berry:

Equal Compensation for Women   (Lowell House, 1994)
The Divorce Sourcebook   (Lowell House, 1995)
The 50 Most Influential Women in American Law
(Lowell House, 1996)

Grateful acknowledgment is made for permission to reprint portions of the following:

"Five Minutes in Hell: Battered Woman Fights Back," by Sherri Winston. Copyright 1994 by Sun-Sentinel, Fort Lauderdale, Florida. Reprinted with permission. All rights reserved.

Men Who Hate Women and the Women Who Love Them by Dr. Susan Forward and Joan Torres. Reprinted with permission of Bantam Doubleday Dell © 1986. All rights reserved.

Family Violence: State-of-the-Art Court Programs by The National Council of Juvenile and Family Court Judges, © 1992. Used by permission. All rights reserved.

"Remember the Children," by Rosemary L. Bray, Ms., vol. v, no. w, September/October 1994. Copyright 1994 by Ms. Used by permission. All rights reserved.

"To Many Teens, 'Guys Beating Girls Just Seems, Well, Normal,'" by Bonnie Weston. Reprinted with permission of The Orange County Register, © 1994.

Shattered Dreams by Charlotte Fedders and Laura Elliot, © 1987. Published by Harpercollins Publishers. All rights Reserved.

"Battered Women Who Kill: The Law Still Denies Us a Fair Hearing," by Brenda Aris, © 1994. All rights reserved. This article originally published in Glamour.

TABLE OF CONTENTS

ACKNOWLEDGMENTS

I am extremely grateful to all of those who shared their stories, recollections, insights, knowledge, books, clippings, thoughts, ideas, and encouraging words; in particular Dr. Bob Henry, Mary Blick, Janet Wiederkehr, Susan Embry, Andy Martinez, Dr. Patricia Murphy, Becca Jean Hughes, Christine L. Bailey, Donna Ferrato, Jane Fraher, Brenda Aris, Clarette Bradley, Rae Jean Bradley, Gary W. Markham of the National Victim Center, and many others. While all of the stories in this book are true, a number of contributors have asked to remain anonymous or to be identified by pseudonyms. I am thankful to them for their candor and willingness to share difficult memories.

Thanks also to everyone at Lowell House, especially my great editor Bud Sperry, and to my husband, Willy Berry.

INTRODUCTION

Last spring while vacationing in Key West, I took a nasty spill off a bicycle and landed on my face. The result, not surprisingly, was a colorful assortment of bruises and scrapes, topped by the biggest black eye I'd ever seen—a classic shiner.

Of course I was embarrassed by the thought that I was such a clod I couldn't stay upright on a Schwinn. But the thing that mortified me most was the idea that people might think my husband had beat me up. I made a point of wearing dark glasses around the clock, and quickly telling my story to anyone who gave my ravaged face a second look. I wanted to make sure nobody would think I was "the kind of woman who would let a man beat me."

What kind of woman "lets" a man beat her? Who is the "typical" violence victim? Is she weak? Helpless? Doesn't she have any friends or family to turn to? Is she too ignorant or impoverished to escape? *Why doesn't she just leave?* This has always been the foremost question in my mind when I heard about women who stayed with abusive partners. Why would any woman live with a violent man, a man who says he loves her, yet hurts her? Why doesn't she "just leave"?

Easy for me to ask. Easy, because I've never been there. I grew up in a peaceful home where my parents treated each other with warmth and respect and rarely so much as raised their voices in argument. I never had a violent boyfriend. I married a gentle man, who recognizes the same boundaries that I do: Yell and scream and cuss if you have to, but never, ever, hit. Hitting is the line you never cross, the line that ruins everything. One strike and you're out. I've never had to cope with violence in any of my homes. So, from this vantage point, it's been very easy for me to ask, "Why doesn't she just leave?"

As I researched this book, I began to see just how naive I was. Domestic violence is not a simple matter. It affects people of astonishing diversity: rich and poor, old and young, black and white, party animals and fundamentalist Christians. The reasons women don't "just leave" are as diverse as the individuals themselves. Some have no place to go. Many *have* left only to be threatened, stalked, or cajoled into returning.

Some are afraid they can't support their children. Some have been so psychologically damaged by years of mistreatment that they are incapable of leaving. Some think they deserve it. And some still love the men who batter them and can't give up the hope they will change; that this will indeed be the last beating, as they have promised so many times before.

Domestic violence is a plague that maims and kills—not only women, but children, men, families. What can be done about it? Fortunately, most victims of domestic violence today do have one or more ways out, if they know options exist and have the capacity to use them. The growing awareness of how pervasive and destructive this disease is in American society, and the outrage that accompanies this knowledge, has spawned a wide variety of programs, shelters, educational endeavors, legal changes, law enforcement initiatives, and other efforts to prevent and halt the growth of this tragic epidemic.

I've learned a lot through writing this book—about the causes of domestic violence, what types of programs are working to stop it, and about the "kind of woman who would let a man hit her." I have to say I'm ashamed of my own narrow-mindedness last spring, when I was more concerned that people would think I was a victim of violence than a klutz who can't ride a bike. Battered women are not weak, self-loathing, ignorant, or pathetic. The strength many have had to draw upon simply to survive is phenomenal.

In this book I have generally used the female gender to refer to the victims of domestic violence, and the male gender to refer to the abusers. This choice reflects the fact that an estimated 95 percent of the victims of domestic violence are female. The book is not intended to be sexist, or to diminish the very real, equally tragic problems faced by the thousands of men who are also abused. It is my hope that those involved in any way with the crisis of family violence—victims, friends, professionals, and others who care about stopping the cycle of violence—will find this information helpful and illuminating.

One of the most fundamental rights recognized in American society is the right of every person to be free from bodily harm. This right belongs to every human being. It is difficult for those of us who have never suffered the horror of a violent home to imagine the pain, the terror, the hopelessness of living with the constant threat of attack in the one place that should feel most safe. Perhaps one day the home will be a peaceful refuge for everyone. In the meantime, dedicated people are working to change attitudes, provide services, and hold abusers accountable. Through their efforts, things are changing—but we still have a long way to go. If educated professionals like me still ask, "Why doesn't she leave?" then there is a great deal of education yet to be done. I hope this book will provide a few answers and a few new questions, such as "Why does domestic violence still happen?" And better yet—"What can I do to help stop and prevent it?"

CHAPTER ONE

WHAT IS DOMESTIC VIOLENCE?

What is domestic violence, anyway? It has been called by many names; wife beating, battering, family violence, domestic abuse. All refer to abuse by one person of another in an intimate relationship. This book discusses only violence between adults in a current or former husband-wife, living together, or dating relationship. The equally complex and tragic problems of child abuse, elder abuse, and sibling abuse involve different issues and dynamics that are beyond the scope of this book. While a home in which one form of violence goes on is likely to suffer from other kinds of abuse, the nature, causes, and types of help available differ.

Domestic violence is not limited to physical battering, but may include other forms of abuse as well. Psychologist and author Susan Forward, Ph.D., has described abuse as ". . . any behavior that is intended to control and subjugate another human being through the use of fear, humiliation, and verbal or physical assaults . . . it is the systematic persecution of one partner by another." An abuser often wears down his partner by unrelenting criticism and fault-finding. This form of psychological abuse is especially cruel, she says, because it is often disguised as a way of "teaching the woman how to be a better person."

Many experts believe that emotional abuse may have longer lasting effects than physical abuse. When a person hears over and over that she is stupid, worthless, or ugly, she may internalize these things and let them become a part of her self-image. "Verbal abuse can be more psychologically damaging in the long run than physical abuse," says Patricia Murphy, Ph.D., a vocational rehabilitation specialist and counselor who helps women rebuild their working lives after suffering abuse. "When we hear over and over that we are worthless and incompetent, we begin not only to believe it, but to hear it repeating over and over in our minds."

Also, emotional abuse is often one of the control tactics an abuser employs to break the spirit of the victim and destroy her perception of her own choices until she no longer believes she *can* change her situation or leave. This is one of the characteristics of the "battered woman syndrome" which is discussed in greater detail later.

As Dr. Forward states in her book *Men Who Hate Women and the Women Who Love Them*, "Once [a] woman accepts an attack on her self-worth and permits herself to be demeaned, she has opened the door for future assault." Dr. Forward describes one woman's healthy reaction to her partner's irrational attack: "I don't know why he thought he could get away with that kind of stuff, but he picked the wrong girl when he pulled it on me. I told him I wasn't going to put up with that kind of treatment, and that if he pulled it again I was going to leave. Well, then he was sweet as pie for a day or two, then he did it again. So I left." Dr. Forward emphasizes the importance of standing up to any abusive treatment as soon as it happens. If the abuse is verbal, there must be at least an unequivocal assertion that you will not stand for this type of treatment. If it turns violent, there should be no second chances until you have removed yourself from the situation and received some assistance. The relationship may still be salvageable, but only with professional intervention.

Therefore, with the understanding that this text refers to violence between couples, "domestic violence" is generally understood to include:

Physical violence. Slapping, hitting, kicking, burning, punching, choking, shoving, beating, throwing things, locking out, restraining, and other acts designed to injure, hurt, endanger, or cause physical pain.

Emotional abuse. Consistently doing or saying things to shame, insult, ridicule, embarrass, demean, belittle, or mentally hurt another person. This may include calling a person names such as fat, lazy, stupid, bitch, silly, ugly, failure; telling someone she can't do anything right, is worthless, is an unfit mother, is undeserving, is unwanted. It also involves withholding money, affection, or attention; forbidding someone to work, handle money, see friends or family, make decisions, socialize, keep property; flaunting infidelity; engaging in destructive acts; forcing someone to do things she does not want to do; manipulation; hurting or threatening children or pets; threatening to abandon; threatening to take children away. It may also include refusing to help someone who is sick or hurt; ridiculing her most valued beliefs, religion, race, heritage, or class; insulting her family or friends.

Sexual abuse. Forcing someone to have sex when she does not want to, forcing someone to engage in sexual acts she does not like or finds unpleasant, frightening, or violent; forcing someone to have sex with others or watch others; criticism of sexual performance; sadism; anything that makes her feel demeaned or violated. This form of abuse may also include forcing a woman into reproductive decisions that are contrary to her wishes; or forcing her to have sex without protection against disease or pregnancy.

Authors/counselors Greg Enns and Jan Black simply define abuse as any behavior that results in the mistreatment of another. Taking a slightly different approach, EMERGE, a Boston counseling program for abusive men, describes domestic violence as any act that causes the victim to do something she does not want to do, prevents her from doing something she does want to do, or causes her to be afraid. In many abusive relationships, different forms of abuse are combined.

While physical abuse is generally considered the most serious form of domestic violence because of the immediate threat to life and limb, this does not mean the other forms should be taken lightly, even if they don't seem "serious." Other forms of abuse often precede physical abuse and function as warning signals. Any time a partner engages in behavior that makes a woman feel demeaned, humiliated, and uncomfortable, whether it amounts to roughhousing, small shoves, sexual domination, or insults, she should tell her partner to stop—and he should be willing to respect her request. Many couples have nasty spats occasionally. The difference in an abusive relationship is, first, the vicious, one-sided character of the attack and, second, that while the abuser may agree to stop the behavior at the time, the first time is never the last—nor is the second or the third. In violent homes, one partner dominates and controls other family members, often to the point of creating a sort of terrorist state in which the threat of harm is constant and unpredictable. Professor Linda Harshman has compared the lives of battered women to the "state of war" that exists without government protection as described by the political philosopher Thomas Hobbes some three hundred years ago: "solitary, poor, nasty, brutish, and short."

It is no secret that violence also happens between same-sex couples, and some studies suggest it may occur more frequently, with as many as one in three couples involved in violent relationships. Most of the principles applicable to heterosexual couples apply to homosexual couples as well, though relatively little research has been done. A brief discussion of the special problems faced by couples in violent same-sex relationships is provided later in the book, and sources with more detailed information are listed in the Resources and Suggested Readings section.

STALKING

Domestic violence is a peculiar crime with its own dynamics and special risks. Even women who do what society tells them is right, and leave at the first sign of violence, often fall prey to continued harassment. Stalking is a particular problem for women who leave, whether its sooner or later. The vast majority of stalking crimes are committed by former husbands or boyfriends against women who have left the relationship. According to a 1997 study by the U.S. Justice Department, one in twelve women has been stalked. Eighty percent of those who are stalked are assaulted, and women are four times as likely as men to be stalking victims.

Stalking involves any pattern of behavior that serves no legitimate purpose and is intended to harass, annoy, or terrorize the victim. The stalker is obsessed with the victim, and can't cope with the rejection and anger he feels when she leaves. The stalker often wants to "take revenge" on the victim, who is blamed for causing these feelings. Typical stalking activities include repeated telephone calls, letters or gifts by mail, surveillance at work, home, and other places the victim is known to frequent, vandalism of the victim's car or other possessions, and physical encounters.

Stalking is a special problem for several reasons. First, it usually escalates. A series of harassing telephone calls may lead to direct threats then to violence. The National Council on Stalking advises that a stalker should be considered dangerous if he has a previous criminal record or history of mental instability; if acts of vandalism or destruction have been committed; if he is unable to control his temper; if there has been physical contact between the stalker and the victim; if he lives in isolation; if he has a substance abuse problem; if he has been in a violent domestic relationship; if he has or is familiar with using guns; if threats have been made to the victim; or if the stalker has felt humiliated by the victim. More information on laws against stalking and safety tips are included later in the book. Most states have enacted specific anti-stalking laws so a stalker can be arrested before the behavior becomes dangerous. In most areas, a good set of laws against domestic violence and stalking is now available. Such laws frequently distinguish between stalking and aggravated stalking; harassment, which requires a regular pattern of conduct; and telephone harassment, which is easier to prove.

Stalking victims can assist law enforcement and prosecutors by keeping a written record or diary of all incidents of stalking or harassment; including the date, time, location, and type of incident; details of reports to law enforcement agencies; and witness information. Some social service or law enforcement agencies provide forms for keeping such records. Law enforcement professionals advise that all stalkers should be considered extremely dangerous, and victims should avoid any contact or discussion with the stalker—get away from them as soon as possible. The police should be notified of any incident of stalking or harassment. It is essential that law enforcement be made aware of the complete history between the stalker and victim. Prior acts should be noted, as these can provide evidence of a "pattern of conduct," which may effect the charges and penalties available, and may also mean the difference between a misdemeanor and a felony charge. Many states now have laws that distinguish between various degrees of stalking, for example, by providing different definitions of "harassment," "stalking," and "aggravated stalking."

HOW COMMON IS DOMESTIC VIOLENCE?

There is no denying that the statistics on violence in families paint a grim picture. Some experts believe domestic violence is increasing. Others believe that there has been a slight decrease, but that more women are reporting abuse. Either way, the numbers prove that it still happens far, far too often. Even by the most conservative estimates, domestic violence is a national tragedy of staggering proportions. Each year, literally millions of women are wounded, crippled, disfigured, traumatized, and maimed by male partners—or they die. Donna Shalala, Health and Human Services secretary, has frequently stated, "Domestic violence is an unacknowledged epidemic in our society." In April 1994, she announced that there are 4 million reported instances of domestic violence every year in the United States. Domestic violence is not only a leading cause of injury, but also an increasing cause of chronic medical and mental illness. According to a study conducted in 1995 in Memphis, Tennessee, 35 percent of the victims studies suffered assault on a daily basis. Forty-four percent had been assaulted by their partner during pregnancy. In the same study, 75 percent of the assailants arrested spent less than 18 hours in jail. Those who stayed longer were detained only for the practical reason that the arrest took place on a weekend or holiday. Sixty-seven percent of the perpetrators were on probation or parole, but none had been sanctioned for repeat domestic violence offenses.

The damage wrought by domestic violence extends far beyond the walls of the home. It exacts a tremendous cost to health care, criminal justice, social services, lost productivity, and perhaps most costly of all, the physical, emotional, and behavioral damage it inflicts on the children who grow up in a home where the monsters are real. Domestic violence is also a major cause of disability, homelessness, addiction, and attempted suicide. Thus, domestic violence commands a substantial proportion of a community's health, criminal justice, and social service resources.

Consider the following statistics compiled by sociologists, psychologists, law enforcement agencies, scientists, private research organizations, government agencies, and other reputable researchers:

- Each year, at least fifteen hundred women are killed by a current or former husband or boyfriend. According to FBI data, four women a day are murdered by a male partner. Over thirty percent (some estimate over fifty percent) of all murders of women in America are committed by intimate partners.

- Studies of women killed by a husband or boyfriend show that 90 percent of the victims had reported at least one prior incident of abuse. The average number of calls to a scene before a domestic homicide is eight.

- Up to 6 million women are believed to be beaten in their homes each year. Four million incidents are reported. The National Coalition Against Domestic Violence estimates that up to 90 percent of battered women never report their abuse.

- Women who have divorced or separated from their abusers report being battered fourteen times as often as those still living with their partners. It is estimated that 73 percent of emergency room visits, and up to 75 percent of calls to the police for domestic violence incidents occur after separation.

- According to the American Medical Association, family violence kills as many women every five years as the total number of Americans who died in the Vietnam War. Homicide is the second leading cause of death for women ages 15 to 24.

- Battering contributes to one-quarter of all suicide attempts by women generally, and half of all suicide attempts by Black women.

- The American Medical Association reports that one out of every three women treated in emergency rooms is a victim of violence. At least one in five has been injured by a current or former husband or boyfriend.

- One million women a year visit physicians and hospital emergency rooms for treatment of injuries caused by beating. According to the National Centers for Disease Control, more women are treated in emergency rooms for battering injuries than for muggings, rapes, and traffic accidents combined.

- In 1992, the U.S. Surgeon General reported that abuse by a husband or partner is the leading cause of injury to American women between the ages of fifteen and forty-four.

- Medical expenses for treating victims of domestic violence total at least $3 billion to $5 billion annually.

- In one western city, domestic violence was the single most reported crime in 1995—more than assault and battery and burglaries combined.

- Ninety-five percent of the victims of battering are female. Rape is a regular form of abuse in about 50 percent of violent relationships.

- Weapons are used in 30 percent of domestic violence incidents.

- Up to 75 percent of battering victims have left or are trying to leave men who will not let them go. A Texas study revealed that 75 percent of the women calling a domestic violence hotline had left their abuser at least five times before.

- On the average, a woman is battered in the United States by a partner every twelve to fifteen seconds.

- Between 25 and 50 percent of all women in America will be physically abused by a partner at least once in their lives.

- Businesses lose about $100 million annually in lost wages, sick leave, absenteeism, and nonproductivity as a direct result of domestic violence.

• Seventy-four percent of abused women who work outside the home are harassed by their abusers at work, either in person or by telephone. Fifty-six percent are late for work at least five times a month because of their abusers. Fifty-four percent miss at least three full days of work a month, and 20 percent lose their jobs because of abuse.

• Some experts estimate that more women leave the work force permanently because of domestic violence than leave to raise children.

• In a series of studies compiled in 1987, between 20 and 30 percent of college women reported being the victim of physical abuse by a dating partner. In a 1990 study, more than one-third of girls in grades 10 to 12 reported at least one incident of physical or sexual abuse.

• Twenty-eight percent of high school students have experienced violence in a dating relationship. The Federal Bureau of Investigation reports that 21 percent of the women murdered in America are between the ages of fifteen and twenty-four.

• Pregnant women are especially at risk. Robert McAfee, M.D., president of the American Medical Association, estimates that more than one-third of pregnant women are abused. Twenty-five percent of all women battered in America are abused while pregnant.

• According to the March of Dimes, battering during pregnancy is the leading cause of birth defects and infant mortality—more than the birth defects caused by all of the diseases for which people are routinely inoculated, combined.

• Fifty to 70 percent of men who abuse their female partners also abuse children in the home. In homes with four or more children, the figure leaps to over 90 percent.

• In one study of violent homes, all sons over fourteen attempted to protect their mothers. Sixty-two percent were injured in the process. Another study found that 63 percent of the males beteween the ages of fifteen and twenty who are incarcerated for homicide killed their mother's batterer.

- More than 3 million children directly witness acts of domestic abuse each year. Battered mothers are more likely than other mothers to abuse their children. Children whose mothers are abused are six times more likely to attempt suicide and 50 percent more likely to abuse drugs and alcohol.

- Studies estimate that 25 to 33 percent of men who batter their wives also sexually abuse their children. Up to one-third of battered women were sexually abused as children, generally by a male relative.

- Between 70 percent and 87 percent of children in homes where their mother is beaten witness the violence. Virtually all are aware of what goes on, even if they do not see the abuse taking place.

- Most men who batter women abuse more than one; in one study, 95 percent of those who sought treatment admitted to abusing more than one woman.

- An estimated 90 percent of men and 80 percent of women currently in prison were abused at some point in their lives.

- About 50 percent of all homeless women and children in America are fleeing domestic violence.

- According to a study conducted in 1991, among the men arrested, prosecuted, convicted, and sentenced for assaulting a female partner, less than one percent served any time in jail. The average batterer taken into custody was held less than two hours.

- In 1970 there was no such thing as a shelter for battered women. Today there are over two thousand service programs, and over thirteen hundred shelters—but there are roughly 20,000 cities and towns in America. Thirty-one percent of abused women who sought shelter in New York City in one year returned to abusive homes primarily because they could not locate permanent housing. Up to 60 percent of victims are turned away in some areas.

- Despite the vast increase in attention to the problem of domestic violence through hotlines, shelters, and public awareness, the number of assaults has remained about the same over the last decade.

WHY IS DOMESTIC VIOLENCE SO COMMON?

The studies that spawned these statistics have proven that abuse knows no boundaries: racial, ethnic, religious, or socioeconomic. It occurs among the very rich and the very poor, the highly educated and the illiterate, in all parts of the world. As stated in a 1994 *Newsweek* article, the phenomenon is as complicated as it is common.

The Battered/Formerly Battered Women's Task Force of the National Coalition Against Domestic Violence (NCADV) says, "Battering is an issue of crime, health, safety, ethics, politics, systems, choices, economics, and socialization. It is an issue of individual, institutional, and cultural significance." As the task force points out, not only must individual thinking and behavior change if battering is to be stopped, but social and cultural values that allow battering and perpetuate it must change as well.

Ingrained social stereotypes support tolerance of abuse in families. Many people still think most instances of battering are "rare" or "minor" and don't warrant outside "interference." Others feel men are inherently aggressive, and women naturally passive, so abuse is inevitable due to "human nature." Some believe that women who nag, get angry, or speak their own minds "provoke" violence and deserve to be beaten. Battering is viewed as a problem caused by stress or poverty, or limited to the "lower classes."

Throughout history, two persistent assumptions have contributed to society's turning away from domestic violence: first, that it was a minor, private, and/or family matter; second, that others were helpless to do anything about it. It is only recently that society has begun to face the unspeakable horror of domestic violence, as images such as photographer Donna Ferrato's portraits of the human beings behind the headlines fill books, magazines, and newspapers with their powerful reminder that these are not statistics—these are people. Yet still we turn away.

In the words of Senator Joseph Biden, "If the leading newspapers were to announce tomorrow a new disease that, over the past year, had afflicted from three to four million citizens, few would fail to appreciate the seriousness of the illness. Yet, when it comes to the three to four million women who are victimized by violence each year, the alarms ring softly."

11

IS THERE ANY GOOD NEWS?

Definitely. One thing is certain: As the shocking numbers and stories are made public knowledge, attitudes are changing. People are becoming aware of the widespread nature of domestic violence, its devastating effect on women, men, children, and families, and the tragic consequences of turning away. Unfortunately, it has taken events like the killing of Nicole Brown Simpson and her history of abuse to jar the public's awareness that domestic violence is a serious crime, and that the consequences are tragic.

The Legacy of the Simpson Case

When O.J. Simpson was acquitted for the murder of his ex-wife and her friend in his criminal trial, many feared that the verdict would send a message to abusers that they can get away with murder. Another chilling lesson of the Simpson case is that even when women do everything right, everything society tells them to, they can end up murdered—unless outside intervention by law enforcement, criminal justice, and other community sources takes swift and firm action to stop the batterer. Nicole Brown Simpson wisely kept Polaroids of her battered face and a letter O.J. had written apologizing for (and thereby acknowledging) beating her in a safe deposit box. She told friends and family members what was happening, and gained their support. She divorced Simpson, and called the police when he came to her home and attacked her. Many feel that if Simpson had been treated as a criminal when Nicole first called the police in 1989—with a harsh fine, mandatory counseling in a long-term batterer's program, and strong condemnation of his behavior by his employers and colleagues—Nicole Brown Simpson and Ron Goldman might still be alive.

And this is the positive lesson that has risen out of this tragedy. Although media coverage of the case was, at times, lurid and overblown, it drew the nation's attention to the fact that domestic violence is a life-threatening crime that must not be taken lightly. Calls to shelters and hotlines have steadily increased as abused women realized that they, too, could be in mortal danger. Dozens, possibly hundreds of new organizations, shelters, and hotlines have sprung up as the magni-tude of domestic violence has come to light. October has been declared Domestic Violence Awareness Month. The law, at the federal, state, and local levels, has changed to strengthen penalties against abusers and close loopholes. Police departments have begun taking abuse cases more seriously, implementing new protocols, improved officer training, and tougher sanctions against batterers. Even entities not generally affiliated with the organized efforts against domestic violence have become involved. For example, in 1997, the Seattle Public Housing Authority established a training program to educate its personnel, police officers, and others who work with domestic violence victims. In 1995, Illinois State University added a domestic violence unit to its residential assis-tant training program. State Farm Insurance, once harshly criticized for denying a woman insurance because she was a victim of family violence, has launched a family abuse prevention campaign.

Also, it is important to remember that while one jury acquitted Simpson of murder, another held him accountable in a civil action for the wrongful deaths of his former wife and her friend. Moreover, discus-sion of the case has made clear that the Simpson case cannot be considered a "normal" case indicating what would happen under the same circumstances with a non-celebrity defendant. As prosecutor Marcia Clark has emphasized, the Simpson case was an anomaly. The defendant, unlike most, was virtually unconvictable. As Clark com-mented in her book, "O.J. Simpson slaughtered two innocent people and he walked free—right past the most massive and compelling body of evi-dence ever assembled against a criminal defendant." The odds of such an outcome in a case not involving a celebrity and sports hero—especially since the outrage, legal evolution, and change in public attitude—are almost nil.

We now know that it is not only the poor, the uneducated, or the underprivileged that suffer the pain of domestic violence. We know that batterers can be successful, handsome, gifted men—even our heroes. We know that wife beating is often treated far too casually by the police. We know that domestic violence is often brushed aside as "a family matter" or "no big deal" by the men who batter, by the criminal justice system, and by the public. We know that women who appear to have ample means of escape through money, intelligence, family, and friends remain trapped in violent relationships. We know that even when they do try to get free and end the relationship, the batterer often won't let go.

Perhaps, most of all, the tragedy of the Simpson family has turned the public eye toward the crisis of domestic violence that has become an epidemic in our nation. America can no longer ignore the fact that domestic violence is extremely common, extremely serious, and potentially deadly. The media have begun to take a broad look at what is going on around the country—both the problem and the solutions. In the first few weeks after murder charges were filed against O. J. Simpson and his prior abuse of his wife, national headlines, hotlines, shelters, and coalitions reported a tidal wave of calls—from victims who want help and from men who want to stop battering.

And this is the good news. People have been touched by the horror of domestic violence, both directly and indirectly. The problem continues, but people are trying—both in their own lives, to escape or repair relationships torn by violence—and in the community, to find out what works, how to use it, and how to make services available to all who need them.

So what can be done about a problem that is so complex, so pervasive? Certainly, understanding what causes domestic violence and which families are most at risk helps. Despite the grim statistics, there is plenty of evidence that progress is being made by those working to "wage peace" on the home front. Two respected national studies showed a slight decrease in domestic violence between 1975 and 1985. There is less of a stigma against those who admit problems in the family and seek outside help, so violence which was previously hidden is being reported more often.

Perhaps the most important change that has taken place toward stopping domestic violence is the way society views the problem. Throughout most of America's history, the old adage "A man's home is his castle" reflected the attitude that the home was sacrosanct, not to be invaded or disturbed. Women were expected to solve the problem themselves or simply keep it behind closed doors.

Vestiges of the notion that the home is surrounded by a "zone of privacy" that shields it from the scrutiny of the outside world remain, but public sentiment is gradually changing as people are made aware of how severe and how common violence in the home has become. Finally, domestic violence is being seen more clearly as a serious social problem. Psychologists, social workers, and law enforcement officials are beginning to view family violence as something that can be treated and explained, but never tolerated. And the prevailing sense among professionals and the general public alike is that domestic violence is *everybody's* problem.

What *does* work? A wide variety of sources from various fields—psychologists, judges, law enforcement, sociologists, activists, social workers, and the abuse survivors themselves—almost universally agree on two points. First, domestic violence must be treated as a crime. The abuser should be arrested and removed from the home immediately, and spend at least one night in jail. For many, therapy of some kind often helps, but most counselors agree that abusive men must first experience some real consequences if treatment is to be effective. They need a powerful, immediate demonstration by law enforcement that their behavior is criminal, unacceptable, and intolerable.

Second, all of the community institutions addressing domestic violence and helping the victims in various ways must join in a mutual effort to communicate, cooperate, and work together to prevent and stop violence in families. This includes both those organizations immediately associated with helping victims, such as the police, hospitals, and shelters, as well as those that become involved earlier, later, or on a more peripheral basis, such as the courts, probation/parole officers, schools, churches, mental health providers, child protective agencies, welfare and public housing services, politicians, private organizations, social workers, and physicians. Victims must receive immediate support and information, as well as continuing service, no matter where they turn first for help.

There are two different schools of thought within the domestic violence community as to which of these two vital responses should get priority. Should the first order of business be to punish and restrain the abuser, or to help the victim? Everyone seems to agree that both of these matters must be addressed in any successful program. Those that work the best seem to give nearly equal attention to both concerns, often through coordinated systems that use the same facilities to accomplish both goals. For instance, an offender may spend a night in jail, then come before the judge to be charged with his crime *and* told of the treatment options available. Meanwhile, the arresting officer takes the victim to a hospital. The officer or hospital staff makes sure the woman receives information on shelters and other services available for her in the community. She is put in touch with people who can help her find support groups, social services, and assistance with the court processes she will face.

When an integrated, ongoing effort is made by a coalition of people and groups to coordinate their efforts and skills, both the system as a whole and each component functions more efficiently. The Miami community has made impressive strides toward curtailing the incidence of domestic violence with model shelter programs and a strong partnership between the police and health care communities and other community organizations. Perhaps because the services that are available grew out of grassroots efforts by women with a great deal of gumption but little money, many communities have found that such an integrated program can be established and run for a surprisingly small amount of funding. This type of system also allows for tremendous flexibility according to the particular needs and structure of each geographic area.

Private individuals and businesses are also getting involved. *Ms.* has pledged to keep the issue of domestic violence in the forefront, with its September/October 1994 issue enclosed in a black cover, listing the names of some of the thousands of women killed by their husbands or male partners since 1990. The magazine also announced its pledge to donate five dollars from each subscription to the Family Violence Prevention Fund. Other private businesses have begun to realize their potential to help stop domestic violence, which also promotes positive public relations. For example, the Marshall's chain of discount stores recently donated a percentage of all sales in its 459 stores on a particular date to the Family Violence Prevention Fund, and gave all proceeds from a specially designed holiday pin to the Fund as well. In 1994, the U.S. Postal Service announced limited public access to change of address information filed by individuals and families.

Later chapters describe what various communities have done to attack domestic violence. Many have seen astounding results. Most of the techniques that have proven effective can be emulated by others. Several, led by the Duluth, Minnesota Project, have expanded to provide training seminars, curriculums, videos, books, and various other materials to communities throughout the country wishing to establish or improve programs of their own. Things are changing, but it took us a long time to get here, and there is every sign that our work is just beginning.

CHAPTER TWO

HOW DID WE GET TO THIS POINT? THE HISTORY OF DOMESTIC VIOLENCE

Domestic violence is as old as recorded history. It has been reported in virtually all societies, and in most countries it has been both legal and socially accepted until very recently. Through time, physical force has been used to keep subordinate groups in their place by the more dominant forces in society. Men have always been physically larger and stronger than most women, and most societies have been male dominated. So its no surprise that women have been common victims of physical assault.

In ancient Roman times, a man was allowed by law to chastise, divorce, or kill his wife for adultery, public drunkenness, or attending public games—the very behavior that men were allowed, even expected to pursue, on a near-daily basis! During the middle ages, a man's right to beat his wife was beyond question, yet a woman could be burned alive for so much as threatening her husband.

This general idea prevailed for hundreds of years. A few enlightened souls began to recognize the brutality of wife beating very early on, though it took centuries before any real efforts were made to curtail the problem. In 1405, French writer Christine de Pizan complained of the harsh beatings and injuries suffered by women at the hands of their husbands, who had no cause or reason to inflict such treatment. Early women's advocate and author Mary Wollstonecraft wrote of the problems of male tyranny in eighteenth century England. Judge William Blackstone criticized the prevailing law in his *Commentaries on the Laws of England*, published in 1799, and urged priority be given to ". . . security from corporal insults or menaces, assaults, beatings, and wounding." Philosopher John Stuart Mill criticized "wife torture" as an atrocity in the nineteenth century. American colonial women organized informal support systems to help battered women escape brutal husbands. When the first organizers of the American women's movement met in the 1840s for the primary purpose of securing the right to vote, the issue of male brutality was also on the agenda. Suffragist Susan B. Anthony is reported to have helped battered women escape their husbands during the same era.

The widespread acceptance of wife beating has often been reflected in popular culture. We have all heard the expression "rule of thumb." It is commonly used in American conversation to describe a general guideline, a rule for everyday, routine use. Yet this innocuous expression has chilling origins—in a past that helps explain why domestic violence is still with us.

"Rule of thumb" refers to an English common law, which was included in Blackstone's codification of the law published in the eighteenth century. Before the rule of thumb, a husband could chastise his wife with "any reasonable instrument." The rule of thumb actually represented some progress toward limiting the amount of force a man could use. It allowed a husband to beat his wife with any stick of his choosing—as long as it was no thicker than his own thumb.

American courts approved this rule in 1824, when a Mississippi court held that husbands could use corporal punishment against wives within this paltry limitation. A typical statement of the early law declared that a man could beat his wife "without subjecting himself to vexatious prosecutions for assault and battery, resulting in the discredit and shame of all concerned."

For the next fifty years or so, court decisions varied. A North Carolina court overturned the rule of thumb in 1864, but a higher court in that state upheld it three years later in 1867, stating, "If no permanent injury has been inflicted, nor malice nor dangerous violence shown by the husband, it is better to draw the curtain, shut out the public gaze, and leave the parties to forgive and forget." An 1874 North Carolina court even took a giant step backward, holding that a husband was entitled to chastise his wife under *any* circumstances. Meanwhile, England passed its first law against "aggressive assault upon women and children" in 1853. The law provided for a fine and up to six months in prison.

An interesting, though isolated, development took place in rural Texas in 1866. Martha White McWhirter founded the Sanctificationist religious group on the belief that no woman should have to live with a brutal, or "unsanctified," husband. Her followers were made up of other women escaping battering husbands, and they founded what may be the first shelter ever established. By 1880, fifty women lived together in a self-reliant group that owned and operated three farms, a steam laundry, a hotel, and several rooming houses. The Sanctificationists sometimes had to defend against irate husbands on the rampage. McWhirter's home still stands in Belmont, Texas, with a bullet hole in the front door.

Alabama and Massachusetts courts handed down rulings against wife abuse in 1871. An unusually enlightened Alabama judge wrote that year in *Fulgham v. State*, "The privilege, ancient though it may be, to beat her with a stick, to pull her hair, choke her, spit in her face, or kick her about the floor, or to inflict upon her like indignities is not now acknowledged by our law." By the early 1880s, most states had laws limiting the amount of force that could be used against a wife, but few provided any penalties for violation. No state actually passed a law making wife beating illegal until 1883, when Maryland finally made it a crime.

Yet few people actually saw violence in the home as a problem. One reason for the lack of concern was the common notion—in British, American, and many other societies—that a woman was not a full human being, but property, first of her father, then of her husband. In fact, this idea was so widely accepted by the seventeenth century that the early American slaveholders adopted the law governing women to establish the legal status of slaves!

Under this system, a wife and husband became legally one person—the husband. By law he had to answer for the misdeeds or debts of anyone in his household, so the law delegated to him the obligation of keeping his family in line. Accordingly, he was allowed, and even expected, to chastise any errant child, servant, or wife. By 1895, a number of states had adopted the Married Women's Property Act, which gave women some rights to own their own property and made a husband's conviction for assault sufficient grounds for divorce. Convictions were hard to get and seldom seen, but the act did help begin to change the concept that women were the husbands' property.

Another roadblock in the law that has prevented battered wives from holding their husbands accountable is the concept of "spousal immunity." This is a legal principle that says wives and husbands can't sue one another for civil wrongs, or "torts." These are acts that give one person the right to sue another for compensation for their losses caused by the misdeeds. Torts include things like trespass, negligence, and assault and battery. Thus, a woman battered by a stranger on the street could take him to court to recover her damages, including medical bills, lost wages, and pain and suffering. But she couldn't sue her husband for the same behavior.

The philosophy behind this rule seems patently stupid: The idea is to preserve harmony in the family unit. As late as 1962, the California Supreme Court threw out a woman's assault case against her husband on the theory that to allow the case to proceed ". . . would destroy the peace and harmony of the home and thus be contrary to the policy of the law." Such reasoning ignores the obvious conclusion that a home in which the family members are beating and suing one another is far from peaceful and harmonious to begin with.

Though relatively uncommon today, appallingly insensitive attitudes were frequently encountered by women who tried to make use of what help was available. As late as the 1970s, it was not uncommon for a prosecutor to base the decision of whether to bring charges against the abuser on the number of stitches required to close the woman's wounds.

Prosecutors joked about the "fifteen-minute rule"—if, after spending fifteen minutes with the victim, the lawyer was ready to beat her himself, he would not pursue the case. In the late 1970s, a Harris poll found that one out of five Americans—including women!—still approved of a man hitting his wife under some circumstances.

Thus, until very recently, the criminal justice system saw its task as limiting the amount of force a man could use against his wife, rather than recognizing spousal abuse as a crime. This very attitude has been one of the greatest barriers in trying to end the brutality that still goes on behind the drawn curtains. Until the 1970s, only the most extreme crimes—like murder—made it to the courtroom. It was common for state laws to be structured in such a way that the very same action, beating a person, was a felony if it was committed against a stranger, but only a misdemeanor if done to a spouse! In most cases, a woman's legal remedies were limited to a provision in a divorce or legal separation decree prohibiting the abuser from contacting or harassing her. It has only been within the past twenty years that any real progress has been made in using, changing, and expanding the law toward greater justice for victims of domestic violence.

Until the 1970s, there were virtually no social services for victims of domestic violence. Haven House, the first contemporary American shelter, was opened in San Gabriel Valley, California, in 1964, but it was one of the very few. People in violent relationships had to depend on the police, mental health professionals, churches, friends, and family if they needed support or intervention.

Other sources of help began to emerge in association with the rape crisis movement of the early 1970s. grassroots activists and social service professionals borrowed the techniques of organizing and counseling to address the similar plight of battered women, creating shelters, hotlines, support groups, legal aid centers, and advocacy projects. The first book on domestic violence was published in 1974 in England by Erin Pizzey. It was called *Scream Quietly or the Neighbors Will Hear* and a documentary film by the same name helped draw attention to the problem when it was broadcast in England and America. Pizzey founded the first shelter for battered women in England, and women's groups began setting up shelters and safe houses in America at about the same time.

Since 1974, over eighteen hundred shelters have been established by grassroots workers in what has been described as one of the most astonishing social reform movements in history. While child abuse had long been recognized as a major problem that received the attention of organized legal, political, and protective groups, the fight against spouse abuse was almost entirely undertaken by the victims themselves. Most of the community-based services that now exist and work in a cooperative effort with government service agencies, the criminal justice system, and other institutions were created by these pioneers.

Volunteers have also set up emergency hotlines, information services, advocacy organizations, and programs for victims, and have successfully pushed for changes in the law. Large social reform organizations soon took note, and became involved. In 1975, the National Organization for Women (NOW) created a task force on battered wives. The National Coalition Against Domestic Violence (NCADV) was organized in January 1978 when over one hundred battered women's advocates from all over the nation attended the U.S. Commission on Civil Rights hearing on battered women in Washington, D.C. The NCADV was established to organize the various grassroots shelter and service programs for battered women around the nation, and to address the common problems of these formerly isolated programs.

In 1980 the Domestic Abuse Intervention Project was created in Duluth, Minnesota. It founded one of the first systems to coordinate the efforts of the police, prosecutors, civil and criminal court judges, shelters, legal advocates, probation officers, social service agencies, mental health professionals, and others involved in efforts to end domestic violence. This program has been a model for other cities and agencies, and has expanded its efforts to include training programs for other communities.

Creative efforts have continued at the grassroots level. In 1987, Rockland Family Shelter in New York established a catalog called the Company of Women, which features a wide variety of products, with special emphasis on goods useful to women, such as a car emergency kit (see appendix). All profits from the sales of goods in the catalog go to support the shelter's wide variety of programs, both in the community and beyond.

The law has, at long last, seen dramatic changes over the past fifteen years, due in large part to the efforts of the same volunteer organizers who lobbied for changes in social attitudes so that domestic violence would be viewed as a serious crime, not a "family matter." Law and police policy changes have made the arrest of batterers mandatory in many jurisdictions. Prosecutors have established systems in which the abuser can be charged and even tried without the victim's direct involvement. Courts have begun imposing mandatory jail sentences, counseling programs, and stiff penalties for convictions or violation of orders. Civil lawsuits by individuals and groups have held both batterers and police who refuse to enforce the law accountable for the damages caused by their actions or apathy, and have helped create more legal tools for other abuse victims to use.

Yet the quality of justice a person receives often depends on where she lives. In many places, attitudes have not changed as quickly as the law. As recently as the mid-1980s, some judges tended to view abuse as a symptom of a bad marriage rather than the cause of it, and a man who admitted to being sorry was viewed as deserving a "second chance." In some jurisdictions, a man who could manipulate his wife into allowing him to spend the night under the same roof could claim that the couple had reconciled, effectively halting or at least delaying a divorce.

Today, in some areas, the legal system, social service agencies, and other professionals work smoothly together in a coordinated effort that efficiently deals with every reported case of domestic violence. In other places, a double standard remains in the vastly different way law enforcement and the judicial system treat the same behavior, depending on whether it occurs on the street or in the home. Abusers are still set free without suffering any consequences for their behavior.

Why on earth should this be so? If anything, it seems *more* shocking, more offensive, to think of hitting someone you love than hitting a stranger. Again, these attitudes have deep roots in the past that have mutated into equally unreasonable presumptions today. One hundred years ago, a woman who left a brutal husband was soundly criticized for abandoning her "sacred family obligations." Today, we ask her why she *doesn't* leave if she is unhappy. The focus is still in the wrong place: on the woman. Society continues to place the responsibility for change on the victim; asking why she doesn't leave, instead of asking why the man abuses her, and why the agencies that are supposed to protect people haven't put a stop to it.

There is no question that, today, most people consider wife beating wrong. We believe that women should have options, that no one should have to live with brutality. Yet the question "Why doesn't she leave?" is still asked over and over.

This attitude is based on mistaken assumptions. We assume that every woman has family, friends, or a shelter in her town with room to take her; a police officer in the neighborhood who will assure her safety; a judge who will punish the batterer and enforce protective orders; therapy programs; child care; affordable housing; job opportunities; medical care; and support groups.

Even the best programs in the country, some of which are profiled in the last chapter, are imperfect. Virtually all suffer from chronic underfunding. Minnesota, which boasts one of the most progressive and generously funded anti-abuse programs in the country, routinely spends less money to help battered women than it does to kill mosquitoes!

And amazing ignorance persists in the attitudes of some. There are people who still think that domestic violence is anything from a necessary evil to an acceptable part of family life. Judge Angela Jewell, former domestic violence special commissioner for a New Mexico district court, tells the incredible story of a man who was arrested for battering his wife. At the police station he kept repeating, "But she's my *wife!*" He was astonished to learn that beating his wife was a crime—he honestly thought that he had the absolute right, as a husband, to hit his wife if he pleased. And this occurred in 1994!

Perhaps changing ingrained attitudes will always be the most difficult task of social reformers. Even something as innocent as a fairy tale can help perpetuate old beliefs. Storybooks still teach young girls that they need only wait for a handsome prince to be assured of true love and living happily ever after. We still hear the expressions, "Kiss and make up," "All's fair in love and war," not to mention, "That's a good rule of thumb."

Yet considering that virtually all of the progress against domestic violence has happened in just over twenty years, there is great reason to be proud and hopeful. Today every state has a domestic violence coalition, at least a few shelters, and laws that make domestic violence a crime. Much remains to be done, but much has been achieved.

CHAPTER THREE

THE PSYCHOLOGY OF
DOMESTIC VIOLENCE

It's always easier to solve a problem that can be identified, analyzed, or isolated when we can say, "This is what causes the problem, this is where it happens, and why." Unfortunately, domestic violence does not easily lend itself to scientific analysis. Victims and abusers come from all races, religions, classes, ethnic groups, socioeconomic levels, occupations, and backgrounds. "Intelligent people let this happen too," psychologist Robert Geffner, president of the Family Violence and Sexual Assault Institute of Tyler, Texas, said in a 1994 *Newsweek* article. "What goes on inside the home does not relate to what's outside it."

Also, appearances of the home to the outside world may be deceiving. Even women who appear to be strong, financially secure, and privileged may suffer from isolation, a history of abuse, low self-esteem, or other factors not apparent beyond the confines of the home.

As domestic violence has at last come to be viewed as a crime and a social problem, scientists in various fields, including psychology, sociology, law enforcement, and medicine, have begun to study violent homes and the people who live in them. Many questions remain, and not all the experts agree on how to interpret and apply what has been learned. But some answers have emerged that have proven very useful in helping to understand the tragedy of family violence, and in determining what can work to prevent and stop it.

In 1991, the American Psychological Association established a task force on male violence against women. The task force has emphasized that the problem cannot be fully understood, let alone solved, by focusing exclusively on individual psychology. There must be changes in the social institutions that have given rise to the problem before any lasting solutions can be achieved. As psychologist Carolina Yahne, Ph.D., observes, "Psychology's tradition of focusing on the individual must not obscure social and cultural dimensions."

THE VIOLENT HOME: DYNAMICS OF THE ABUSIVE RELATIONSHIP

Those in violent relationships may also fight about the same "flash-point" topics as non-violent couples—money, housekeeping, parenting —but do not draw the boundaries that healthy couples do. Social scientists and others studying domestic abuse have discovered certain risk factors that help predict which homes are more likely to become violent, and which individuals have greater tendencies to become abusers or victims. These studies are extremely valuable in helping prevent those prone to abuse from becoming involved in it, and in understanding what ingredients go into making an abusive home.

But these generalizations must be approached with care. The scientists themselves stress the need for caution in using these models, because they are imperfect and prone to misunderstanding, as with any method that tries to reduce the complexities of human behavior to neat formulas. It is essential to remember that the lists of factors predict only characteristics that mean domestic violence is more *likely* to happen. They do not mean that all homes in which the factors are found will become violent, or that those without them never will be. As we all know from the media, as well as from our own experience, domestic violence happens in "ideal" families, in which all members have education, money, and professional success. And plenty of large, blue-collar, financially strapped homes remain peaceful and loving.

Richard J. Gelles, director of the family violence program at the University of Rhode Island, has studied and written extensively on the issues surrounding domestic violence. In an analysis entitled "Men who batter: The Risk Markers," released in 1994, he and his colleagues identified eleven risk factors for future abuse in the home. The highest risk factor is previous involvement with domestic violence. This, more than anything else, serves as a red flag to warn of probable future violence. Other factors include:

1. The man is unemployed
2. The man uses illegal drugs at least once a year
3. The man and woman are from different religious backgrounds
4. The man saw his father hit his mother
5. The couple cohabits but is not married
6. The man has a blue-collar occupation, if employed
7. The man did not graduate from high school
8. The man is between eighteen and thirty years old
9. Either person uses severe violence toward children in the home
10. Income is below the poverty level

Gelles reports that homes with two of these ten specific factors have twice the violence of those where none of these factors are present. In homes with seven or more of these factors, violence is forty times more likely than in homes without any.

It appears that unemployed men batter their wives at twice the rate of those who are employed. However, while the incidence of violence in low-income families seems to be significantly higher, the statistics may not be accurate because of the far greater amount of secrecy surrounding violence in middle- and upper-income families. Such families are also more likely to seek counseling or other private help.

Yet much also depends on the individuals in the home, and their own unique way of relating to one another. The relationship between a man and woman caught in an abusive relationship is very complex. The single most important factor, present in all such relationships, is one partner's need to feel he or she absolutely controls the other. For most couples, the violence begins with relatively minor incidents and escalates in both frequency and brutality over time. Some spend several years in an idyllic closeness, then things begin to deteriorate. Others start the cycle of abuse very early, often while they are dating.

Newer marriages seem to have a higher risk of violence, although it can occur at any stage. The structure of the marriage also seems to be significant. Families in households where decision making is shared are less likely to be violent than those in which one partner makes all the decisions.

Abuse usually starts with degrading behavior, insults, put-downs. The man begins to convince the woman she is causing unhappiness in the relationship, and that she needs to change. Isolation often comes next, along with jealousy. He insists on knowing her every move, under the guise that he loves her so much he can't stand to be apart from her. The jealousy often includes not only other men, but family, work, and friends as well—anyone who takes her attention away from him, even momentarily.

The verbal abuse usually escalates over time. An abuser often projects his own failures and faults onto the victim. A typical example is screaming at her in public for embarrassing him. He may keep her continually occupied with catering to his needs so she is constantly exhausted. Some batterers encourage their partners to abuse alcohol or drugs, so they will become dependent in yet another way.

Often, he will make her financially dependent by insisting on controlling all of the family finances. She is required to turn over her paycheck, quit her job, sell her car. Transportation is often a big issue. Even very wealthy women have been kept penniless, denied money for such necessities as medical bills, made virtual prisoners. A friend recently told me about meeting a woman who was herself a millionaire—yet she had become trapped in a relationship so violent that she had suffered a broken jaw and broken ribs before she finally escaped.

Abusers often refuse to allow their victims money for new clothes, haircuts, and personal maintenance, and in turn criticize their appearance. They may convince their partners to commit illegal acts or run up huge bills in their own names in order to make them more insecure and dependent. Abusers wage an insidious campaign to convince women they are stupid, worthless, and the cause of everything that's gone wrong. Often all these steps progress before physical abuse begins. By this time, the woman is so demoralized that she is, quite literally, a hostage. Her self-image and self-confidence have been shattered. Her spirit is broken. Her sense of reality has become so warped that she does not have the emotional equipment to leave even if she does have access to shelters, friends, family, and other support services.

Hard to believe? For those of us who have never been mistreated in this way, it is almost beyond comprehension that such things go on between people who have pledged to love and care for one another. But it happens—and it happens with chilling frequency.

Carol Jarvis, a twenty-eight-year-old high school teacher, astonished long-time friends when she returned to her native California after spending several years in Texas—where she had been trapped in a terrifying relationship with a brutal man. "My friends knew me as smart, gutsy, accomplished, always the leader," she says. "They couldn't believe that I had become involved with a man who battered me. But he was so good to me at first, and the abuse really crept up slowly—starting with put-downs and small acts of unkindness. Plus we moved out of state, so I was away from everyone I knew. I had no friends, family, no one around I felt I could talk to about what was going on when he started beating me. It got to the point where I was truly in fear for my life. I had to construct an elaborate plot to get away. I stashed some money, organized the things I would take with me, and waited until I was sure he would be at work all day, since he often came home for lunch. I left as soon as he was out of sight and just kept heading west. I didn't feel safe until I crossed the New Mexico state line."

Fortunately, Carol reconnected with friends and family in her hometown and built a satisfying life with a loving man. With this support, she regained her confidence and became the successful woman they remembered, returning to work in teaching and social services and rekindling her old love of the theater. Many formerly abused women report gaining a new lease on life—if they can survive, plan carefully (as Carol did), and break free.

What about mutually abusive relationships? Do they exist? Of course there are relationships in which both partners exhibit violent behavior, but according to those who have studied all types of domestic violence, they are rare. In a relationship based on power and control, only one partner can dominate. It appears that when two abusive people get together, the relationship usually ends quickly.

Some couples occasionally brawl, but the dynamics of their relationship do not match those of what experts traditionally call domestic violence, in which one partner clearly dominates. As psychologist and author Lenore Walker, Ed.D., has explained, battering is not a "fight" that involves two people. It doesn't arise from a rational disagreement between people. Often, violence will be triggered by something utterly insignificant, such as knocking a paper cup to the floor, forgetting to turn off a light, or nothing at all. Often, the abuser will wake a sleeping woman up to beat her.

In some abusive relationships, the woman will try to defend herself by fighting back. However, this is not a form of mutual combat, but rather a fear-induced reaction to being attacked. The mutually combative relationship, involving "fair fights" between the parties, is both very unusual and distinct from the typical abusive home.

Fighting back usually proves either ineffective or deadly, because most abusers become more enraged if the victim tries to fight back. Also, the man generally has an edge in size and strength, so a victim who tries to use physical force against an aggressor is frequently beaten more brutally or killed. Additionally, police who are called to a scene in which both parties show signs of injury often arrest both, although this is changing in many areas as police receive training on the dynamics of abusive relationships. A battered woman often finds that the only effective way to defend herself is with a weapon, which can land her in prison for the rest of her life, even in cases that appear to fit the traditional requirements of self-defense. This separate issue is discussed in chapter 6.

WHY DOES DOMESTIC VIOLENCE HAPPEN?

One of the most perplexing questions about domestic violence is *why?* Most people today agree that men do not have the right to beat their wives, and that those who do are committing a heinous act. We realize that it is dangerous and emotionally destructive for children to grow up in a violent home. We condemn family violence, and praise the shelters, hotlines, and volunteers that try to help the victims. We recognize it as a social problem. We want the problem to go away, and wonder why it does not.

Dr. Walker has been one of the pioneers in the study of domestic violence. Currently director of the Domestic Violence Institute in Denver, she has been collecting and analyzing information since the 1970s, and has conducted extensive research on the psychology of battered women and the dynamics of abusive relationships. She has authored many books on domestic violence, including several editions of her landmark work, *The Battered Woman*. One of her most famous discoveries, now accepted by most experts, is the cycle of violence.

The Cycle of Violence

Dr. Walker found that in about two-thirds of violent homes, there are three phases the couple goes through over and over, in a circular pattern. The aspects of the violence may vary from home to home, but the cycle almost always has these ongoing components. First, tension builds. The man becomes edgy, critical, irritable. The woman may go out of her way to try and keep the peace during this period, "walking on eggshells" to try and pacify him. She avoids anything she fears may set him off on a tirade.

Meanwhile, he becomes gradually more abusive, often with "minor" incidents such as slapping, verbal abuse, and increased control techniques. The woman allows this behavior in a desperate attempt to keep the abuse from escalating. Yet docile behavior tends to legitimize his belief that he is all-powerful and has a right to be abusive. She continues to try to control the environment and the people around him, and her isolation increases as she tries to keep things on an even keel. This uncomfortable stage may last from a few days to a period of years. Usually, both can sense the impending loss of control and become more desperate, which only fuels the tension. Many women feel that the psychological anguish of this stage is the worst.

Then comes the second stage, the violent outburst with acute battering. Often the man will fly into a rage and become violent for no apparent reason, or a stated reason that seems petty or irrational, such as his wife's cooking. Anything can be the catalyst for the explosion, and the woman may not even be involved—she may be asleep or just walking in the door. The man flies into a savage, destructive rampage, a total loss of control. Men in this stage are extremely irrational. They often turn on anyone who intervenes. This is one reason police are sometimes reluctant to answer a domestic violence call, and another reason for good police training.

After the brutality comes the loving contrition. It is a period of profound relief for both partners. The man is remorseful and apologetic, or, at the very least, nonviolent. He may beg forgiveness, swear it will never happen again, and go out of his way to be kind, tranquil, and loving. He will often promise to change, bring his wife gifts, shower her with attention and romantic gestures. As one woman said with the contempt of hindsight, "He thought he could beat me, then take me to bed and have sex with me, and that would make everything all right."

This phase explains a great deal about why women stay with abusers. A woman will often believe the man is sincere, that this is his "real" character, which he may himself believe at this time. She sees what appears to be an ideal and loving partnership. Her dreams are fulfilled, and she wants to believe it can work. Many women feel that they are the sole source of the abuser's emotional support, and feel responsible for his well-being. Dr. Walker believes this phase may be the most psychologically victimizing, because it perpetuates the illusion of interdependence—he depends on her for forgiveness, she depends on the "real" man coming back.

As the cycle repeats itself, denial plays an increasingly important role. The woman may also believe that this really will be the last time, that her partner will change. But unless something changes—such as intervention by someone outside the home—the cycle will start again, and the abuse will almost surely become more severe. These relationships rarely change for the better on their own.

Behavior scientists have long known that one of the best ways to change behavior is through intermittent reinforcement—occasional, unpredictable rewards. A batterer who intersperses abuse with loving acts, courtship, and gifts is unwittingly using one of the most powerful techniques for convincing the woman to stay with him. Behavior that is intermittently reinforced is often the hardest to stop.

Learned Helplessness

Learned helplessness is a psychological term first identified under this name by psychologist Martin Seligman of the University of Pennsylvania and used extensively by Dr. Walker and others working with battered women.

Dr. Seligman studied both animals and people who had been placed in environments where they were trapped without the possibility of escape, and then subjected to random, unpredictable torment. In one experiment, dogs were locked in cages where they received occasional electric shocks from the floor. At first, as would be expected, they tried to find a way to escape. Eventually, however, they completely stopped trying to find a way out and instead developed coping skills to try and minimize the discomfort. These activities included things that would otherwise be considered unhealthy or bizarre, such as lying in their own excrement for insulation from the shocks and curling into uncomfortable positions on the area of the floor where the shocks were the weakest. Eventually, the coping mechanisms completely replaced the normal escape responses. Even when the doors were opened so the dogs had an immediate means of escape, they did not leave the cages, but instead kept using the coping responses. They had to be retrained to learn the normal escape response. Once they did, the coping behaviors disappeared.

With humans, thoughts play a larger part in the way people deal with stressful situations, but the responses are similar. Constant degradation, unpredictability, and insecurity in the face of ever-increasing violence is bound to distort the way a person views the world. A woman who appears to have control over a situation—a car in the driveway and an unlocked door—but who has been "trained" to believe that she does not have choices, is more likely to try to cope than to escape.

"Learned helplessness" is a somewhat misleading term because the person does not actually learn to be helpless. Rather she learns that she cannot predict the effect of her behavior, so she must develop new coping skills. People experience great anxiety in situations where they do not know what is expected of them or what will happen from one moment to the next. Therefore, she is likely to do what will give her the most predictability within a known situation, and to avoid things that can send her into the unknown. The familiar demons become less threatening than those that are unknown.

The control skills used by a batterer have been found by researchers to strongly resemble the brainwashing techniques practiced by Nazi concentration camp soldiers and prisoner of war guards. They include many of the behaviors identified by Amnesty International as psychological torture, including isolation, monopolization of perception, induced exhaustion and debility, threats, occasional indulgences, demonstrations of complete power, degradation and humiliation, and enforcing trivial demands.

Of course, most batterers have no formal awareness of the techniques they are using, yet they know how to use isolation, torture, and violence to destroy the will and spirit of another human being. As Dr. Richard Gelles stated in a 1994 *Newsweek* article, "There's no better way to make people compliant than beating them on an intermittent basis."

Victims of this kind of relentless torment understandably live in a constant state of terror, which also contributes to learned helplessness. They do not believe that any action they take will be effective in stopping the violence, and their fear becomes so all-encompassing it often crowds out other reactions, such as anger, that would be natural under the circumstances. The fear is not irrational; it is based on repeated brutality, and a very real fear for their very lives. At the same time, their partners are terrified of abandonment and willing to do anything to trap their women. It is common for battered women to believe that their abusers are capable of coming after them and finding them no matter where they go.

Different Homes and Different Dynamics

These models are extremely helpful in understanding how domestic violence happens, and especially in explaining why women often believe they cannot leave. Again, however, it is important to remember that the dynamics are somewhat different in each family. In many, both a cycle of violence and learned helplessness are present. In others, it seems one or the other is present, but not both. It is likely that in those families where the beatings occur more frequently, with little or no remorse or respite for a honeymoon phase, learned helplessness plays a greater role. Some experts believe that the honeymoon phase would be better characterized as a period of acceptance, because many men show no remorse after the beating, and instead adopt a strong position of blaming the wife for "bringing on" a "justified punishment." Not surprisingly, such men have the least chance of benefiting from therapy or counseling, and seldom seek help unless ordered to do so by a court.

In other families, beatings may happen as infrequently as every two or three years, with long periods justifying the label, "honeymoon phase." Yet these abusers proceed into an equally long tension-building phase, in which they may become sullen, angry, demanding, and verbally and emotionally abusive.

In addition to the psychological patterns and family dynamics that go into making a violent home, there are many individual, as well as practical, factors that contribute as well. Financial fears are often crucial, especially when a woman has been kept out of the work force or prevented from getting education or training. Many women find themselves in a position in which they feel they will be damned if they do and damned if they don't. People keep saying "Why don't you leave?" and yet women on welfare or public aid are also criticized for "milking" the system. There should be no shame in turning to social supports when they are needed—that is precisely why they exist—yet society sometimes unfairly ostracizes those who take advantage of the programs created to help them.

WHAT MAKES A MAN ABUSIVE?

Unlike victims, most abusers tend to share quite a number of common traits, background factors, and behavior patterns. Virtually all of the experts in the various fields who have studied the dynamics of domestic violence and the abuser personality agree that the goal of the abuser is power and control over his partner. Also, abusive men almost universally deny or minimize the abuse and blame the woman. As one psychologist commented, "Abusers always make excuses. None are valid." A batterer tells himself, his friends, the police, prosecutors, and his victim that she was the instigator, that she brought it on, that if not for her "bad" behavior, he would not have "had" to beat her. Acts of violence may be preceded by the absurd admonition, "Don't make me hurt you."

Men who batter tend to be highly dependent on female partners for emotional support, though most subscribe to the traditional notion that men should not express emotions, and to do so indicates weakness. Thus, the man who adopts a macho stoicism that erupts into violence may actually be among the most emotionally needy. The abusive man tries to take away his partner's power, while at the same time giving her the ultimate power to grant or deny him happiness by expecting her to make everything in his world perfect. No woman can live up to the expectations of a batterer, because they are, by definition, impossible. When she "fails," he becomes enraged. This also explains why the point of separation is often the most dangerous: Abusive men have a terrible fear of abandonment, and become desperate when they feel they could lose their partner. Over and over, studies find that the men who exhibit dominating behavior are in fact extremely insecure, vulnerable, and dependent. They tend to be unreasonably jealous, both of other men and of anyone or anything else that takes a partner's attention away from them—family, friends, work. One batterer threw a religious candle that had special meaning for his wife through the screen of her computer after he became irrationally convinced that she was having an affair with another man via the Internet. Another grabbed his girlfriend by her long hair and cut it off because he believed another man was admiring it.

Abusers often have trouble accepting responsibility for their own behavior, abusive and otherwise. They feel guilt and shame when they lose control, yet try to justify, minimize, or deny their behavior. They often come from families that were isolated and cold, if not actually abusive, in which they learned to mistrust outsiders and keep family business strictly private. Many were raised to equate respect with fear. About half have chemical dependencies of some kind, and many exhibit mental or personality disorders such as lack of empathy, depression, general hostility, and feelings of victimization. They tend to invest their whole beings in their families, and virtually all are in some kind of pain.

Researchers have found that many violent men lack basic social skills, though they appear to function well outside the home. They interpret innocent situations that arouse their jealousy as having been done with hostile intent on the part of their wives—for example, when they see their wives talking with other men at parties. They lack the ability to trust, often because they did not have a secure attachment with a parent. They believe they can only gain security against abandonment through control.

Those who abuse adult partners often grew up in homes marred by violence between the adults, against the children, or both. However, it is essential to remember that growing up in a violent home does not guarantee that a man will become abusive. Many violent homes produce children who grow up to be kind, gentle adults. Many, many factors go into making up the personality of the man with the potential to be brutal. The difficulty lies in identifying what these factors are, and what combination produces the violent individual. The patterns that do exist do not cover all abusive homes. For example, Dr. Gelles has found that men with less education and a lower income are more likely to be abusers, but notes that some white-collar men also beat their partners.

Dr. Walker has discovered that most batterers have a poor self-image and low self-esteem, traits that are often found in battered women, as well. Many abusive men are severely depressed. She, too, has noted that many have traditional ideas about male superiority and stereotypical sex roles. They tend to be chronically jealous, react abnormally to stress, and some are compulsive drinkers.

Some psychiatric researchers are experimenting with Prozac and other antidepressant drugs to help abusers. Many do exhibit symptoms of clinical depression, and early trials with these drugs hold some promise. But most therapists agree that neither drugs or therapy alone will cure an abuser—there must be accountability, and acceptance by the abuser that he is responsible for his actions. He must understand that his actions are wrong, and he must recognize the need to change.

Another troubling but interesting factor that has been discovered by psychologists studying batterers is the high incidence of head injuries among these men as children. One study found that a history of head injuries may increase the likelihood of abuse by six times. However, researchers are quick to point out that biological factors do not cause abusive behavior. Again, this is but one factor in a complicated mix, and does not operate as an excuse for violent behavior. A recent article in *Psychology Today* compared domestic violence to "a very strange onion." It is a product of many forces, operating at many levels, between the individual abuser and his environment. Biological, cognitive, psychological, behavioral, and cultural forces may all play a part in shaping the man who batters.

Some psychologists who have studied men who batter divide them into two or three groups, depending upon their patterns of abuse— whether they are intermittent or nearly constant—and their personality traits. Family psychologist and behaviorist Neil Jacobson, Ph.D., of the University of Washington, has studied the physical reactions of couples in violent relationships as they discuss topics that generally lead to violence. He found that in one group of batterers, about 20 percent of those he studied seem to get inwardly calm when they become abusive. Their violence is not triggered by rage or emotion. Most of these men identified in Dr. Jacobson's study witnessed extreme violence between their parents.

The National Centers for Disease Control (CDC) in Atlanta has been conducting a detailed study on what actually helps batterers stop abusive behavior. The study has classified three types of abusers. First is the traditional batterer, who follows the cycle of violence. Second is the episodic batterer, who erupts into violence on rare occasions. Third is the rapid cycler, whose violent incidents escalate rapidly. This is the group that is often violent outside the home, and includes those who get into bar fights, and commit sexual assaults and other violent acts. The third type is the least likely to benefit from counseling.

Other psychologists identify a small but dangerous group, similar to the CDC's third category, as men who have an antisocial personality disorder and are frequently violent with others outside the home as well. Several leading scientists, using different theories and methods, have found the same number of men, about 20 percent, that are somehow different from the others in their reactions, their behavior outside the home, and high degree of danger—not only to their female partners, but to others as well. This seems to be the main characteristic that sets this group apart. The vast majority of batterers are only violent at home, against their wives and often their children.

Both those who have studied abusers and those who have lived with them almost always recognize a "Dr. Jekyll and Mr. Hyde" aspect to the man's personality. Abusers often seem to be two different people. Many are successful on the job, handsome, well-liked, charming, and kind in public. Usually, both sides are seen in the home, but only the pleasant, "regular guy" is seen by outsiders. Abusers often work hard to hide their battering from the outside world. "He'd hit me where it wouldn't show, or if it did, he wouldn't let me leave the house until the marks were gone," says one woman who was married to an abusive man for over twenty-five years.

Many abusive relationships also have another side, one that is very positive, romantic, and loving, whether or not they follow the cycle of violence with its characteristic honeymoon phase. Couples in abusive relationships sometimes have the sense of having a very deep and special connection. Ironically, this positive side of the abuser's personality actually may contribute to the continuing violence in two ways. First, friends of the couple who have never seen the man's "Mr. Hyde" persona may not believe the woman when she tells them he beats her. Second, she herself falls prey to his loving side, which often makes its strongest appearance after an attack, when he is apologizing, trying to make it up to her, swearing it will never happen again.

Some experts also believe abusers have a kind of "radar" that enables them to spot women they will more likely be able to abuse. Both professionals and abuse survivors have pointed to this odd quirk over and over. It does make sense that a man with a strong need to control a partner, one who has traditional ideas about the dominant role of the male in the family, would tend to seek out a partner who, at least on some level, exhibits traits of passivity or vulnerability.

There is a persistent myth that stress turns men into abusers; that men under pressure from financial strain, emotional upheaval, unemployment, or other difficulties hit a breaking point and start lashing out at whoever is handy. While it is true that stress often contributes to the tension that leads to an outburst in a violent man, stress does not make otherwise peaceful men suddenly become abusers. The explosive combination of a need to control, dependency, domination, and the other ingredients that make up the abuser personality must already be in place before stress ignites the fuse that leads to battering.

An otherwise stable, nonviolent man does not become an abuser because of difficult circumstances. Men do not batter because they're insecure, angry, facing financial difficulty, poor communicators, or feel trapped in an unhappy marriage. Plenty of men with these problems never beat their mates. Most batterers are selectively abusive. At least 80 percent are not violent outside the home. Rather than turning their anger toward the real source of their frustration, such as the company that laid them off or the driver who hit their car, abusers select the people they believe they can control.

A batterer has his own warped agenda, in which he places the full responsibility for his happiness or unhappiness on the woman in his life. He feels that by controlling "his" woman and "training" her to do what he wants, all his needs can be met. Obviously, a woman living with such a man is in a no-win situation. No matter how hard she tries, she can never make the world perfect for him. Yet he expects no less.

Ironically, while violence can certainly be an effective way for an abuser to gain short-term control over his partner, it usually fails in the long run, because most women *do* eventually break free of abusers—or are killed. Thus he ultimately brings about the one thing he fears most: abandonment.

THE BATTERED WOMAN

Unlike abusive men, battered women share few common characteristics. Low self-esteem, a poor self-image, and a childhood marred by abuse or neglect are found in many abuse victims, but not all. Women with little education or work experience, who married young, who have small children, or who have limited earning capacity may be more susceptible to the practical, economic constraints of an abusive home. Yet women with high-powered, lucrative, successful careers and plenty of friends, money, and prestige also fall prey to abusive partners. It happens to women of remarkable talent, fame, and achievement, like Tina Turner, who endured nearly twenty years of brutal abuse from her husband Ike before walking out in an unfamiliar city with thirty-six cents in her pocket. Sometimes victims who are educated in the dynamics of battering even recognize the cycle, see the typical behavior of the victim in themselves, yet still believe the abuse is their fault.

Psychologists who have worked with battered women say that the stereotype of the victim as fragile, passive, docile, and self-deprecating is often inaccurate. In many abusive homes, the woman is by far the more functional of the partners. Many do stand up to violence, try anything they can think of to try and stop it, but discover they cannot.

Furthermore, most battered women do not stay. Up to 75 percent of those reporting abuse *have* left and are being stalked, harassed, and assaulted by former husbands or boyfriends. Yet many women do remain or leave and then go back; it often takes a battered woman several tries to leave a relationship for good. A popular (and degrading) myth is that women who stay must be masochists who enjoy being abused. This is one factor the experts agree is *not* common in battered women.

One very rational reason why women stay is fear. A battered woman is more likely to get killed when she tries to leave than at any other time in the relationship. Sherry, a social worker now in her forties, says that her first husband only beat her when she threatened to leave him. She was still in her teens when they were married, and they lived in a remote rural area. She had no car of her own, so she had to play the role of loving wife until he was away and she could arrange for a family member to come pick her up. Her story is very common.

Abusers often tell their victims, "If you leave, I'll see that you never see your kids again." Abusive men are almost never awarded sole custody of their children, but women who have not had the opportunity to learn about the law often don't realize this. Some of the most evil abusers use their own children as a weapon against their wives or girlfriends, threatening or actually abusing the children if the woman does not meet their ideal standards. One survivor recalled that her abuser threatened to kill or injure not only her, but her children and other family members as well if she tried to leave him. He also refused to let her work outside the home, and controlled what little money she earned sewing for others. Yet she was still asked why she didn't leave him sooner.

Social factors must also be considered. Most women are raised to believe that the woman is the primary caretaker of the family, the member responsible for "holding things together." We are also taught from the days of childhood that "Love conquers all." Many women believe on some level that if only they love a man enough, they can "save" him and he will change. Those who stay learn that he will not.

Women who find themselves in an abusive relationship with a man they know was mistreated as a boy often feel sorry for him, and want to help him heal. Such nurturing comes naturally for most women, and fits the role most were taught. Yet with an abuser, it will never work. The only thing that will help him is to hold him accountable and insist the abuse stop. To allow it to continue only perpetuates the misery.

Again, it is difficult to separate the psychology behind abuse from the cultural and social influences that shape us all. Many women still feel they must have a man to be a whole person. Social pressures also subtly encourage women to stay with their abusers. Despite the fact that only about 10 percent of American families today consist of the traditional mother, father, and their natural children living under the same roof, this remains the ideal to which we aspire, and anything else seems less desirable. Our culture places a great deal of importance on "having a man." Ridiculous rumors about a desperate shortage of men, such as the myth that circulated a few years ago that the likelihood of marriage for a woman over forty is about the same as a terrorist attack, feed not only the fear of loneliness but the disproportionate importance of being a part of the traditional family. Especially if an abusive relationship follows the cycle of violence that includes a honeymoon phase, some women come to believe it's worth putting up with the abuse because there's nothing better available. Others believe that their children will suffer if the parents divorce, and that any father is better than no father at all. Research and experience have shown that such assumptions are wrong, yet they persist.

Women in violent relationships often use a special coping mechanism, a particular species of denial called "minimizing." They downplay the serious nature of their circumstances, tell themselves: It's no big deal; nothing's wrong that I can't fix; I can hold things together. The victim's family may also deny or minimize the abuse, as a coping mechanism of their own.

Virtually all experts agree that if family violence is ever to be stopped, prevention is key. Dr. Gelles suggests several specific changes in social attitudes that could help achieve this goal, recognizing that these require fundamental, long-term efforts. First, elimination of norms that tolerate or glorify violence as acceptable—spanking, media violence, acceptance of guns, capital punishment. Second, reduction of contributing stresses such as poverty, inequality, discrimination, unemployment, and lack of basic human needs. Third, reduction of social isolation— more integration of families into community and kinship networks. Fourth, changed concepts of sexist roles delineating "men's work" and "women's work." Fifth, breaking the cycle of violence in the family by the elimination of physical punishment and other means of teaching children that violence in the home is acceptable.

Financial pressures are also a very real obstacle for many women who want to leave, but question their ability to provide for themselves, and especially for their children. In the first year after divorce, a woman's standard of living usually drops, some estimate by as much as 73 percent, while a man's improves by up to 42 percent. Forty-five percent of all families headed by single mothers live below the poverty line. The persistent wage gap between the earnings of men and women, the problems faced by working mothers, and the glass ceiling that shuts women out of more lucrative positions still plague women in the work force. Even among professionals, many families today need two incomes to maintain a comfortable standard of living.

Yet most women who leave, even those with limited job skills, find ways to make ends meet and build a new and much better life for themselves and their children. When women are freed from the demands and exhaustion of simply surviving in an abusive relationship, their energy can be put to better use. Many experience the freedom to find their true calling for the first time, and amaze themselves with what they learn they can accomplish. More and more services are becoming available to help women who are suddenly single, not only to survive but to flourish.

It appears that some professional women, or those married to white-collar males, may be less likely to leave than their more impoverished counterparts. Dr. Lenore Walker has studied battered women at all socioeconomic levels and has found that a poor woman is more likely to have contact with community social service agencies, and to be more aware of the help that is available. She may also have prior experience using such services, and finds a much lower stigma attached to seeking help in her community than a middle- or upper-class woman.

In contrast, women who are themselves professionals or are married to men who are successful, respected, and visible in the community are less likely to seek outside help for several reasons. Many fear that no one will believe them, or that a powerful husband will be defended by those with ties to him. This is a rational fear; police officers in some communities have complained that men with power or political ties do not get prosecuted after arrest. This image of the husband as all-powerful also feeds the perception that the wife cannot leave, and if she does, he will track her down or use his connections to bring her back.

Also, affluent women are more ashamed to admit to problems in the family, fearing they will be condemned or ostracized by the social community. Mary Blick, R.N., an obstetrical nurse in a prosperous, small midwestern city works in a hospital that serves a large number of middle- and upper-class women, plus a group of public-aid patients. "The women from white-collar homes are very unlikely to say that they are abused," she says. "They're ashamed. The public-aid patients are more apt to admit to being battered, and usually do so earlier, because they are screened for abuse when they visit our free prenatal clinics. Many private physicians don't ask about abuse unless there is some indication of a problem and, even then, many don't screen for battering. So our public-aid patients actually get better screening, care, and services when it comes to abuse."

Also, the white-collar world tends to have an insular effect. Charlotte Fedders, a battered wife who was married to a high-powered government lawyer, writes in her book, *Shattered Dreams* that other families she knew looked fine from the outside, she had never encountered family violence, and she couldn't imagine any other husband hitting his wife. This reinforced her isolation, and her belief that she must be a terrible wife who somehow brought her problems on herself.

One survivor from a middle-class family discussed her reaction to persistent inquiries of "Why didn't you leave?" from those who learned after she was divorced that she had been battered for many years. "Number one is pride. You have all this self-recrimination. You don't want to admit to anyone that this goes on in your home. Number two is that he's such a nice guy to the outside world, nobody would believe you if you did try to tell them."

Some experts say the risk of being battered has little to do with the woman and nearly everything to do with who she chooses as a mate. Professionals who work with battered women report treating professors, models, professional athletes, heiresses, lawyers, doctors, actresses, royalty, psychologists, and business executives. The only trait all share in common is that they are female.

Karla M. Digirolami, managing director of Digirolami Associates, a consulting firm specializing in assisting public agencies, nonprofit organizations, and the corporate and business communities in domestic violence training and program development, has written that there is no profile that will predict whether a woman will be battered, and that any self-esteem problems observed in battered women are likely the result of the battering by a partner who has so degraded, criticized, and manipulated his partner that she has come to question her competence or value in the world. She urges us to consider the remarkable degree of strength and resiliency it takes to calmly show up at a job, child's school function, or other everyday event and perform as if life is normal only hours after surviving unspeakable brutality in one's own home.

However, scientists have learned that women who stay in abusive relationships for long periods tend to share certain personality traits and risk factors. According to Robert Geffner, Ph.D., these may include low self-esteem, a background of an abusive family life, alcohol or drug abuse problems, passivity in relationships, dependency, and a high need for approval, attention, and affection. The more of these factors an individual has, the more likely she will be a candidate for an abusive relationship. Yet women who have few or none of these characteristics also become abuse victims.

Dr. Lenore Walker has found that many abused women have a poor self-image and low self-esteem. They also tend to have traditional ideas about what constitutes a woman's achievement, and base their feelings of self-worth on how they view their capacity to be a good wife and homemaker, even if they have an outside career as well. Many abused women were battered or neglected as children, many were victims of incest. These women had little or no concept of normal family intimacy developed in childhood that they could bring to adult relationships. Being hurt by those who were supposed to love and protect is nothing new.

Yet girls raised in loving, peaceful families also grow up to be abused women. One of my friends has often expressed her frustration over her inability to understand how her sister could have become an abused woman, when the family was stable and close, and the other siblings would never tolerate abuse from a partner. "Something in her is different, or something happened to her in her life that affected her in ways we don't know about," she says. "I guess all we can do is keep telling her she shouldn't take it, we're here for her when she needs our help and is ready to accept it."

Women who are candidates for learned helplessness often share common traits in their histories. Through her research, Dr. Walker has identified five factors from childhood and seven from adulthood that can help predict and identify learned helplessness in individuals. The five childhood factors include:

1. Witnessing or experiencing battering in the home
2. Sexual abuse or molestation as a child or teenager
3. Critical periods in which the child experienced a loss of control due to such things as the loss of the alcoholism of a parent, frequent moves, or situations such as poverty that caused shame
4. Stereotyped, rigidly traditional sex-role training
5. Health problems or chronic illness

The adult factors that usually occur during the battering relationship are:

1. A pattern of violence, especially one that follows the cycle of violence and/or an escalation in the frequency and severity of abuse
2. Sexual jealousy
3. Other jealousy, mistrust, possessiveness, and isolation
4. Threats to kill or injure the woman
5. Psychological torture (as defined by Amnesty International)
6. Knowledge of other violent acts by the man, including violence toward children, pets, other animals, or inanimate objects
7. Alcohol or drug abuse by the man or the woman

Post-Traumatic Stress Disorder and the Battered Woman Syndrome

People who experience severe and unexpected trauma or repeated, unpredictable exposure to abuse often develop psychological symptoms that may affect their ability to function long after the original trauma is over. They may believe that they are essentially helpless, that they lack the power to change their situation. They often develop coping responses that take the place of the type of active response that would normally be expected under the circumstances—for instance, escaping a painful situation. The world stops making sense, and the person becomes literally incapable of trying to change it; she chooses only the responses she believes will protect her from further suffering. This can lead to a learned helplessness response, as discussed throughout the chapter, or another syndrome, called post-traumatic stress disorder (PTSD). This type of psychological injury is often seen in people who have suffered prolonged isolation and mistreatment in an abnormal situation, such as combat veterans and hostages. PTSD may be brought on by a single, extremely traumatic event. Yet its consequences are often more severe in people such as battered women, prisoners of war, abused children, and hostages because of prolonged terror and abuse.

The battered woman syndrome (BWS) has been considered by Dr. Lenore Walker as a subcategory of PTSD. It is marked by significant changes in the way victims of the syndrome think, act, and behave.

For a clinical diagnosis of the battered woman syndrome, Dr. Walker states that four criteria must be met:

1. A traumatic stressor exists, which is a source of extreme stress outside the scope of the unhappy, but common experiences most people face in life, such as the death of a loved one, illness, or the breakup of a relationship. Spouse abuse is accepted as such a traumatic stressor.
2. The individual experiences past-traumatic events again without intentionally thinking about them, in the form of nightmares, flashbacks, or intrusive thoughts about the previous trauma. When this happens, the person feels a loss of control and a sense of powerlessness.
3. There is a numbness of emotions and an avoidance of anything that reminds the person of the abuse. Not surprisingly, this can lead to problems in relationships with others, isolation, and a loss of interest in other people and social activities. Victims come to believe that their abuser will find out everything they do and think.
4. The presence of any two or more specific symptoms indicating a higher than normal arousal response, such as generalized anxiety, panic attacks, phobias, sexual problems, hypervigilance to cues of further violence (indications of being easily startled, such as jumping when touched), suspiciousness, sleep problems, irritability, and outbursts of anger.

Dr. Walker explains that it is essential to recognize the battered woman syndrome as a terrified human being's normal response to an abnormal, dangerous situation. It is not a form of mental illness.

Another interesting theory, noted by psychologist Susan Forward, suggests that women who stay in violent relationships may be suffering from what is known as the "Stockholm syndrome." This is a syndrome that was first identified by sociologists who studied a group of people who had been held as hostages during a bank holdup in Sweden. Oddly, when the crisis was over, the hostages defended their captors, and projected positive motives onto them for their crimes. The sociologists found a tendency in such people to do this in order to try and find safety in a dangerous situation. This could help explain why battered women sometimes buy into their abuser's statements that he is trying to make her better, punishing her for "her own good" so that she can become a better person.

People suffering from these disorders are not considered mentally ill, though many psychologists feel that professional counseling is important to help the victim fully recover and begin to enjoy life again. Usually, when a woman gets free of the abusive home, the "abnormal" coping behavior disappears, although she may suffer other long-term effects of having been traumatized.

Looking at the psychological effects of prolonged battering adds a whole new dimension to the question, "Why doesn't she leave?" A woman living in an abusive home may be subjected to both intermittent reinforcement and learned helplessness, two of the most powerful control techniques, either of which could be sufficient to distort her perception of reality to the point that she is completely unable to do what is generally considered to be "normal" behavior. This enhances the common belief among abused women that there is something wrong with them. PTSD can cause severe difficulty in coping with everyday challenges. Psychologists have described PTSD as one of the most accurate diagnoses to explain common aftereffects of domestic violence. It is not a form of "craziness," but rather a normal response to abnormal life events. Yet it can render a person incapable of accessing her inner resources to make a change.

A woman living with a batterer is caught up in a very complex relationship that can trap her emotionally. The "honeymoon phase" of Dr. Walker's cycle of violence can be every bit as insidious as the violence. A woman who wants to hold her family together is presented with the ideal man—the ardent lover, the generous provider, the Prince Charming of her girlhood dreams. It is easy to see how she can become blinded by the false hope that this time he means it, he really will change. Then the tension starts building again.

Even when the honeymoon phase is brief, or where there are merely short respites from violence, it allows the woman an opportunity to become numb to the reality of the situation. As the cycle continues, the woman becomes physically and mentally exhausted. The control tactics can virtually destroy her ability to think clearly. Her perceptions are distorted to the point where she believes she is incompetent, she deserves to be abused, and that she can't leave.

Battered women who manage to keep an optimistic outlook may have an even more difficult time breaking free. They often keep hoping, praying, and trying to change themselves, convinced that the relationship will get better and the abuse will stop. One woman compared loving an abuser with the love a mother feels for her children—even when they're "bad," you still love them. Having come from an unstable background, this woman found it especially difficult to leave her abuser when he offered her two young sons attention and affection and 95 percent of the time made her happier than she had ever been. He worked two jobs to support the family, and still found time to clean the apartment and take the boys to the park. But when his brutality surfaced, he became a monster who left her with a broken eardrum and scars covering her body. When she finally left him for good, this woman acknowledged that she was better off, even lonely and living in a homeless shelter.

What about women who *do* get out? Is there one particular event that triggers their decision to leave? Many do leave at the first sign of violence. For others, there is a last straw, some specific action or information that changes their perception of the situation. Often, it is a direct threat to their children. One woman decided to leave when her husband began beating her as she held their two-month-old baby.

Another heard her husband making inappropriate remarks about sex to their thirteen-year-old daughter, and when she confronted him, he threw an iron skillet at her head—at which point she left forever with her purse, her daughter, and a little over a dollar in change. One woman began taking steps toward leaving when her eight-year-old son started making degrading, disrespectful remarks to her—just like he heard his father doing.

Other women take action when they suddenly realize their life could be in danger. One began packing after a friend showed her a news story detailing the gruesome murder of a woman by her abusive husband and bluntly stated, "This could be you." *Time* reported that in the week after O. J. Simpson was charged with the murder of his ex-wife and her friend, calls to domestic violence hotlines across the nation surged to record numbers. In Los Angeles, calls increased by 80 percent. Sometimes a dramatic event is required for a woman to realize the potential meaning of "Til death do us part."

For some, a new sense of empowerment from getting a job, earning a degree, or improving their financial resources triggers the change. Some concrete achievement gives them the confidence that they can survive on their own. The first time a woman stands up to her abuser and demands he stop may give her a sense of power, something to build upon until she has gathered all the resources she needs to leave.

Sometimes it happens when an acquaintance or physician sees the scars and bruises and expresses horror, or doubts the old story about walking into a door. Some seem to hit an emotional rock bottom, then slowly find the light at the surface that draws them out. "I felt dead inside—I couldn't fight back, and I couldn't feel sorry for him any more," said one woman.

Not all women pack up and flee the moment this new reality hits them. But most take some positive step that signals a turning point—calling a hotline, seeking counseling, filing for divorce, picking up a book on domestic violence at the library. The most important aspect is the altered view of her life, which many compare to an awakening, that leads to the first step taken toward change.

Dr. Gelles found that women who sought help or left violent men tended to experience more frequent or severe violence, experienced less violence as children, and usually had more education or job skills than those who stayed. Yet all who have studied family violence caution against oversimplification, and stress the fact that many factors go into the making of a violent home: personal, cultural, social, learned behaviors, the environment inside and outside the family, expectations, and history.

Women who suffer abuse over long periods of time can be injured in many different ways. Death and severe physical injury are not unusual, with battering now the number one cause of injury to all American women between the ages of fifteen and forty-four. Extreme psychological damage is also possible, and may be so severe that it is utterly debilitating—especially when post-traumatic stress syndrome occurs.

Even women who have left violent relationships early, and who appear to have none of the more severe problems, report various aftereffects that mar their ability to enjoy life. Many suffer from a vague fear of nonthreatening situations, overreaction to minor disturbances, or the feeling of being stalked by a known or unknown menace. Many remain anxious, jumpy, sick with fear, and terrified of men for months or even years after getting the abuser out of their lives. When they are able to form new relationships with men, many react with involuntary terror at innocuous or even affectionate gestures, such as when the man walks up behind them and touches them. Therefore, most experts recommend some form of therapy as beneficial for any woman who has suffered domestic abuse.

COMPLICATING FACTORS IN THE ABUSIVE RELATIONSHIP

Domestic violence occurs in all kinds of homes. In some, other factors, such as geographic location, race, immigrant status, or sexual orientation, present special complications that change the picture in some way. Many of these families face special challenges.

Rural Women

Women in rural areas are presented with a host of unique circumstances. In addition to a lack of special services for domestic violence victims, such as shelters, many suffer from a lack of basic amenities such as reliable telephone systems, 911 service, reliable roads, available transportation, sources of child care, social services, even gas for vehicles. Those who have spent their lives in rural settings or small communities often feel uncomfortable or intimidated by larger cities, and may be reluctant to travel to seek help. In some areas, the criminal justice system remains mired in a "good old boy network" that condones inefficiency, backward attitudes, and resistance to change.

Women in farm or ranch families may also be concerned for land or livestock that depend on them for care. Sparse population means a long distance between neighbors, and contributes to psychological feelings of isolation. Just getting around may be difficult and, in many places, mobility ceases in bad weather. Migrant farm workers face all of these problems, in addition to the stress and isolation of constantly moving, long hours, poverty, substandard housing, and language barriers.

Yet grassroots organizers in rural areas continue the pioneer spirit of their forebears in new ways. The strong women who settled outlying areas and adapted to the harsh conditions provide an inspiring heritage that is still evident in many country communities. Volunteers in rural areas are usually sensitive to the special needs of the women they serve. Community spirit tends to be strong when people decide to work on a problem together, although most programs have only a few volunteers who must wear many hats.

Cooperation between various public and private agencies is especially important in rural programs, as is training that stresses what has changed, and what works, in other communities with similar needs and problems. Communication and rapport among different individuals and groups seem especially important in the neighborly yet skeptical atmosphere of many small towns. One advocate from a small southern rural community reported that the volunteers spent a good deal of time just "hanging out with the good old boys," building relationships that ranged from tolerance to friendship. As in most settings where people with diverse views must work together, rapport and a constant building of trust are essential. Local power structures need to be shown that ending violence in homes is an important, common goal, that domestic violence is indeed a serious problem in the eyes of their fellow professionals as well as the people of the community, and that something has been done about it in similar areas.

Rural communities often take pride in self-reliance and may be reluctant to seek government funding for local projects, so local involvement and support become especially crucial. One rural Virginia group effectively used a community development approach to set up a shelter in only three months. It approached individuals, civic clubs, merchants, and other local groups for both financial and volunteer support. Even the most conservative groups came forth with help, and together the community provided a house, renovation materials, food, clothing, utilities, furniture, and human services. Not only did the town experience pride in its ownership of the project, it also became aware of the problem of domestic violence and its importance, as well as the need for continuing education and attention.

Older Women

According to an AARP report, older women who are abused by their husbands or partners face the problems of both battered wives and abused elders, yet may be falling through the cracks in both the elder abuse and domestic violence communities. When the AARP planned a forum to bring together professionals from both areas to discuss how to constrain this problem, a small article in the AARP forum seeking input from older battered women drew an alarming response. More than five hundred letters arrived during the first month, including letters from women in their 80s who had suffered abuse for as long as 50 years. Many reported that they had sought help from various professionals, including the police and the clergy, only to be told the abuse was their fault. Abused elders are more likely to continue to live with their abusers than younger victims. Older women of color reported additional barriers and greater difficulty getting help.

Following the forum, the AARP urged that certain changes be made to make assistance more available to older women, including shelters that take into account the special needs of older women, with special attention to rural communities and multicultural considerations; better outreach and dissemination of information to older women through such places as senior centers, health clinics, and public benefits offices; coordination between the elder abuse and domestic violence communities; and advocacy programs to provide a supportive sister-to-sister or "buddy" network between recently and formerly battered women.

The AARP Women's Initiative has developed a directory of services for older battered women, "Spouse/Partner Abuse in Later Life: A Resource Manual for Service Providers." The manual, which provides information on domestic violence and offers strategies for outreach, detection, and intervention as well as program development and a listing of resources, is available from the AARP Women's Initiative (see the appendix).

Battering in Black Relationships

In her book *Chain, Chain, Change: For Black Women in Abusive Relationships*, Evelyn C. White says that the experience of domestic violence is different for Black women. She explains that in the African American culture, women are often viewed as both subhuman and superhuman. They are expected to be monoliths of strength, yet are scorned as inferior. These stereotypes can contribute to a woman's feelings of confusion, insecurity, and inferiority caused by abuse. Unfortunately, Black women, perhaps more often than battered women of other races, often see the abuse as something to be ashamed of, rather than something to overcome. White urges Black women to look at the situation differently, and to realize that no amount of good cooking, love, or attention will stop an abusive man.

Many Black women have a tendency to put the needs of others before their own—especially the needs of their male partners. White points out that Black men are more scarce in the community than Caucasian men due to the higher incidence of early death, plus unnaturally high rates of unemployment and incarceration. Black women may be more likely to endure an abusive relationship to keep a man. White emphasizes that remaining in such a relationship does neither partner any favor. She states that it is important to hold a partner accountable for the injuries he inflicts, both to end the woman's own pain and to stop him from engaging in behavior that is destructive to her, the family, and himself. She urges women to move beyond a victimized status, to take responsibility for themselves, and to make their partners do the same.

Also, the presence of racism, especially in institutions designed to deal with domestic violence such as law enforcement, courts, and social service agencies may add to the tension and frustration. Some research suggests that women of color are less likely than White women to use shelters and similar services, relying instead on family, friends, or the health care system. Other societal factors unique to the Black experience may also be partially to blame. White says that Black men often experience a sense of powerlessness in society, which contributes to an abuse of power in the family.

Black author Rosemary Bray, writing in Ms. about growing up in a violent home, describes how her father used to say that "nobody was ever going to run all over him." Yet, at that time, she says, White people were free to run all over him, and by the time the changes of the 1960s began, his hopes and possibilities were behind him. All that remained was his family—the only people he believed he could control.

Recent statistics indicate that domestic violence in Black homes is declining. Yet it is still far too common. Black women are three times more likely to be murdered in domestic violence than white women. Evelyn White urges abused Black women to talk about the pressures they feel and share experiences with other Black women who have endured—and overcome—similar issues. Support groups that meet at shelters or other social service centers in predominantly Black areas can provide this type of interaction.

Other Minorities

Battered women in other minority groups also face special problems. Cultural factors, ethnic traditions, and isolation may contribute to abuse in relationships. For example, Jewish women sometimes face both stereotyping within their own community as well as anti-semitic attitudes and accusations. Traditional Jewish religious law may also pose obstacles for a woman seeking separation or divorce, yet wishing to remain a part of her religious sect. Many of the groups listed in the appendix provide special materials, information, referrals, and assistance targeted toward minority women, including Latinas, Jewish women, Asians, and Native Americans. Domestic violence coalitions in states with large populations of specific ethnic groups often provide special services and materials as well. The Duluth Domestic Abuse Intervention Project, for example, publishes a wealth of materials about violence in Native American families. Additionally, articles and books dealing with the special needs of minority women are listed in the Resources and Suggested Readings section.

Immigrant and Refugee Women

Women who are not legal U.S. citizens are sometimes reluctant to seek services because they believe they will be sent away or turned over to the Immigration and Naturalization Service (INS). However, shelters and medical providers generally keep information provided to them confidential, and police seldom turn in a woman reporting domestic violence to the INS. A woman need not be a citizen or legal permanent resident to get a protective order. In addition to shelter workers, court personnel, and legal aid providers, immigrant women may be able to get help from an immigrant advocacy group. Public aid, housing, food, and other services should also be available regardless of a woman's status, though laws may vary from state to state. An immigrant woman can also get a divorce, although this may affect her residency status, depending upon the circumstances. Under the 1994 Federal Violence Against Women Act, special protections are provided for aliens, including suspension of deportation for battered spouses and children. Any woman concerned about her current status and how various steps she may wish to take could affect that status should consult an immigration attorney or other qualified advisor. The National Coalition Against Domestic Violence produces a pamphlet especially for immigrant and refugee women. The National Network for Battered Immigrant Women trains service providers to help battered immigrant women identify lawyers who will work pro bono (without charge) to help them gain legal status to remain in the United States. For more information, contact the National Immigration Project at (617) 227-9727. The address and telephone of the NCADV, and other organizations that can help, are listed in the appendix.

Battering in Same-Sex Relationships

Many of the experts studying the widespread nature of domestic violence believe the problem may be even more common among gay and lesbian couples. The National Coalition Against Domestic Violence estimates that battering may occur in as many as one in three same-sex relationships.

According to a report published by the National Lesbian and Gay Health Foundation, battering in same-sex relationships is similar to violence in heterosexual relationships in many ways. Abuse in homosexual relationships can be physical, sexual, or emotional; it often occurs in a cyclical fashion; it can be lethal; its purpose is power and control of one partner over another; routine intimidation may be used to gain power; the abused person feels isolated; and the victim often believes it is his or her fault.

However, important differences exist. Gays and lesbians in violent relationships usually have much more difficulty in finding appropriate support. Those who do use existing services must necessarily reveal their sexual preference to others, although most shelters and related services will keep information about those who seek help confidential. However, this may still mean confronting a major life decision an individual may not be prepared to make. For those who have not yet "come out," the threat of publicly revealing a partner's homosexuality, especially to parents, employers, and relatives can give the abusive partner another weapon for control.

Social attitudes against homosexuality also make it difficult for battered gays and lesbians to find support and compassion. Stereotypes and bigotry against homosexuals persist. Even within the homosexual community, there may be a reluctance to acknowledge social problems, which could further fuel prejudice and homophobia among the hetero-sexual community.

Isolation is a special issue for abused gays and lesbians. In an area where there are few other homosexuals, the abused partner may feel very alone. Even in areas with large gay populations, the community tends to be small enough that people know one another, so it is difficult to find support yet maintain privacy. There is also a persistent myth that batter-ing in same-sex relationships is mutual "fighting," as opposed to one partner dominating and battering the other.

Fortunately, information and special services for gays and lesbians in violent relationships are becoming more abundant. Several books deal-ing with the unique circumstances faced by battered gays and lesbians are now available, and a number of organizations, including the National Coalition Against Domestic Violence and other local and national groups, offer assistance. Additional information is listed in the appendix and Resources and Suggested Readings section at the end of this book.

Battered Men

What about men who are battered? Certainly some men are physically abused by partners, especially in gay relationships, and some are battered by women. According to the U.S. Justice Department, as many as 24,000 men per year report being physically assaulted by intimate partners. Yet this accounts for only two to five percent of the battering in abusive rela-tionships, so the emphasis of study and services has been, understandably, on battered women. However, the suffering of abused men should not be ignored simply because their numbers are relatively small.

The limited amount of research that has been conducted shows that while psychological traits of battered men and battered women are simi-lar, there are key differences that make the nature and severity of the abuse different for men. Male victims suffer fewer physical injuries from abuse, at least in heterosexual relationships, simply because most women can't hit as hard as men. Also, it appears that men are less likely to stay in abusive relationships for a long period. This is partially due to social and cultural factors, such as boys being raised to be self-reliant, the pri-mary child-rearing responsibilities being placed on women, and the greater financial resources generally available to men.

Yet, the dynamics of the relationship in which men are abused appear to be similar to that of the more common male-abuser–female-victim relationship. Abusive women tend to be controlling, possessive, unpre-dictable in their outbursts, and very jealous. Some believe that while physically abusive women are comparatively rare, many more psycholog-ically or emotionally abuse their male partners, which can be as devastating, if not as immediately dangerous.

Men tend to suffer the same torments as women as long as they stay in abusive relationships, including shock, unexpressed anger, misplaced guilt, and agony over whether to stay or go. One man who spent three years with a woman who was both emotionally and occasionally physi-cally abusive reported suffering many of the same aftereffects common to women who have left, such as fear, mistrust, and the inability to estab-lish another intimate relationship. Those who stay generally stay for the same reason women do—fear, dependence, or a desire to keep the family together for the children. Men too can be beaten and tortured into a state of learned helplessness, as the tragedy of war has shown.

When abused men leave, their experiences tend to be much different that those of their female counterparts. They are less likely to tell anyone the truth about the breakup, and must face sexist attitudes from many sources. Police tend to disbelieve the male victim or expect any man to be able to protect himself from any woman. In our society there is still criticism of men who seek help for "personal" problems and, again, there is the lingering perception of domestic violence as a "family matter."

Men who do speak up risk scorn, gossip, and the public spotlight. Because such abuse is relatively unusual, or at least unreported, the cases that do come before the public eye are often sensationalized. Consider the case of Lorena Bobbitt, who cut off her husband's penis, claiming he had abused her for years and raped her earlier in the day. The story was exploited worldwide. TV actress Shannen Doherty has been accused of assault by a former boyfriend, and this, too, made international headlines.

The media frenzy that often accompanies reports of male abuse is detrimental not only to the victim, but to other men who become reluctant to seek help, and especially to women, who are portrayed as equally likely to be perpetrators as victims—a gross distortion of the real picture.

Unfortunately, there are few services for battered men, and some end up in homeless shelters, which may or may not offer additional assistance. One shelter for battered men opened in Great Britain in 1992, but closed its doors before long, presumably due to few users. Communities with a large gay population are beginning to establish services for gay males, but the heterosexual man abused by a female partner may find little help available. Also, due to the way boys are socialized in this culture, an abused man will often be ashamed and embarrassed to seek help from law enforcement, social service agencies, or other sources. Of course, private psychologists and counselors can provide confidential help, and most social service agencies are open to all who need them. More and more male support groups are being established to help men with a wide variety of problems. Admitting personal difficulties and seeking help no longer carries such a strong stigma of weakness or failure.

The suffering of abused men should not be taken lightly, and all services to victims of abuse should be free of sex discrimination. Yet it makes sense that the majority of resources and programs are geared toward women, when they account for 95 percent of the victims. In the final analysis, it comes down to the simple right of all people to live lives free of brutality, and this right should be applied equally to everyone by those working to end domestic violence.

CHAPTER FOUR

SOCIAL ASPECTS OF DOMESTIC VIOLENCE

Much of what goes on outside the home also has a hand in shaping the conditions that allow domestic violence to continue—and those that work toward its demise. A wide range of social and cultural forces help shape the attitudes of individuals. Chapter 2 outlines the role history has played in both perpetuating domestic violence and setting the stage for change. Today's world continues to affect our opinions and behavior in both positive and negative ways.

Some believe people today have become desensitized to violence by the common occurrence of all types of brutality. We are surrounded by violence on the street, in the media, on the news, in sports, in war, virtually everywhere. The pervasiveness of violence outside the home may make it more acceptable in the home as well.

The way children in American culture are raised is also an important factor. Despite the changes of the past few decades, our educational, religious, military, and recreational institutions still tend to encourage boys to be aggressive, authoritarian, and to refrain from showing emotion. Such conduct is considered "manly." The sports culture had been accused of having a hand in encouraging violence. Certain sports do emphasize physical force and domination of opponents. Yet others believe that sports provide a healthy outlet for male aggression.

At the same time, girls are raised to be passive, submissive, and gentle—traits traditionally considered feminine. Women's roles have changed dramatically over the past century, yet women are still denied equal access to many of the opportunities available to men. Women still suffer from discrimination on the job, and only earn an average of seventy-four cents for each dollar earned by men. There are very real financial barriers to economic stability for many women, and many in abusive relationships stay because they do not believe they can support themselves and their children independently.

Cultural attitudes toward domestic violence itself also contribute to its proliferation. We are trained to respect our neighbor's privacy, which gives us a good excuse to look the other way when we suspect something ugly may be going on behind the drawn curtains. We tell ourselves we're "minding our own business" when we ignore crashes and screams, perhaps even police cars late at night.

There are many social factors and institutions that contribute to society's behavior and attitudes toward domestic violence, in both good and bad ways. A few of the more important influences are discussed below. The civil and criminal justice systems, which of course play a huge part in both social attitudes about domestic violence and what is—or is not—done to stop it, are discussed in the next chapter.

SUBSTANCE ABUSE AND DOMESTIC VIOLENCE

What about drinking and drugs? Many women report that their partners only become abusive when under the influence, leading some to conclude that substance abuse causes domestic violence. But the experts agree that while there is often a connection between the two, alcohol or drugs do not *cause* domestic violence. That there is some relationship between alcohol abuse and violence is clear, but what the relationship is remains puzzling.

Alcoholism and drug abuse do increase the risk of domestic violence.

But as with the other factors that contribute to chances of violence happening in a home (like unemployment, for example) they are *separate* problems. Many abusers never use drugs or alcohol; many who are addicted never become abusive. Men who batter women while under the influence of intoxicants have to be abusive people to begin with. Alcohol or drugs can remove the inhibitions that keep them from beating their partners when they're sober, and do tend to increase the risk of severe injury or death during battering episodes. But they can't turn peaceful people into abusers without the traits that make a person violent already in place. Above all, intoxication should never be accepted as an excuse for battering.

Undeniably, the connection between substance abuse and domestic violence needs further study. A team of physicians who worked with the Memphis police department in conducting a 1995 study of domestic violence calls found that two-thirds of the assailants had used a combination of cocaine and alcohol on the day of the assault. The team recommended greater attention to the connection between substance abuse and battering, including evaluation of the batterer at the scene or after arrest by police. Many physicians emphasize that integration of legal intervention and counseling to stop substance abuse by perpetrators is overdue.

THE MEDIA

The entertainment and news media have been alternately cursed and blessed in recent years for their treatment of domestic violence issues. Certainly this powerful institution can be an extremely valuable tool for disseminating information on services, reporting crimes and consequences, educating a broad segment of the public, raising money and volunteer support for shelters and other organizations, and shaping public attitudes.

Battered women's advocacy groups have launched their own media campaigns to make victims of abuse aware of their legal rights and remedies, to educate the public about domestic violence, to publicize hotlines and shelters, and to warn batterers that family violence is a crime. Newspapers that move stories of domestic violence to the forefront contribute to a public perception that it is an important issue. In 1994, New York City Mayor Rudolph Giuliani launched a poster campaign using photographs provided by Domestic Abuse Awareness, Inc. to educate subway and bus passengers about domestic violence. Television stations frequently air programs that portray the gritty reality and potential consequences of domestic violence, and broadcast public service announcements at appropriate times, such as during the Super Bowl (various reports show that, for some reason, Super Bowl Sunday is the most violent day of the year).

Of course, there is a flip side. The downside of extensive media coverage cannot be ignored. Abusers very often use death threats to control and terrorize their victims, and many report being told that what happened to Nicole Brown Simpson or other women who died will happen to them if they don't "shape up" or "behave themselves." Movies and music videos in particular have been criticized for mixing violence with sex and portraying women in inaccurate, inappropriate ways.

But today, the scope of the media is nearly boundless, with new newspapers, magazines, and cable TV channels appearing almost daily. The best way to deal with negative or false messages is usually to counter them with the truth. Publicity about domestic violence, what it is, the damage it causes, and, perhaps most important, what works to stop it, can be an extraordinarily powerful tool for change. Popular media figures, such as Malik Yoba, of the TV drama "New York Undercover," have become involved. Yoba did a 1997 radio spot in which he urged listeners of a popular Los Angeles radio talk show to refrain from violence against women and each other and offered suggestions for more positive ways to channel negative energy. Actor Ben Savage donated his time to narrate the video for children entitled, "It's Not OK: Let's Talk About Domestic Violence," produced by the American Bar Association in conjunction with the Walt Disney Company. Actor Danny Glover has lent his support to help raise funds for the Family Violence Prevention Fund.

High-profile court cases also draw attention to needed changes in social and government policy. After a battered woman named Tracy Thurman won a landmark civil rights case against the police department that failed to protect her and a TV movie was made chronicling her story, policies and practices changed in police stations across the nation. Much of the news regarding domestic violence issues does not get the publicity it deserves, but anyone can help remedy this by writing letters to the editors of local newspapers, contacting television stations about stories, and making other small efforts. The public appetite for a good story is insatiable, and reporters are always looking for a scoop.

There is a tremendous emphasis today not only on protecting victims and punishing offenders, but on changing the attitudes that permit violence against women to continue. The efforts of ordinary people who spoke out, wrote letters, campaigned, and worked deserve credit for getting us this far. Such efforts can continue to move us toward the day when domestic violence will be a part of our history—not our future.

THE INTERNET

According to Robert E. McAfee, M.D., past president of the American Medical Association, every 12 seconds a woman suffers from some sort of violence or abuse at the hands of her spouse, boyfriend, or significant other. McAfee, who has characterized domestic violence as terrorism in the home, notes that more years of life are lost to violence in American society than to heart disease, cancer, and stroke combined.

The Internet is a remarkable resource for information, guidance, and shared ideas on domestic violence. Many of the organizations listed in the appendix have their own web sites with links to other sites with related materials. Additionally, more and more state and local coalitions are developing sites to help individuals and other groups connect with local sources of information and assistance.

For those without personal access to the Internet, many public libraries offer free use of their computers to access the world wide web, as well as brief classes that teach the basics on how to use the vast array of resources on the Internet. Bookstores, community centers, schools, and computer shops also offer classes, many free of charge.

HEALTH CARE

According to Robert E. McAfee, M.D., past president of the American Medical Association, every 12 seconds a woman suffers from some sort of violence or abuse at the hands of her spouse, boyfriend, or significant other. McAfee, who has characterized domestic violence as terrorism in the home, notes that more years of life are lost to violence in American society than to heart disease, cancer, and stroke combined.

In 1985, U.S. Surgeon General C. Everett Koop described domestic violence as a public health menace. The impact of family violence on the physical, emotional, and mental health of its victims is almost impossible to calculate because so much of the damage goes untreated and unreported. Even if only the reported and reliably estimated violence is considered, the statistics are devastating. Remember, domestic abuse is the leading cause of injury to women between the ages of fifteen and forty-four. Between one-fifth and one-third of women who are treated in hospital emergency rooms are there because of battering. Between 20 percent and 50 percent of the women admitted to hospitals for emergency surgery have been hurt by a male partner.

According to the American Academy of Orthopedic Surgeons, "Violence is a disease with many causes, and the medical community is uniquely positioned to have an important role in reducing its prevalence and the pain and suffering that results. Because the incidence of violence continues to increase, it is imperative that physicians increase their efforts to curb this epidemic."

Battered women have unique needs that require special attention from health care professionals in prevention, screening, and treatment. Yet many physicians have little or no training in the area of domestic violence. Two emergency medicine specialists I spoke with—a doctor and a nurse—complained that their efforts to get the dean of a major medical school to require more specific training on domestic abuse in the curriculum for all medical students have fallen on deaf ears.

However, there is every indication that positive changes are occurring in the medical community, as both individual care providers and organizations become more aware and sensitive to the unique needs of domestic violence victims. In 1994, the American Academy of Facial

Plastic and Reconstructive Surgery (AAFPRS) entered into a unique partnership with the National Coalition Against Domestic Violence to assist victims of domestic abuse who have suffered facial injuries and need surgery to repair the damage from assaults. The service, called the National Domestic Violence Project, founded by plastic surgeon Dr. Lori Hansen, provides reconstructive surgery for victims of abuse without charge. As of early 1996, some five hundred women had been helped. Such surgery can free women from the constant reminder of the violence they have suffered, and help to restore their self-esteem. A toll-free number has been set up for use by advocates and victims (see appendix). The Project will refer victims to participating physicians in the victim's local area, whenever possible.

More and more emphasis is being placed on the danger of strangulation in domestic violence cases. Choking is peculiarly common in domestic violence cases, far more so than in stranger assaults. What form of control could be more intimate than controlling a person's ability to breathe? Strangulation is both a serious warning sign that this is an extremely vicious abuser and a potential medical crisis that must be monitored closely. A victim who has been strangled may exhibit only mild injuries at first, then die within 36 hours as internal swelling increases.

An attempt by an abuser to strangle his victim is taken very seriously by most prosecutors. Such cases can be prosecuted as aggravated battery with intent to cause great bodily harm, which is a felony. Officers need to be trained to understand the medical aspects of such injuries—such as the fact that marks on a victim's neck may not appear for several hours after the assault—and to ask the right questions, such as whether she became dizzy, saw stars, or lost consciousness, in order to correctly define the crime. Medical personnel, too, must be aware of the peculiar nature of strangulation injuries. A victim who does not seem to be seriously injured yet speaks in a raspy voice, has red eyes or broken blood vessels in her cheeks, or has trouble catching her breath may have suffered extremely severe injuries which will manifest over the next day or so as internal swelling occurs in the neck. Some physicians are routinely ordering cat scans for all choking victims, and/or admitting them to intensive care units for 48 hours of close observations. In some areas, physicians are presenting seminars to teach police officers how to recognize symptoms of strangulation in a victim that is too hurt or terrified to give an account of what happened.

The emergency room is the first place many abused women find themselves after an outburst of violence. Sensitive treatment and communication is especially critical at this stage. Bob Henry, M.D., an emergency medicine specialist who has worked in Albuquerque, New Mexico, for twenty years, believes that one-on-one intervention is essential.

In his practice, a specific procedure is followed when a domestic violence victim enters the emergency room. First, a nurse screens the patient and reports the nature of the injuries to the doctor. Next, Dr. Henry calms the patient with a bit of casual conversation and asks what happened. The patient usually states that she and her husband or boyfriend had an argument or that he beat her up. "These patients show an incredible mix of emotions," he says. "They're usually crying, and experiencing embarrassment, anger, fear, and frustration. Their emotional suffering is often worse than the physical pain. I tend to see relatively minor injuries in my practice, primarily bruises and cuts. But they feel so demeaned in many ways, similar to rape victims."

After examining the patient and treating her injuries, Dr. Henry makes notes and documents injuries. He is careful to note the cause of injury on the medical report as assault by husband or boyfriend when the patient so states. While medical reports are not given to the patients, they are made available to the police, the district attorney, or the patient's private attorney. Dr. Henry has never personally been questioned by a district attorney or called to testify in court on a domestic violence case, though he has testified in a number of rape cases.

The woman is asked whether she has called the police, and while the majority still report that they have not, Dr. Henry has found that the number of victims who do seek to press charges has increased to nearly 50 percent over the past five years. If the woman hasn't yet reported the crime but wishes to do so, the hospital calls the local Domestic Abuse Intervention Unit (DART) of the Albuquerque Police Department, and a specially trained police officer comes to the hospital.

Dr. Henry also asks whether the abuser is at the hospital (which he rarely is, in the doctor's experience) and whether this has happened before. Most report that it has. "I believe we see just the tip of the iceberg," he says. "Women rarely come in the first time they are assaulted, unless their injuries are very severe."

Dr. Henry also asks his patients if they are going to return to the home upon being released from the hospital. If they have another place to go—such as patients who show up with a friend or relative—they will be discharged. If not, the situation becomes trickier. "We have two options in that case. The local women's shelter has been a marvelous ally. We call to see if they can take the patient, and I don't recall a single instance in which someone has been turned away. We get a cab or the police to take her there. But it's more tricky if children are involved. If there are children still in the home with a dangerous man, we call child protective services, who investigate with the police. A social worker and an officer usually go get the children. Or we can call adult protective services, especially if the victim is an older person. But we can only offer this help when the woman wants it."

One of the greatest frustrations faced by health care professionals lies in deciding how to help the patient who admits being battered, yet declines offers of help. "In this case, we call psychiatric nurses who come in and meet with the patient, and act as a liaison with the doctors," he explains. "Sometimes we're so busy and overwhelmed, it's hard to get our empathy across and spend the time with the woman that she needs. The nurse can sit down and talk to her, and try to come up with a treatment plan that will at least get her some counseling and support." The final backup is provided by a hospital social worker, who can help develop a discharge plan that may include site visits to the home. If a woman has been sexually assaulted, the rape crisis center may also be called.

New Mexico physicians have another alternative to which they can turn as a last resort when a patient is distraught and believed to be in great danger. "Under the mental health code, all I have to do is document that a patient is emotionally impaired, and we can hold her at the hospital until some form of intervention arrives, with hospital security standing by. It's a valuable tool in extreme cases."

Dr. Henry has been the chair of the emergency medicine department in his hospital for fourteen years. He is disturbed by statistics that suggest physicians very often misdiagnose or fail to recognize domestic abuse in a high percentage of cases. "At least in emergency medicine, the physicians and nurses take a very active approach to screening for domestic violence, and we do a lot of intervention. I think most health care professionals have the capability and capacity to determine abuse has occurred and to intervene in the vast majority of cases. In emergency medicine, we've always been very aware of the indications of abuse. It's very difficult to miss the signs if you're aware of what to look for. The victim is usually crying, withdrawn, and frightened. Her injuries tend to have a characteristic pattern, including multiple contusions all over her body that indicate an assault rather than a fall or other type of injury. There are subtle cues you learn to pick up, too. I think it's relatively rare to see someone who has just been beaten up and not know. Occasionally, there will be an aberrant situation in which it's hard to tell what's going on. But these cases are rare."

Dr. Henry believes that direct, one-on-one intervention and follow-up are essential. "We tried handing out brochures for awhile, but found them out in the parking lot. We need to involve all of these resource people, and give them time to work with the patient. Once I know or have a high suspicion that a woman has been battered, I alert them and let them delve into how to best help the patient. We have to be sure her safety is a priority before she is released."

Hospital personnel often follow up to check on a woman's safety after she is released and to remind her of her options. "Sometimes we arrange for a nursing visit two or three times after the woman leaves to make sure she is in a safe environment. First and foremost, she needs to be told that this is not her fault. Along with the embarrassment, anger, and frustration, so many of these women feel guilt. Sometimes on a busy night, where someone is having a heart attack in the next cubicle and someone else is bleeding across the hall, I simply can't take the time to sit down and talk with a victim at length. But I always make a point of telling her that the abuse is not her fault."

Beyond these preliminary steps, Dr. Henry has to rely on his own instincts to determine how to best help each woman. "I see a lot of the same women in here over and over. You have to try and decide what will work with each individual. Sometimes a very gentle approach is required; but others need someone with a take-charge attitude to give them the tough facts so they'll accept help. Sometimes I tell a patient that if she returns to her abuser, I will see her in here again, or see her dead. It's a balance you have to have throughout emergency medicine. Emergency room doctors are great manipulators—we have to manipulate patients and other doctors and get coercive sometimes to get our job done. I'm fortunate to have great partners, and a wonderful community support system."

Though Dr. Henry has not extensively studied the social and psychological research on domestic violence, his own experiences tend to parallel most of the commonly accepted findings. He believes 99 percent of his domestic abuse patients are women, and has seen only two to three male abuse victims in his twenty years of emergency practice.

Likewise, Dr. Henry often sees the cycle of violence in his practice. "I ask women how their partners are treating them now, and most report that they are remorseful, loving, and sorry—which naturally makes many of them go back, which starts the whole process over again. I see some women over and over, though not as many now that more support services are available. There are certainly no cultural, ethnic, or economic boundaries. Domestic violence tends to be universal." Like obstetrical nurse Mary Blick, he believes that women in white-collar families and in small communities or rural areas tend to be less likely to report abuse than lower-income women living in cities. "There is more anonymity in a big city hospital," he says. Also, he notices a good many of his patients have a very distorted view of the reality of their lives. "Many are psychologically incapable of leaving unless they get intervention and support."

Dr. Henry says the greatest change he has witnessed in his years of emergency practice is the increase in community awareness and resources for his domestic abuse patients. "All we had for many years was the shelter. Now, there are many services, and they are coordinated very well. I can see why the integrated efforts are so important." Dr. Henry is involved in one such effort, conducting a training class to teach police officers how to recognize signs of potentially life-threatening strangulation injuries in domestic violence victims. Yet he sees room for improvement. "We aren't all aware of what the others in the system provide, or well versed about other aspects of the overall problem. For example, I never deal with batterers in my practice, so I really know nothing about them beyond the basic behavior patterns that affect my patients, such as the likelihood it will happen again and the way they coerce the women into returning."

He also feels that services should be more accessible to victims. "It's too cumbersome—too hard for the victims to get into the medical system," he says. "They have to be hurt so badly that they really must have immediate treatment, or they have to have reached that turning point where they are ready for attention and help in changing their situation." He believes that many of the women who come to the emergency room with fairly minor injuries do not necessarily require medical attention. Instead, they are seeking intervention, a way to get into the network of services available.

There should be an easier way, he believes, for women to access both medical treatment and other services. "I believe that the vast, vast majority of abused women do not seek medical care," he says. "We estimate that at least 90 percent of all maladies are self-treated, mostly because of the expense and difficulty many people find in getting to a hospital or clinic."

Dr. Henry has also served as medical director of the Albuquerque Ambulance Service since 1976, and believes that there is much room for expansion of services to domestic violence victims on the scene. "Currently, paramedics can give victims only two choices—go to the hospital or sign a letter of refusal. But with today's computerized communication systems, better mobility, and state-of-the-art equipment, paramedics and nurse practitioners can work under the supervision of physicians and begin to offer more services. New ways of using localized clinics and mobile services can make health care—and connected services—more available, affordable, and accessible to victims."

Physician education is also placing more emphasis on domestic violence. Dr. Henry, who studied before emergency medicine was a recognized specialty, says he received no training on domestic violence in medical school. He is now involved in the teaching program at the University of New Mexico (UNM) medical school. "Those of us who helped usher in the specialty had to learn through conferences and study on our own," he says. "There was no board specialty until 1980, and no residency program at the UNM medical school until 1985. But all that has changed. The UNM program, now one of the most sought-after in the country, places a great deal of emphasis on domestic violence, and it is covered extensively on the written and oral parts of the board exams. The American College of Emergency Physicians is very active in studying what actually goes on in the trenches, and has produced a position paper on treatment of domestic violence victims, with more study and work in the area going on all the time."

Dr. Henry, like many professionals who work with victims of abuse, expresses frustration in trying to help victims, while at the same time understanding the nature of their psychological circumstances and carefully avoiding placing any blame on the victim. "I know it happens to people from all cultures, walks of life, and economic levels," he says. "But it seems there would have to be something that makes a woman more susceptible, more liable to be victimized. I believe that low self-esteem does play a large part, and I realize that many of these women are incapable of leaving, and that to do so could be dangerous. But I can't help wanting to yell, 'Get out!' "

BATTERING AND PREGNANCY

Domestic violence poses a special risk to pregnant women. Battering often escalates when something changes in the violent home, and pregnancy—especially the first—may trigger an increase in abuse. According to a recent report in the *Journal of the American Medical Association* (*JAMA*), as many as 37 percent of all obstetrical patients may be abused while pregnant.

Physicians who ask patients about abuse can make an enormous difference in their lives. At the 1996 meeting of the American College of

Obstetricians and Gynecologists, the attending physicians were encouraged to routinely screen for abuse by carefully framing a series of brief questions designed to open the door for abused women to seek help, learn about resources, and shake off the stigma that may have kept them from asking for the assistance they need. The doctors were also advised that patients who often miss appointments, especially pregnant women, may be under the control of an abuser, and should be questioned further rather than automatically labeled "noncompliant."

Pregnant trauma victims need specialized care for two reasons. First, the physical changes a woman experiences during pregnancy may require adjustment in the usual methods of diagnosis and treatment. Second, the survival and recovery of the other patient—the fetus—depends on the health of both of the patients. Battered women are four times more likely to have low birth weight babies, and twice as likely to miscarry as other women. Abuse of pregnant women is a leading cause of infant mortality and birth defects. Yet prenatal and obstetrical health professionals have only recently begun to emphasize the importance of screening pregnant women for this risk, and such screening is not yet routine.

As a registered nurse with a certified specialty in obstetrics, Mary Blick only began asking patients about abuse after attending a March of Dimes seminar in 1993. "I was shocked to learn how common the problem is. Within the first day or two after returning to work after the seminar, I asked a woman who had come in with preterm labor about abuse. She told me her boyfriend had battered her, and she had taken out a restraining order against him."

Injury can trigger premature labor and other problems in the early stages of pregnancy. Women who are admitted to the hospital before their due date are given special attention. "Most of the time it comes to light when they come in with preterm labor," she says. However, Blick and many other obstetrical health care workers have begun screening all patients for abuse as a part of the general admission assessment. "I just ask them point blank, 'Does anyone hit you in your home?' or 'Does anyone ever hurt you?'" she says. "We have to ask a lot of very personal questions, so it's not hard to fit in one more. I do make sure to wait until the woman is alone. The biggest problem sometimes is getting the husband or boyfriend to leave, now that all the admission forms can be completed in one place. Some men won't leave, some even answer all of the questions for the woman and won't let her speak for herself. Since I've had the training to recognize that this may be a sign of the type of controlling behavior that occurs in abusive relationships, I make a special point of talking to the woman later, whenever possible, or sending our hospital social worker or pastoral care counselor to see her."

Blick described one couple that really worried her. The woman was from a Central American country, spoke only Spanish, and her husband would not allow her to take English lessons. He had a dominating manner, stayed with his wife throughout the screening and admissions process, and answered all of the questions for her, rather than interpreting. Blick was concerned for the woman's safety, but could not get an opportunity to speak with her alone. She had to wait until the woman was checked in, then she called the social worker.

The hospital where Mary Blick works employs a full-time social worker who visits any patient who may be at risk. She explains the services available in the community, and makes referrals if needed. Occasionally, a patient may be sent directly to a shelter or safe house if she is afraid to return home when she is discharged. Yet the social worker is not available around the clock, and her services must be requested by someone in direct contact with the patient.

Blick also expressed her concern that the hospital has no formal policies requiring screening for domestic violence. "After the March of Dimes presentation, I discussed what I learned with the other nurses at a unit meeting, and emphasized the importance of screening for abuse. But a lot of the nurses still don't ask. There isn't a specific question about violence on the assessment form, and the hospital doesn't have any specific protocol or policy on this issue. We do ask about the home environment, but that can be interpreted in different ways." She explained that for most of the fifteen years she has been working with obstetrical patients, the emphasis was placed on screening for drug or alcohol abuse. "After the March of Dimes seminar, I realized I hadn't been screening as I should have. A lot of health care workers still aren't."

Blick also feels that more screening should occur earlier in a woman's pregnancy. "We don't see patients until they're ready for delivery or have a preterm problem. Many women aren't questioned about battering during their prenatal exams. Earlier screening would really help. A woman in danger could at least be warned about the risk to herself and her baby and be told about the resources in the community so when she's ready to leave, or if she has a crisis, she will know she has somewhere to go."

Blick is frustrated by her patients' reluctance to admit they are battered. "We try to do all we can, but we can't offer professional intervention and safety assistance unless the woman admits it. Many claim to have fallen down the stairs. A few probably did, but now that I know the other signs, especially in the batterer's behavior, I know a lot of the injuries come from a direct assault. Even when they do acknowledge abuse, many go back. All we can do is talk to them, tell them about services, encourage them to file a police report, and make sure they know the man won't necessarily find out. We make sure they're familiar with the help available, and deal with related issues, like urging the young women to finish high school, that sort of thing."

This lack of required screening by all health care providers is one of the most often cited problems in the overall medical care of abuse victims. According to one survey, only half of the medical schools in the United States and Canada provide any special training on domestic assault, and those that do seldom require more than one ninety-minute session. Some estimates place the number of battered patients correctly diagnosed by physicians as only one in twenty-five. Even in cases identified as assaults, three out of four doctors do not ask the patient about her relationship to the assailant. Up to half of the nation's emergency rooms have no protocol for dealing with domestic violence victims. One hospital emergency room found that when it added a line on its intake chart requiring routine screening for domestic violence, the number of recognized cases doubled in one month.

Many recommendations have been made by organizations such as the American Medical Association and other family violence professionals as to how the health care profession could improve its response to the victims of family violence. Education is at the top of every list, both direct education for health care professionals at the undergraduate, graduate, and continuing education levels, and public education through community programs. All facility staff should be trained in interview techniques, risk assessment, safety planning, and procedures for linking medical services to other community resources. All staff, especially nurses, should be trained to identify abuse victims and invite them to share their stories, with assurances of privacy. All facilities should have protocol for the screening and treatment of domestic violence victims. Battering should be treated as a serious health problem, and any past or present abuse should be recorded on the patient's medical history—again, with special attention to confidentiality.

Patients should be referred to appropriate social services, and given choices where different kinds of services are available. Emergency and urgent care facilities, in particular, should provide patients with information on battered women's rights and services available in the area. Doctors and nurses can often establish a rapport with a patient to help empower her to seek help, to reassure her that she is not to blame, and to raise her self-esteem by reminding her that she is a valuable, worthwhile person. The overuse of tranquilizers to mask the constant anxiety of living with the threat of abuse should be avoided. However, this area is controversial. Many battered women suffer from depression, both during the relationship and after they leave. Antidepressant drugs such as Prozac have helped some pull out of their desolation and go forward with their lives. "I couldn't have made it through this without the help of my good friends and the antidepressant drugs," said one woman who recently broke free of an abuser. Most agree that such drugs should be prescribed with caution, and any use which would make a woman more likely to tolerate or stay in an abusive situation avoided.

Some hospitals have taken innovative steps in working with victims of family violence. The Children's Hospital in Boston, for example, started a program called AWAKE: Advocates for Women and Kids in Emergencies. AWAKE offers support services including counseling, help finding emergency shelter and housing, court assistance, referrals for legal and medical care, and support groups. It also consults and conducts training for health care professionals.

The medical profession is gradually becoming more actively involved and organized in its efforts against domestic violence. In 1991, the American Medical Association (AMA) announced a campaign to combat family violence as a public health menace. A national conference on family violence was held in March 1994 which was organized by the AMA and attended by professionals in the health and justice fields, including nearly one hundred groups representing physicians, lawyers, law enforcement, parents, teachers, social service agencies, and others concerned about domestic violence.

The importance of prevention was one of the topics emphasized at the conference. It was recommended that physicians become more involved in the prevention of domestic violence, with training in how to intervene a part of every doctor's education. Reviving the practice of home health visits was also encouraged as a means of helping families get the services that are available. Violence was recognized as a disease with many causes, an epidemic the medical community is uniquely positioned to help reduce. The conference attendants drafted a set of strategies for addressing the needs of the victims of family violence, including the recommendation that communities across the nation create "family violence coordinating councils" with the single goal of protecting and supporting victims of family violence. They also proposed development of an effective assessment process for patients which would promote the safety of all family members. The AMA has stated its commitment to helping stop the epidemic of domestic violence. A follow-up meeting is scheduled for the spring of 1995.

DOMESTIC VIOLENCE AND WOMEN AT WORK

Abuse has a tremendous impact on women as workers. As the statistics set out in chapter 1 indicate, women who are abused have a very difficult time maintaining their work identity and keeping their jobs. Violent men often resent a woman's job because it is an area they cannot control. Abused women miss many days of work due to both physical injury and psychological coercion. They have far greater problems with lateness, interruption, distraction, and harassment on the job than other workers.

Dr. Patricia Murphy, a vocational rehabilitation specialist, counsels women on rebuilding their work lives after they have suffered various kinds of abuse. "Abuse survivors have many different problems that affect their identities and abilities as workers," she explains. "Many suffer from post-traumatic stress disorder. This can cause problems with memory and concentration, personality problems, sleep disorders, and a distorted perception of the future. Not all abused women exhibit symptoms of PTSD, but the victims suffer from other disorders as well that can interfere with their ability to function in the workplace. Some have substance abuse problems, others are in denial about their mental and physical injuries. Many have been permanently injured and may not be able to do the kind of work they were once able to do."

In her book *Making the Connection: Women, Work and Abuse*, Dr. Murphy quotes former U.S. Surgeon General C. Everett Koop, who said, "It's an overwhelming moral, economic, and public health burden that our society can no longer bear. Battery is the single most significant cause of injury to women in this country." Dr. Murphy points out that the physical injuries these women suffer may produce lifelong disabling effects, continuous pain, and chronic discomfort that interfere with a woman's work options and performance. Spinal injuries are common in victims of domestic violence, as are head injuries. "Head injury, in particular, can cause many diverse problems—physical, cognitive, behavioral, and emotional. Plus, women who deny or minimize abuse are often misdiagnosed as mentally ill when in fact they suffer from PTSD or the effects of head injury," she explains. "Medical and psychological injuries must both be addressed, yet many women can't afford complete medical care, and even those shelter budgets that provide for medical attention are seldom sufficient to provide for a complete examination. Few doctors or nurses are specifically trained to treat these populations of abuse survivors."

The distortion in a woman's view of her life caused by living in a violent home can have a serious effect, as well. "Continued abuse can result in denial of pain—one of the body's most important defense and alarm mechanisms," she says. "Also, women in abusive homes often don't see doctors and dentists for the preventative care necessary to stay healthy."

Dr. Murphy also feels the legal system needs to pay more attention to the impact of abuse on women's losses in their work lives. "The no-fault divorce process has effectively excluded the battered or raped wife from compensation for her injuries within the divorce process." Murphy sees the implementation of no-fault divorce laws as perhaps one of the most important changes in the work lives of women in this century. "Courts mandate that all spouses who appear able to do so should seek employment. Yet many of these women have never worked outside the home, and their work in the home has not been valued. A forty-year-old woman may be no more advanced in her work life than an eighteen-year-old. And the special circumstances of battered women are not considered. They need rehabilitative support. Battered women often exhibit fear, passivity, learned helplessness, depression, and low self-esteem. This kind of trauma can interfere with a woman's ability to solve problems and cause her to turn to self-destructive coping mechanisms. The battered woman syndrome can obviously lead to vocational impairment that precludes a woman from fully participating in the work world."

Domestic tort law allows the victim to sue outside the divorce process in a civil suit, and may help fill the gap left by no-fault divorce, by providing her with a means of getting financial compensation for her injuries. Dr. Murphy notes that vocational analysis and expert testimony on a woman's ability to work and earn money is sometimes allowed in such a suit. "Vocational impairment should be an element of damages, but testimony by experts on this issue is still rare. The value of unwaged work should also be considered, as should hedonic damages to compensate a woman for her loss of life enjoyment, pain and suffering, loss of life expectancy, and loss of ability to pursue her chosen vocation."

She points out that while no amount of money can make up for the damage to a woman's humanity caused by abuse, money can help pay for therapy, rehabilitation, and vocational training, and a damage award can send a message. "Abuse survivors, like all victims of war, deserve war reparations," she explains.

Dr. Murphy stresses the importance of work in the lives of abused women and abuse survivors. "Work can be a lifeline for self-respect, role models, and contacts with friends who can help. On the other hand, the loss of a person's work identity, which often accompanies abuse, is a sort of death, a soul murder."

SOCIAL SERVICES

Through the grassroots efforts of the battered women's movement, a wide variety of services are now available for everyone damaged by domestic violence—the victims, the abusers, and the children. All states now have domestic violence coalitions (see appendix) that provide assistance, information, and referrals. Yet where a battered woman lives can make a world of difference in how she is treated by police, courts, and other institutions, as well as what services are available and how accessible they are. Fortunately, help for those in abusive relationships is becoming more abundant and more effective. Coordination of efforts between the various helping agencies—police, shelters, courts, and others—has greatly improved overall, so more of the available services are streamlined and communicating with one another. Even small, rural communities are beginning to establish shelters and safe house networks, counseling programs, and other services. Many of the older programs with proven track records have begun producing low-cost training materials and conducting seminars to teach people in other communities how to use the same techniques in their own areas.

Battered Women's Shelters

There are over eighteen hundred shelters for battered women in America today, and countless other safe houses (private homes) or temporary facilities in churches, community centers, and YWCAs across the nation. The shortage of shelters for battered women and their children is still desperate. In 1996, there were only about eighteen hundred shelters nationwide. For every two women accepted, five were turned away. And for every two children sheltered, eight were refused. The locations of shelters are usually kept secret to protect the residents from angry husbands. Telephone numbers are listed in local directories under "Shelter," "Social Services," "Women's Services," "Crisis Intervention," or similar headings. Numbers are also posted in areas such as women's bookstores, libraries, Laundromats, bus stops, and other public places.

Shelters are best known for what their name implies—emergency, short-term housing for women in a crisis. Shelters usually allow residents to stay for thirty days. The average length of stay is about two weeks.

First and foremost, shelters save lives. Yet most shelters, and the organizations that run them, provide far more than crisis intervention. For example, the Women's Community Association in Albuquerque, New Mexico, provides a shelter for battered women and their children free of charge; a twenty-four-hour crisis hotline; emergency transportation; food, clothing and medical attention; individual and group counseling; employment and housing referrals; legal advocacy; counseling for children; battered women support groups; and parenting programs. For a low fee, it also offers a twenty-four-week program for abusers, which includes a crisis hotline; group, individual, children's, and partner counseling; and parenting programs. All services of the Women's Community Association are also offered in Spanish.

While the Albuquerque shelter offers more services than many, especially those in smaller communities, nearly all shelters provide some kind of individual and group counseling, as well as referrals to other agencies. These services are generally available to women who are not staying in the shelter, as well as those who are. Other shelters may offer housing assistance, legal assistance, and on-site help with public aid and other social service applications. Most shelters today are part of a larger system of services that work together to help a woman face the complex array of legal, social, and personal needs she encounters when fleeing an abusive marriage. Sometimes court or victim advocates visit shelters to let women know their rights, and to help them pursue prosecution of the abuser and/or obtain a protective order. Research by law enforcement agencies has shown that when more shelters are available for battered women, fewer male partners are killed by women defending themselves.

Some abuse survivors and the professionals who work with them believe the support of other women who have survived abuse is the single most important key to recovering from the damage caused by violence. Women who meet in shelters very often develop a sense of sisterhood with others who have suffered in similar ways. Women who share housework, child care, and a common plight often find a strong bond that leads to ongoing support and friendship lasting well beyond the duration of the shelter stay. Many lifelong friendships have been forged beneath the roofs of emergency housing facilities.

Today, most larger cities have shelters or safe houses, and many programs centered in cities serve outlying areas as well. In Albuquerque, for example, the Women's Community Association serves a tri-county area. Through two outreach sites, the program has expanded its services to accommodate a vast, sparsely populated rural area, including transportation of victims to the shelter at any time of the day or night. "Sometimes we have to drive 150 miles to go get someone at three o'clock in the morning, but if that's what it takes, we'll do it," says Catherine Chaney, director of the programs. Women's shelters are also beginning to address the common problem of substance abuse among battered women, rather than enforce blanket rules that those who use alcohol or drugs will be evicted. Women may react differently to traditional treatment methods, most developed for men, and need a different kind of treatment. Their practical problems must also be considered. For example, a woman who can't get child care and misses a meeting as a result might be told she is in denial, when she is not. Female alcoholics suffer more stigma than males, and abused women often face a double stigma—they are asked why are they using, and why don't they leave. The right question would be how can we help her stop and leave. A victim who conquers her substance problem is more likely to stay out of an abusive situation.

The University of New Mexico has begun research to determine what works for women with both domestic violence and substance abuse problems. Working with the Women's Community Association, the study seeks to identify the resiliency that keeps the survivors out, and what aid from the community, peers, and treatment programs best helps them stay both sober and free. As part of the study, one shelter plans to implement a program that will offer resident special substance-abuse counseling.

Support is also essential for women who have left a shelter for alternative housing, those trying to make this transition, and those who have never been in a shelter. Many shelters and social service agencies provide such support as counseling and group therapy, information and assistance on such issues as housing, and referrals to all who need it.

Diverse needs should also be recognized in addressing the question of how to help battered women. As the NCADV's Battered/Formerly Battered Women's Task Force emphasizes, there are many ways abuse survivors work to empower and heal themselves, and while traditional mental health approaches do work best for some, the importance of alternative methods such as art, spirituality, political involvement, study, and physical achievements should not be discounted.

The services provided by shelters is invaluable. Women who stay in a shelter or safe house are more likely to leave their abusers. Even the most basic shelters serve not only as a refuge, but as a community where women find support, encouragement, and an end to isolation and helplessness. Shelters often serve as a point of entry into the system of services for women who are leaving abusive marriages, whether or not they stay at the shelter. Police in many cities provide transportation to shelters for women fleeing the scene of a domestic assault.

Most shelters receive some funding from the state, local, or federal government. Some states use part of the fees charged for marriage licenses to fund shelters. Others contribute from fines charged as part of abuser sentences, or charge fees to abusers in related counseling programs. All, however, must rely on private sources as well.

Shelters are chronically underfunded, understaffed, and incapable of serving all of the women and children who need them. In some cities, as many as six out of seven must be turned away. Most shelters must rely, at least in part, on volunteer help and donations. Many former shelter residents go on to volunteer or work in a paid capacity for the shelter, and find such work a rewarding part of building a new life.

In many areas, better assistance to victims is needed after the initial escape, for example, after her time limit at the shelter runs out. This is when many women return to their abuser because they feel they have no place else to go. Ironically, many victims feel safer if they return to a dangerous home than if they must continually be on the lookout for a stalker.

COUNSELING

Most professionals agree that mental health counseling can be beneficial to any family member who has lived through the trauma of domestic violence. Many believe that for perpetrators and children, it is almost essential. For victims, the role of psychological counseling is more controversial.

Mental Health Treatment for Abused Women

In the past, it was not uncommon for even psychiatrists and psychologists to take part in the "blame the victim" mind-set. Women were commonly diagnosed as masochists, in keeping with the notion that any woman who didn't leave must enjoy being abused. Psychiatrists and other medical professionals have also been known to diagnose "hysteria" and prescribe tranquilizers. Sometimes women were told they had a personality disorder. Fortunately, as mental health researchers and society in general have learned more about the real nature of domestic violence and the dynamics of the abusive relationships, such practices are becoming uncommon.

Yet many people are troubled by the suggestion that seems inherent in recommending mental health treatment to an abused woman. Telling a woman she needs counseling seems to imply there is something wrong with her, something she needs to fix in herself. This is of special concern to some of the professionals involved with court programs that order both batterers and victims to complete a program of therapy. The benevolent intent of these programs is seldom questioned, and most victims find the counseling helpful. But the mandatory nature is somewhat troubling.

Others, however, believe everyone who has been through trauma or difficult change of any kind can benefit. I tend to agree. Counseling does not have to focus on changing something that is "wrong." On the contrary, it can help a person see that she is perfectly fine, that she deserves a good life and has the inner strength to find it. It can help her access her own healing abilities, and reassure her that her feelings are normal.

One of the most common and highly recommended forms of therapy for abused women is group therapy that involves others who have shared similar experiences. This type of counseling is often available in shelters, as well as through public and private organizations. Some of the groups are formally structured and led by professionals, while others use trained volunteers or simply represent a gathering of women who want to share feelings, ideas, and encouraging words. "Some of my best therapy has been helping other women," says Jane Fraher, who found the "aftershocks" of the abusive relationship she endured for three-and-a-half years almost as difficult as the actual relationship. "When I go to my support group and the new women say how they admire my strength and courage, I know I'm helping someone else get to where I am now." Guides are available for those wishing to start self-help groups (see Appendix and Resources and Suggested Readings section).

For most women, the healing process begins as soon as they get free. A great many battered women exhibit amazing resilience, and literally blossom when they are able to focus all the energy formerly used in simple survival on efforts to start a new life. This does not mean guidance of some form is not beneficial, but for many it is not really necessary.

For others, especially for those who have suffered years of abuse or have themselves been abusive to their children, some form of help in restructuring a shattered life may be essential. Women suffering from post-traumatic stress disorder, which can have long-term, devastating effects that seriously impact their ability to work and form new relationships, often testify that they simply couldn't have rebuilt their lives *without* therapy. Depression is also a frequent problem for women who have been abused, and plus traditional therapy and drug treatment (which must be prescribed by a physician or psychiatrist) have been beneficial to these women. Even those who do not experience severe distress often report residual problems that can interfere with their enjoyment of life and new relationships.

Also, many battered women have a history of abuse both during the relationship and prior to it, as children, for instance. This can establish a pattern of other behaviors and characteristics in a woman, such as low self-esteem and mental "tapes" that play over and over, telling her she is weak, is not good enough, has to please others first and herself second. Counseling can help replace these learned thought patterns with more positive messages. Therapy can be helpful in this and other components of building a new life.

Women who need counseling can find help from shelters (many have long-term support services), community mental health providers, churches, medical providers such as hospitals and HMOs, and private counselors. Some psychologists specialize in working with abuse victims. Private counselors sometimes conduct support and therapy groups as well, often charging on a sliding fee scale based on the participants' income. Some groups address recovery issues in general, while others use a specialized approach to treat specific problems. For example, as a vocational rehabilitation counselor, Dr. Patricia Murphy conducts career and life planning support groups for abuse survivors in Santa Fe, New Mexico. Her groups help women learn or regain the skills they need to be confident and successful in their careers, and to establish plans for their futures.

When choosing a counselor, it is important to find someone with whom you feel comfortable speaking openly and intimately. Some women prefer female counselors, and there are many excellent therapists of both sexes. The most important criteria is finding someone who makes you feel better, more hopeful, more certain you are healing. Don't feel disheartened if you have to visit several people before you feel this rapport. Ask for recommendations from others with similar experiences. There are two red flags that should make you not only run, but report the counselor to your local mental health association: Anyone who tells you you deserve abuse or should accept it; or anyone who approaches you sexually. This type of behavior is always inappropriate in a counseling context.

Batterer's Programs

Over the past twenty years, many community mental health agencies have developed treatment and education programs for abusive men, often with the help of other such groups that have been through a trial and error period and learned what types of help are most likely to be effective. Many of these programs started in conjunction with new approaches to domestic violence in the criminal justice system. Today, men who plead or are found guilty of battering are often required to choose between treatment or jail.

The approaches of these programs, and their success rates, vary. Generally, the longer programs, which require abusers to attend therapy sessions for at least six months, have better results over the long term than those that require only a few sessions. Some combine group and individual counseling, some break the program down into separate components such as education, dynamics of the violent relationship, and anger management. Many require screening for substance abuse, and separate treatment for alcoholism or drug abuse if necessary.

There do seem to be three points that virtually all experts agree are necessary for successful treatment of abusers. First, the man must admit to his responsibility for the abuse. He must realize that it was wrong, accept that he cannot control other adults with equal rights, and want to change his behavior. Second, there must be some demonstrated consequences for the abuse. Many programs require all abusers to spend at least one night in jail, some longer, depending on the circumstances of the case. Even one night behind bars can make a strong impression. Third, there must be accountability that continues beyond the mandatory treatment period—through continued group support, court monitoring of a longer term of probation, or a court order strictly prohibiting harassment or violence and providing strict penalties for violation.

Any abuser's program will be most effective if it starts promptly after arrest and lasts several months or longer. The Duluth, Minnesota program, recognized as one of the best, lasts twenty-six weeks. Sixty percent of the men who go through the program have not been charged with assault again, according to a follow-up study. Men who enter programs under court order, with sanctions for unexcused absences and automatic jail time for quitting continued abuse, seem to achieve better results. Also, the earlier this intervention happens, the greater the chance of success: a man who gets into counseling after the first or second assault is more likely to reform than one who has been battering and getting away with it for twenty years.

An ongoing study on batterer intervention that works, conducted by the National Centers for Disease Control in Atlanta, has confirmed the long-held view that the earlier intervention occurs, the easier it will be to change a batterer's behavior. The study has also found that substance abuse treatment must be combined with violence treatment where it is required, and that programs that allow the batterer to choose any counselor are not effective—it takes 6 months to 2 years of work with a trained counselor. Some programs are beginning to use peer sponsorship, similar to that used by Alcoholics Anonymous, which hasn't been studied extensively, but appears to be helpful for some.

Programs for abusive men have several advantages over incarceration alone. Sentencing of abusers has the greatest effect if it includes both sanctions and treatment. A man who feels guilty and remorseful after the battering will often be responsive to counseling if he can start while still in this part of the cycle. He can keep his job, and if the woman wants to maintain the relationship, the couple can have a better chance of a safe and successful attempt to salvage it.

Couples Counseling

There is a great deal of controversy surrounding the question of whether a family torn by violence can ever really be mended. Psychologists, social workers, sociologists, and survivors all have differing opinions. Some simply say get out—do whatever it takes to get free, and give up the relationship. Dr. Lenore Walker has concluded after years of research and therapy, including couples therapy, that battering relationships rarely change for the better. Even when both people truly want to change, she believes that the inherently unequal balance of power is resistant. Violence tends to become ingrained in the relationship, although it may abate in frequency or severity. She feels that the best hope for ending the violence is to end the relationship.

Many women believe that if they are willing to work hard enough, things can change. But there is no way a woman can change an abusive man's behavior by changing her own. "Batterers are violent for their own personal reasons, not because of anything their women do or do not do," Dr. Walker explains. Others have found that while physical violence may be stopped, the psychological abuse generally continues after a brief respite.

Couples counseling, in which both abuser and victim attend therapy sessions together, is illegal in some states because of the suggestion that the woman is partially to blame and needs to fix something in herself; the philosophy that she has some power to change the relationship; and the risk of additional violence, harassment, or intimidation inherent in bringing the couple together. Many feel that at least a limited period of absolute separation is crucial if the abuse is to stop. Also, a court order requiring the abuser to have no contact with the victim is included in most cases in which a batterer is found or pleads guilty.

When an unequal power balance remains, couples counseling cannot work. Most professionals agree that a couple should never attempt counseling or mediation together until the abuser has completed a program on his own, refrained from abusing his partner for a significant period of time, taken responsibility for his past wrongdoing, and committed himself to building a relationship based on equality and respect.

Yet some family therapists, like Virginia Goldner and Gillian Walker, believe battering can be successfully stopped in some families through couples counseling that tries to rebuild the relationship—while not letting the batterer get away with anything.

In reality, many women keep returning to abusive relationships, with the ongoing hope that they can keep the good part and end the battering. Goldner and Walker do not feel their program is for everyone, and have strict requirements for couples who wish to enroll. First, the violence must absolutely stop. Safety is a priority, and some couples are required to live apart for a period. Second, the abuser must take complete responsibility for his actions. Finally, there must be a strong and loving side to the relationship.

Goldner and Walker believe that allowing a woman who wants to save the relationship to do so in a professionally controlled setting helps remove the shame she feels when she goes back, restore her dignity, and avoid secret alliances between the couple. Women are freed to begin asserting more power and pushing for new terms in the relationship. Men are required to spend time alone, to learn they can survive without relying on their wives to cure their loneliness and fill all their needs. They are also taught to recognize the steps that end in violence and how to take charge to stop the progression. Women are required to develop outside interests and build a life of their own as well. Goldner and

Walker believe that rather than a "honeymoon phase," the ties that bind people in abusive relationships are based on acceptance. They found that many women in such alliances were neglected as girls, and the men were often abused as boys. This can lead to a sense of two lost souls finding each other, the one person who can be trusted, at least until the stresses of real life intrude on this secure world and shatter the illusion.

Couples counseling remains controversial, but many professionals believe that with a lot of work, a strong desire to salvage the relationship on the part of both parties, and a strict requirement that the violence stops and the abuser admits his accountability, some families can rebuild a peaceful home. Jackie Moise, probation and parole officer, says that judges need to order family counseling for all members if the family is going to stay together. All must understand what roles they are playing, and how the cycle of violence is perpetuated. Also, all must be committed to change and participation. The story of one couple who successfully rebuilt their lives through long-term dedication and commitment is told later in this chapter.

THE CHURCH

Different churches follow drastically different doctrines regarding domestic violence. Some fundamentalist sects believe that divorce is a sin, and will always counsel a couple to stay together, regardless of the situation.

But most churches today recognize that a violent marriage is far from a holy institution. In 1992, the U.S. Roman Catholic Bishops produced their first official statement on spousal abuse. They issued a document proclaiming that the Bible does not require a woman to submit to an abusive husband or stay in an abusive relationship. The bishops condemned sexism and stated their concern that certain biblical passages have been taken out of context to justify wife beating. The bishops urged the parishes to educate their members about domestic violence and offer refuge to battered victims, as well as help to abusers.

Other churches have long been leaders in the effort to end domestic violence. Some of the first shelters were established on church property, and many still offer emergency services as well as counseling and assistance of various kinds. The clergy can offer personal support, counseling, help in coordinating community efforts, and teach that violence is morally wrong. Many churches help distribute materials about violence and local services. The church has traditionally been one of the most important influences in shaping the values of young people and teaching respect for others. The Center for the Prevention of Sexual and Domestic Violence, a national organization listed in the appendix, provides materials and training for clergy and religious institutions with the goal of preventing domestic violence and child abuse.

Some victims feel awkward discussing intimate family matters with clergy members who have known them since childhood, or have established a relationship with the whole family, including the abusive husband. Some clergy, too, find this difficult as they may perceive competing interests. Women who face this problem but desire counseling or support from the church may find it helpful to ask their own or another minister, rabbi, or priest for a referral to someone outside the immediate community who can provide spiritual counseling within the same denomination, but without the personal history.

Like other services, clerical counseling varies greatly. Some religious practitioners provide extremely helpful support, spiritual guidance, and assistance, while others may be of little or no help or actually detrimental. Much depends on the individuals involved and the program offered by each church. As with other counseling, it is generally best to try anything that seems helpful, but be willing to change if it does not seem to be working—and run as fast as you can from anyone who tells you to accept abusive treatment, no matter what reason is given.

SCHOOLS

Educational institutions at all levels can help put an end to domestic violence by teaching that abuse is wrong, that it is detrimental to all of society, and that there are better ways to resolve personal disagreements than with fists. Many schools have begun teaching peaceful methods of dispute resolution. School nurses and guidance counselors can provide information and advice to children from violent homes. High schools, especially, have become aware of the growing problem of violence between adolescent couples, and some of the programs that were started with prevention in mind have expanded to focus on intervention as well, as rates of dating violence and rape soar.

Many of the efforts in the field of education have been made by battered women's groups at the grassroots level. In Boston, an improvisational theater group puts on skits for area high schools as a joint project of a local women's shelter and a men's therapy group. A four-week course on the prevention of family violence was developed in Louisville, Kentucky, and adopted by other public school systems in Illinois, Arkansas, and Ohio. Several of the national and state coalitions have developed brochures especially for teens who live in violent homes or are involved in violent dating relationships. In Pittsburgh, Pennsylvania, a course called Violence-Free Healthy Choices for Kids is run by the Women's Center and Shelter of Greater Pittsburgh and is a required course in conflict resolution for fourth and fifth graders in five schools. The group also offers a three-day dating violence prevention program for adolescents that distinguishes abusive behavior from healthy relationships.

Many believe that the education and prevention of domestic violence should start much earlier than high school. It has been suggested that a public awareness campaign to reduce domestic violence should be structured in a way similar to the recent programs to reduce drunk driving, or the D.A.R.E. programs to prevent drug abuse. All children should be educated both in preventing violence in various contexts and in how to avoid becoming victimized.

Schools can also provide counseling for children traumatized by violence in the home. School guidance counselors at all levels can help children deal with the trauma of living in a violent home. One man who grew up in an abusive home says he always thought of school counselors as purely academic advisors, but when his home life became unbearable in junior high and he felt he had no one else to turn to, a school counselor helped him tremendously.

Volunteer programs are also provided by many high schools and colleges, which give credit to students who serve internships assisting at shelters or other social service organizations.

ONE WOMAN'S STORY: A WOMAN WHO STAYED

Like many abused women, M'Liss Switzer grew up in a home marred by tragedy, neglect, and abuse, in which she was made to feel worthless and incompetent. When she met the man that would become her husband, she felt valuable and appreciated for the first time. Things were wonderful for the fourteen months they dated—then, on their wedding night, he hit her for the first time. A twenty-year pattern of abuse was to follow.

Chuck Switzer, too, had been abused as a child. Like many men, every time he beat his wife he apologized profusely and swore it would never happen again. But he was locked into a pattern of taking his anger at himself out on her. Typically, he blamed her for pushing him beyond his limits, for anything that went wrong in his world. Chuck and M'Liss fell into the common cycle of violence, marked by tension building, a violent attack, then a period of remorse and kindness.

As the years went by, M'Liss became more and more convinced that the violence was indeed her fault. When she tried to talk to friends or members of her family, she was confronted with attitudes of indifference or even accusations that she was the cause of the violence.

In her book *Called to Account: The Story of One Family's Struggle to Say No to Abuse*, M'Liss describes one of the greatest frustrations of an abusive relationship: the fact that it is good, loving, and comfortable except for the episodes of abuse. Yet she compared the marriage to living in a terrorist state, in which a woman's whole life can become dedicated to keeping things on an even keel and avoiding anything that could cause an outburst.

M'Liss understood the importance of keeping a sense of at least partial control over her life, and though she does feel she was brainwashed, she finally decided to take action, with the goal of forcing Chuck to seek help.

She invited two couples she knew and trusted as friends of the Switzers to be there when she told Chuck she had filed charges. They stated to him that they would support her. This turned out to be a smart move. Predictably, Chuck became angry. The others helped him calm down, and the couple separated.

The Switzers were fortunate to live in Minnesota, a state with a strong cooperative system of impartial laws; a competent police force; a dedicated judicial system; and a strong family-based domestic abuse counseling program that included individual and group therapy, couples counseling, children's groups, and family sessions. The program, Minneapolis' Domestic Abuse Project (DAP), also used different types and combinations of therapy as time progressed.

Like many other women, M'Liss was amazed to learn in group therapy that others had lived with the same terrors and experiences in the context of different families. Her group was composed of some women who were divorcing their abusers and some who were trying to work it out. One thing all the women shared was a sense of self-blame. Over and over she heard, "If I had or hadn't done this..." Her feelings are expressed in *Called to Account*, "We accuse ourselves, our husbands blame us, society condemns us. As unreasonable as it seems, abused women are denounced as the ones responsible for the violence by themselves, by their husbands, and by society."

One of the main tasks of the therapist is to dispel this myth. In therapy M'Liss learned about Dr. Lenore Walker's cycle of violence, and saw that it applied to her marriage. The therapist recommended calling a "time out" early in the tension-building phase to try and diffuse tension, and to work out a personal protection plan. The women helped one another obtain protective orders, and take other necessary steps. They encouraged each other to stick to their guns, stay strong and determined, and not give in to men pleading to come home. The group also provided a forum to express feelings others might not see as clearly, such as their resentment at having to be the ones to shoulder the burden of strength, do all the work and, in some cases, flee the home.

Meanwhile, Chuck attended a men's group. They, too, learned about the cycle of violence, and that violence is learned behavior, usually in a violent family, and further influenced by our culture in which brutality is accepted on the playground and the athletic field. The "macho image" men are pressured to emulate discourages them from developing a softer, gentle side. They learned that while the choice to be abusive is theirs alone, their history and cultural context may help explain why they made this choice. The men learned how anger is often used to mask other feelings, such as fear, hurt, inadequacy, and confusion. They were taught that while it is difficult for abusive men to admit and accept responsibility for their violence, it is essential they do so if they have any hope of changing. They also learned to watch their own cues for tension building, and to take time out. While the men were held fully accountable for their wrongdoings, there was also a focus on the good and potential that can exist in the abuser.

M'Liss emphasized that such programs are no quick fix, but involve a long, drawn-out, and often painful process. It required a great deal of soul-searching, in which she had to gradually accept the possible price of her decision in a positive, yet realistic manner; to think carefully about what the future may hold. She found that the separation, though temporary, freed a lot of her energy to do this.

She also found, as many others have, that it can be very good for a man who has never lived on his own to have the full responsibility of taking care of himself. Chuck grew during this period, and learned to appreciate what M'Liss had been doing for him. The experience also increased his confidence and gave him time alone to plan, set goals, and adopt reasonable expectations for coming home.

M'Liss experienced other benefits of therapy. One exercise the women were asked to do involved writing a letter to someone they were angry with, not necessarily their spouse. She chose her older sister, who had raised M'Liss after her parents died, and had been resentful, abusive, and unloving. She finally confronted her sister, who apologized and admitted she had been unkind. Thus another relationship was healed as an indirect result of the program. A similar project for the men's group resulted in Chuck rebuilding a relationship with his mother and making peace with his father, who had been brutal to him as a child.

M'Liss, like many other battered women, had been programmed to judge herself as a success or failure based on how well she lived up to the expectations of others. She learned she had to change the "tapes" that played over and over in her head and controlled her feelings about herself. Both she and Chuck learned the necessity of reprogramming these "tapes" that control reactions.

The program also stressed the importance of each person building friendships and interests outside the marriage, and advised each to take at least one night a month to go out with friends. M'Liss learned the importance of a support group composed of close friends, professionals, and caring clergy. They were encouraged to keep the growth going when Chuck moved back, and to keep attending counseling sessions. The continued therapy helped them establish new methods of dealing with difficulty and conflict, such as family council meetings in which everyone could share schedules, divvy up chores, and air gripes. The change was not easy, especially dealing with confrontations. "He had to lose his life in order to find it," M'Liss says.

The couple's children had displayed problems seemingly unrelated to their parents' conflicts. This is common, with behaviors such as shoplifting, delinquency, and eating disorders frequently occurring. The Switzers learned that the problems usually are interrelated and the children, too, can benefit from counseling. They were also surprised to learn that misbehavior can be a good sign, demonstrating that the children no longer feel they need to tiptoe about for fear of triggering their father's violence. The Switzers progressed to family therapy, which they found painful but also very healing, especially for Chuck.

M'Liss emphasizes that therapy is not a panacea, but can give a family a new set of tools for meeting their challenges. As a part of their maintenance program, she and Chuck help others now enrolled in the program. Though the Switzers stayed together, M'Liss emphasizes in her book that divorce should not be seen as failure; rather, accepting abuse is failure. She also stresses the importance of support from friends and family members—but only those who are trustworthy and able to keep a confidence. She also feels that a successful outcome depends on both people changing. The man must be willing to do whatever it takes to stop the violence; the woman has to regain a sense of empowerment and self-respect.

The Switzers' experience proves there are no easy answers. Even with all the services offered, it took a tremendous amount of perseverance just to make use of them. M'Liss says she "wore a groove" in the road driving her children and herself to the various sessions. But, in the end, M'Liss says every hour she spent working on herself and her family was worth the time. Both she and Chuck went on to become group leaders at DAP.

ANOTHER WOMAN'S STORY: A WOMAN WHO LEFT SOONER

Sarah Engels typifies the woman you would never expect to be abused. A tall, strikingly attractive woman, she presents an image of strength, confidence, and success. Yet Sarah found herself in a relationship that typified the dynamics of domestic violence.

Sarah had enjoyed the benefits of a good education, with a bachelor's degree plus graduate credit, and an interesting, varied career. She was a teacher for many years, then she went to work in the alumni affairs department of a major university raising revenue. She supervised forty volunteer boards, wrote for the alumni magazine, and did other work that comprised an average work week of over sixty hours. She thrived on the job's challenges, yet the exhausting pace, along with personal difficulties, eventually began to take its toll. When a family-owned commercial truck dealership began floundering, she took over the management of three departments. Within two years, she streamlined operations and made the company profitable again. Once the company was back on its feet, Sarah wanted a change in both career and location, but was unsure of her next move. "I had been through a divorce several years before, my mother had passed away, and I was having some health problems. At work, I was under the gun more than ever. I was feeling depression, anger, and a general malaise that wasn't like me at all, so I started seeing a counselor."

Neither Sarah's parents nor her ex-husband had ever abused her, but alcohol had been a problem in both homes. Sarah's parents had been distant and emotionally detached. She went into therapy wondering what she should do next, and learned to grieve, to deal with her unfulfilled dreams, and to get on with her life. She felt her therapist helped her a great deal, and led her to find a new direction that involved getting out of a situation that no longer worked for her. "I wanted to get out of the big city, away from the stress of my high-pressure job, the problems that continued with my family, a whole situation that seemed toxic to me. I had cleared up my health problems, and felt very strong. I decided to go to graduate school in counseling, and located a good university in Idaho, in a clean and beautiful environment."

Sarah had saved enough money to live on while she pursued her degree, and set out with high hopes. But once in Idaho, she had second thoughts about attending the graduate program. "I loved Idaho, but I was beginning to realize that my heart wasn't totally in going to school; I'd just used it as an acceptable reason to get away from Houston. I really wanted some time to relax and take stock of my life before I found the right direction."

During her relocation, Sarah had become acquainted with John, the man who moved her furniture. "This friendly and charming guy came in and gave me a big rush. I had just started the university orientation program, but I was feeling that I had made a decision that wasn't really right for me. Since I had been in the trucking business and he knew the area, we found plenty in common to talk about. He asked me to dinner after he unloaded my things. We went out and had a really nice time."

Over the next few weeks Sarah saw John occasionally when he was in the vicinity, though he was on the road most of the time. When he was gone, he would call her three or four times a day. "I know now that this was too much, he was probably trying to keep track of me all the time," she says. "But I was feeling renewed and independent, and I liked him. He seemed trustworthy. I hadn't been in a relationship for five or six years, and needed someone in my life. I left myself open, and now I think he picked up on the fact that I was vulnerable, even if I didn't know it."

As Sarah was coming to a final decision not to pursue graduate school, John asked her to accompany him on a three-week drive on a route that would take him through beautiful country. "I thought, why not?" Sarah says. "I had worked all my life, with little chance for fun and adventure. I had the time, some money saved, and John and I had fun together. We were always carefree and laughing, the chemistry was great, that was all there was to it. So we went and had a wonderful time. The trip was very relaxed, though I did check in with a friend every couple of days, because she was worried about me going on a journey with a man I didn't know that well."

Shortly after their trip, John asked Sarah to move to Carson City, Nevada, with him, where his children from a prior marriage lived and he felt his job prospects were better. He spoke of its mountains, beautiful lakes, and clean air. Sarah liked the idea of living in a smaller town. She found out she could attend a similar graduate program there if she decided to continue with school, so she agreed to move.

"I can see now that there were signs early on that John had problems, but since I had never been involved with someone like him, I didn't see them," Sarah says. "He knew my situation, that I had no friends or close ties in either Idaho or Nevada."

Sarah soon noticed a change in John. "The minute he no longer had to pursue me, things were different. His level of stress escalated. I don't know if his first marriage was violent, but there was always some crisis with his ex-wife, and a lot of screaming over the phone."

John's job opportunities in Carson City didn't pan out as he had hoped. "He either couldn't or wouldn't keep a job, and stopped going on the road," Sarah recalls. "He started getting paranoid and jealous. I would go to the grocery store, and he would demand to know where I'd been, saying he was afraid something had happened to me. He didn't want me to make new friends or talk to my old ones, and found fault with everyone except me—at first. It all happened so fast—things started changing before we moved, but really got rolling as soon as we got to Nevada. The minute we were in the house, he came up with all of these rules, like no one comes in unless he is home, and we had to go everywhere together. None of it made sense to me."

Sarah had learned that John was badly abused by both parents as well as his siblings as a child, and that all of the ten children in his family had grown up with emotional problems. She thought his strange behavior was temporary because he was still insecure about their relationship, and because no one had ever really cared about him. She believed that once he was convinced she truly cared for him, he would calm down and act the way he had at first. "I tried to be gentle, use humor to get him to relax," she recalls. "I asked him how he thought I got to be this age without someone taking care of me all the time."

Part of her hopefulness and rationale came from her own background. "I'd learned in therapy that some abused and neglected people practically have to be hit on the head to feel anything, and I had seen some of this in myself. Although I wasn't abused, I had been neglected. I remember a lack of feeling from very early on. My parents were subtle in their behavior—no affection—but they were very authoritarian and verbally critical. John seemed to push the button on some of these old feelings I had inside that made me want to please everyone and get attention, and to make it all right with Daddy."

But things got worse instead of better. "He got more and more paranoid and angry. He was completely self-centered, constantly complaining that there was something wrong with the food, or that we didn't have sex enough even when we had plenty. He would come through the door and be set off by absolutely nothing. He would lie all the time—even when the truth would have served him better. He was so compulsive about it, I began to wonder if he even knew the difference. I had experienced problems in relationships, but nothing like this. I had always been with people who were truthful and more trustworthy, and I didn't know how to act with him. I can see now that his behavior was completely irrational, but back then I was always walking on eggshells, trying to placate him."

Over the seven months she lived with John, Sarah saw the toll the relationship was beginning to take on her. "I started smoking just to have something to do during his long tirades. My energy level was down and I was sleeping more than usual. I didn't feel well, and I was looking for a job, but hadn't found anything. He wanted to keep me isolated, make me stay home all the time."

John's tirades would start with an outburst of yelling and swearing, directed at some real or imaginary enemy. "If I didn't go along and agree with him, pat him on the back like a three-year-old, he would turn his rage against me, telling me I was supposed to be on his side. He would call me 'bitch' and 'whore', other names I've never been called before, accuse me of all kinds of crazy things. He would ask me if I thought I was better than him, then turn around and call me stupid. He never hit me directly, but he did increasingly violent things. He hit my cat, grabbed a book out of my hands, burned my furniture with cigarettes, and smashed pictures. He was terrified I would leave, and of course, the irony is that he drove me to do just that—it was a self-fulfilling prophecy."

John's tirades would go on for two or three hours. "He would get a crazy look in his eyes and go completely out of control," Sarah says. "Then he would be exhausted and remorseful. I tried several times to sit him down and tell him that I couldn't deal with his anger. I told him in no uncertain terms that I would leave if this didn't stop. A couple of times, he seemed to understand—it was as though another person came into his body and became rational for awhile."

After these outbursts, John would make an effort to control his temper for several days. "But he was a time bomb, and I never knew when he would explode again," Sarah explained. She was beginning to believe she was in danger. "I was starting to realize that you can't be rational with an irrational person," she says. "He demanded I 'pay him back' for money he'd supposedly contributed, when I had supplied all of the furniture and bought a second car for him to use. I gave him most of the money I had saved, and I was beginning to feel very used."

John's last explosion was the first—and the last—time that he physically attacked Sarah. "He was in a rage, and I tried to sit him down and talk rationally, as usual. He started hitting my cats again, and I tried to leave the room. As I walked by him, he grabbed me by the tank top I was wearing and yanked the fabric so hard he tore it right off of me. That was it. I remember telling myself, 'Sarah, you may be a very smart girl, able to deal with a lot, but this is beyond what you can handle.' I stood up to him and told him to get out. I put on a strong front, but I was scared to death. But he loaded some clothing and belongings into his pickup, then left in the car. I knew he would come back for his things, and I didn't know what to do next."

Sarah changed clothes and called a paralegal she'd become acquainted with for advice. "She had been in a similar situation, and was afraid for me. She told me to stay put, she would call the police, then she called me back right away and said they were on the way."

Carson City had been John's home town for many years, and Sarah later learned that the police were familiar with John and his temper. However, before they arrived, John returned and flew into another rage. Sarah calmly told him she was going for a walk, and left until the police arrived.

"The officers were wonderful. One stayed outside with me, while another took him inside to get his things and made sure he left. I got a restraining order the next morning, which was very easy. But as I stood in the office filling out the forms, I kept thinking, 'I can't believe this is me.' "

Sarah received continued attention from the police until she left town several days later. "They told me to leave my porch light on, and they would patrol the street. If anything was wrong, I was to turn off the light as a signal. They also helped me program my telephone to automatically dial 911. They really gave me a sense of security."

John, however, had disappeared and the sheriff could not locate him to serve the restraining order. John called Sarah every day, but she refused to talk to him. He even had his young children call her and cry on the phone for her not to leave. "It was pathetic," she said. She listened to John just once, when he talked about getting counseling, and urged him to go. Yet she received a message on her answering machine from a counselor who wanted her to come in for couples counseling the next day with John. She didn't return the call, but John's calls continued.

Finally, she reported his calls to the police, who advised her to tell him about the restraining [protection] order, which had not been served because John kept changing his location. When she did, the calls stopped. Sarah also found the community support she received heartening, though she knew few people. "Everybody was so helpful. The moving people knew him to be a 'hothead', with a long history of this kind of behavior, and said they were sorry this had happened. They provided an unmarked vehicle to move my things. I had to sell a lot of my furniture to raise the money to move what I was going to keep, and even the used furniture people went out of their way to help me take care of business and get out of town."

Six days after John's last outburst, Sarah left Carson City. She told no one of her destination. "I was lucky that I had a vehicle, and enough money from selling the furniture so I could get out fast. I was also lucky that I had been through counseling before. I knew I could make rational choices, that it was all right to leave people I cared for when I couldn't live with them. I had done it before and survived."

Sarah relocated to Arizona, where she now works on the staff of an art magazine. She is content with her new life, but still jumpy about things like hang-up telephone calls. She reflects on the relationship with some regret, but sound wisdom. "I got one letter from John, which was forwarded from the old address. He said he was getting counseling, he loved me, he just needed time by himself, lots of mea culpas. Yet he never took responsibility for his actions, never saw the gravity of what he did to the relationship. I can't give any second chances to someone like that."

Like many women, Sarah caught herself placing some of the blame on her own supposed shortcomings. "I know the problems were all his, yet I thought, if I have so much going for me, if I'm so strong, how could I be so stupid? But women are raised to think they can make everything right. We take responsibility for trying to help others, even when we simply cannot."

Sarah was astonished to learn how closely John's behavior fit the typical pattern of most abusers. She now knows she was not part of the problem, nor could she be a part of the solution. "I know it wasn't my fault. Yet I still wonder how I could have let this happen. But I know now that he is mentally ill. I knew I was in a crazy, toxic situation, and I had to leave or I could go crazy too. His violence was bringing out responses I didn't know I had in me. But I had a choice—we all do. Women must know this. It may not be the ideal choice, but I would tell any woman who finds herself in this type of situation to run for her life—it only gets worse."

ANOTHER WOMAN'S STORY: A WOMAN WHO LEFT LATER

From an outward appearance, Charlotte Fedders seemed to have the classic American dream, the storybook marriage. At the age of thirty-nine, her husband, attorney John Fedders, had worked his way up to the powerful position of chief enforcement officer at the U.S. Securities and

Exchange Commission. They lived in a mansion, raised five boys, and traveled the circles of Washington's power elite. Yet while they were still newlyweds, John hit Charlotte so hard he broke her eardrum. And the beatings—as well as emotional abuse—continued until Charlotte finally divorced him nineteen years later.

In her book *Shattered Dreams*, Charlotte described her strict, yet affectionate and privileged Catholic upbringing. Unlike many battered women, she was neither abused nor neglected as a child, though her father dominated the family and had a volatile temper. However, her upbringing was very traditional, discouraging individual thought and rewarding conformity. Charlotte was taught to be dependent, to accept her father's word as gospel, and to feel guilty for any breach of the rigid code of conduct. Obedience and respect for authority were prime virtues, and her religion taught her to turn the other cheek, accept injustice, forgive, and endure. She and her sisters were sheltered and insulated, "prepared to be princesses," she explains. She attended a Catholic women's college where she studied nursing, and only dated one other man before meeting John Fedders.

John was everything Charlotte had been raised to admire in a man. He was tall, handsome, ambitious, and also a devout Catholic, raised with traditional values. From the day they met, Charlotte says her life revolved around him. And from that first day, he began trying to control her.

When they were still dating, he sometimes criticized her in front of her friends, who teased her about being "blinded by love." From the time they married, John insisted they live beyond their means. Although Charlotte did very well as a nurse, earning high praise and a good salary, her world centered around John. He insisted she turn over all her earnings to him. She was also responsible for all the housework, and their homes always had to meet his obsessive standards, which sometimes included an actual "white glove test."

Yet Charlotte wrote of good times in which the couple shared great joy. As she says in *Shattered Dreams*, "When things were bad they were very, very bad, but when they were good they were perfect." John exhibited typical Jekyll and Hyde behavior. He also followed the common pattern of controlling Charlotte emotionally through brutal criticism and authoritative behavior before he started battering her. Like many battered women, Charlotte started making mental lists of things that were likely to set John off, and blamed herself when he abused her.

On one occasion, Charlotte left John for several days and returned to her parents' home. But although her father tried hard to convince her to leave John, she felt guilty and worried that she would be shunned by other Catholics, since her church still considered divorce a sin, though this was the late 1960s.

Charlotte returned to John, but things did not improve. She learned that anger did not trigger the abuse; on one occasion he beat her without provocation while she was pregnant. She also noticed that John's mother was also obsessive about having a spotless house, and tried to exert complete control over everyone. John's behavior reflected his upbringing. He was becoming more controlling, critical, and obsessed with power and discipline in the home. While he did not routinely batter his sons, he forced them to follow rigid household rules, demanded athletic prowess and manly stoicism. Punishment was harsh for any transgression, and usually involved beating with a wooden fraternity paddle.

Throughout these periods, Charlotte said their sex life remained the healthiest part of the relationship. John still went through periods of kind, normal behavior. Yet he would sink into black moods for no apparent reason and withdraw into silences that sometimes lasted weeks. Charlotte found these silences to be the hardest part of the abuse to endure, and described them as psychological torture.

John also moved the family frequently, and seemed to become more dictatorial with each new, larger house. The ritualistic rules increased, and some areas of the homes were off-limits to the family. Charlotte became more and more isolated as John gave her no privacy, screened her mail, and refused to give her any help with the home or children, so she was constantly exhausted. She received one savage beating simply for writing a check without John's approval.

Yet the cycle of violence continued. John took her on a wonderful trip to Europe at one point, and was especially loving and supportive when the couple lost a young child. Yet the violence always returned. Charlotte would run to her sisters and pour out her sorrows, then she and John would make up and she would pull away from them, not wanting to be reminded of the bad times. Naturally, this put a strain on her relationship with her sisters.

Finally, however, Charlotte began to pull out of her isolation. The catalyst for the change was as simple as joining a book club in which she and other women would meet to discuss books they had read. For the first time in many years, her opinions were considered valid and worthy of listening to. The book club gave her a support group that encouraged her and built her self-esteem. John disapproved, but she handled him and kept going. For over two years, there was no violence. Then, after an especially bad beating when Charlotte called the police, who did nothing, she fell into a serious depression that left her immobilized. In *Shattered Dreams*, she describes her feelings as "deadened."

Charlotte had sought therapy several times throughout her marriage, but had found little help until she consulted a female therapist during this especially black period. For the first time, she was told that John's behavior was unacceptable.

Like many women, the final turning point came when Charlotte thought her children were in danger. John reacted in sudden anger at one of their sons, who had left his skates in the wrong place. He threw the skates at the boy, who got a black eye. Charlotte left and decided to get a divorce. She recalls, "You may not have enough self-esteem left to know you deserve better, but you know your kids do." As she told John in a letter asking for a divorce, "No woman deserves to be beaten by her husband, not ever . . ."

Reconciliation and therapy were attempted, but it didn't take long for the old control and violence to appear. When Charlotte left for good, the publicity, as well as the court battles, were ugly. John claimed he could not afford to pay adequate support to allow Charlotte and the boys to meet their expenses. Although he could have earned far more in the private sector, he refused to give up his prestigious government job. At one point during the trial, after testimony on the years of brutal abuse, John decided he wanted to reconcile. The judge halted the proceedings and suggested they "go to dinner and talk things out."

Yet the publicity had a positive side. Charlotte received many encouraging letters and calls from other battered wives, many of whom were educated, wealthy, or professionals. But the trial was extremely long and difficult. John did everything he could to drag it out, and to resist paying reasonable child support, eventually driving Charlotte into bankruptcy.

During the trial in early 1985, John Fedders admitted on the witness stand to beating his wife fifteen times over the course of their marriage. He said, "There was no justification for hitting Charlotte . . . I am forever remorseful about it . . . Yes, I demeaned her. I did a lot of stupid things."

The *Wall Street Journal* carried the story, and Washington society was shocked. Typically, Charlotte was the one who was interrogated. She had to explain to the press over and over why she stayed with him.

Charlotte's divorce seemed to be finalized at last, but after *Shattered Dreams* was published, John sought a share of the book's royalties because of his "participation in the story." Amazingly, a court master awarded him a 25 percent share. Mary McGrory, an outraged reporter for the *Washington Post*, compared the ruling to awarding Adolf Hitler a share of the proceeds from *The Diary of Anne Frank*. Subsequently, the decision was overturned by a higher judge.

Today, Charlotte still struggles to make ends meet, but knows she and her children are free and strong.

ANOTHER WOMAN'S STORY: ONE WHO LEFT TO BECOME A LEADER

Prosecutor Sara Buel is an especially brilliant example of the many former victims who have risen to become leaders in the fight to end domestic violence. Buel's credentials combine the prestige of an honors degree from Harvard Law School and practical training from the school of hard knocks—literally. With this combination, Buel is uniquely qualified to present herself as not only an expert, but a symbol of hope for others in need of help. Buel never intended to reveal her own background as a battered woman until one day when a fellow prosecutor advanced the stereotype that smart women don't become victims of abuse; that it would never happen to a woman like her.

When Buel left her abuser, she struggled desperately to make ends meet, collecting welfare, paying the price of poverty for safety. Through firsthand experience, she learned that women often return to abusive men because they find they cannot support their children alone, because the men, who control the money, threaten to use all their resources to take the children away, and because they have been conditioned to blame themselves for the failure of the relationship, to believe that there is a magic formula they can find to stop the violence.

With the help of a federally-funded job training program, Buel escaped welfare and began working in a legal services office where she eventually advanced to the role of paralegal and began assisting domestic violence victims. It took her seven years of hard work to earn her undergraduate degree while continuing to work helping battered women. Then, fueled by her anger when colleagues tried to tell her she wasn't Harvard material, she not only won acceptance at Harvard but was given a full scholarship. While there, she started a pro-bono advocacy program for battered women which is now Harvard Law's largest student program, with 25 percent male volunteers. When Buel graduated cum laude in 1990, she sent a copy of her transcript to a junior high teacher who once told her she wasn't smart enough to be in the school's secretarial training track, with the suggestion she not judge the future of twelve-year-old girls.

In addition to her duties as head of domestic abuse prosecutions unit of the Norfolk County District Attorney's Office, the indefatigable Buel teaches a class on domestic violence at Boston College Law School; crisscrosses the country training judges, advocates, police officers, and medical professionals; speaks to various groups working to end domestic violence; and has served on the multidisciplinary ABA Commission on Domestic Violence. An article in *Psychology Today* called Buel "possibly the country's sharpest weapon against domestic violence."

Buel is not only a tireless worker, she is an optimist who believes that with the conviction of whole communities to put a stop to domestic violence, it can end. She emphasizes the importance of ending silence about spousal abuse, more sensitivity among probation officers to the

safety needs of victims and monitoring of offenders, mandatory treatment of at least a year's duration for batterers, sanctions for those who do
not comply with probation and protection orders, greater use of advocates to follow cases, and improved training for police in investigation
and evidence gathering in domestic violence cases.

CHAPTER FIVE

CHILDREN, ADOLESCENTS, AND DOMESTIC VIOLENCE

B attered women are not the only ones who suffer devastating and permanent injury as a result of abuse. Children who grow up in violent homes are tragically affected in many different ways—from the womb through adulthood. Dr. Richard Gelles, one of the leaders in the study of domestic violence, has been quoted as stating that the worst thing that can happen to children is to grow up in an abusive family.

CHILDREN IN ABUSIVE HOMES

Children living in homes in which there is violence between adults are two to three times more likely to be abused than other children. Even if they are not direct targets of violence, they suffer terribly. Children are often injured in the cross fire of the violence, when furniture and other large objects are thrown or overturned. Young children are especially at risk and sustain the most serious injuries, including broken bones and concussions. Older children often try to intervene, and one study found that 62 percent of sons over fourteen who tried to intervene were hurt trying to protect their mothers. Girls frequently try to shield younger siblings from the violence, and may delay leaving home for college or work. Also, battered mothers are more likely to use harsh or abusive punishment than mothers who have not been abused.

Children who aren't physically injured still suffer severe trauma from growing up in a violent home. Each year, millions of children witness their mothers being emotionally abused, physically battered, even sexually assaulted by their fathers or other men in the home. Even parents who try to shelter their children from the violence are seldom successful. Children hear screams, see injuries, live in an atmosphere of terror and tension. And they learn that this is what home is like. That humiliation, disrespect, and beating are normal in a home. That violence is the appropriate way to solve problems. One police officer reported hearing a three-year-old boy say to his mother, "If you don't stop that bitch I'm going to shoot you." An eight-year-old boy began beating his six-year-old sister—just as he had observed his father doing to his mother.

The damage to these children is appalling. A mother who must focus on her own survival or grapple with the depression and other problems that accompany battering is unlikely to be available to her children for their emotional support. Children in violent homes live in a constant state of uncertainty and instability. In one study of children living in battered women's shelters, 85 percent had been sent to stay with friends or relatives during the previous year, and 75 percent of those over fifteen had run away twice. Psychologists and social scientists who have worked with children who witness battering have found that a high number suffer from guilt, anger, depression, anxiety, shyness, nightmares, aggression, disruptiveness, irritability, problems getting along with others, and "acting out" with parents and siblings.

Children may blame themselves for the violence, or devote all their own energy to whatever they think will keep their parents from fighting. They also exhibit poor health, low self-esteem, poor impulse control, difficulty sleeping, and feelings of powerlessness. Problems at school often include difficulty getting along with others, fewer interests and social activities, misconduct, and poor academic performance. They are at risk for drug and alcohol abuse, inappropriate sexual behavior, running away, isolation, suicide, and extreme loneliness and fear. Some become withdrawn, others rebel. Most feel that they have a shameful secret to hide, that they are somehow different than other children. All suffer in some way.

Most human learning is based on modeling—not on what we are told, but on what we see and emulate, especially in childhood. Adults frequently underestimate the level of suffering and damage inflicted on children who witness domestic violence. Some studies even suggest that children who are exposed to violence early in life experience altered brain development—for example, exaggerated reliance on the primitive "fight or flight" response which causes hypervigilance, difficulty sitting still and concentrating, and learning problems. Preschoolers have been diagnosed with post-traumatic stress disorder, and boys as young as two have been observed expressing inappropriately aggressive behavior. Young children from routinely violent homes have been found to have elevated blood pressure and pulse rates as much as ten points higher than others.

Both physical and intellectual growth may be slowed in children from violent homes. It is not difficult to see how this should be so, considering that some of the most widely-known and accepted psychological research, characterized by Maslow's hierarchy of needs, shows that human beings must feel a sense of safety before self-esteem and self-actualization may take place. Some psychologists have found that even indirect exposure (hearing rather than seeing) a single episode of violence between parents can be very traumatic for a child. And some say that the younger a child is, the more profound the impact, because young children have not yet learned the coping mechanisms that older children and adults use.

Boys and girls differ to some extent on the specific psychological or social handicaps they develop and the age at which they occur, but all are at risk for a wide variety of problems. Boys may learn that men have the right to beat women. Girls may learn that it is appropriate for women to accept abuse. It is no surprise that children from violent homes have seldom learned constructive ways of resolving conflicts and tend to choose either passive or aggressive strategies when trying to resolve disputes rather than more assertive, constructive, and effective methods. Children from such homes also show problems with empathy (identifying with the feelings of others) and trouble developing intimate relationships.

Children who grow up in violent homes often suffer from physical symptoms such as colds, sore throats, insomnia, and bed-wetting more than others do. In most cases, the symptoms disappear soon after the children are removed from the violence, though some children who have witnessed battering, especially over a long period of time, have been found to suffer from a form of post-traumatic stress disorder.

I recall the anguish of a friend, years ago, who felt torn between her desire to get free and remove her children from the influence of her husband, a man who was violent perhaps once every two or three months, and her fear that she would not be able to adequately support her children. She was also reluctant to remove them from the comfortable farm home they loved, and deprive them of the parenting of a man who was, the vast majority of the time, kind to her and to them. Two events finally helped her leave—furthering her education, which had the positive effect of boosting her self-esteem and confidence in her earning capacity, and watching her oldest son begin to emulate his father's abusive ways.

Abused women often recognize the trauma their children endure, yet they feel that they are in a dilemma. Others mistakenly believe that it is better for the children to keep the family together. Many abused women were neglected as children, and fear they will harm their children if they have to take a job or work longer hours to support them on one income; that they could lose custody; or that they will be depriving them of stability. In fact, children are much better off in a peaceful, loving, one-parent home than a violent, threatening two-parent home. Yet it is easy to see how a woman might have these fears. "I was shuffled around from relative to relative when I was a child," one woman explained. "Even though I had to put up with a lot from my husband, I was determined that would never happen to my kids. Until he threatened to kill my daughter—then the way I saw things changed." Though some women stay for the sake of the children, it is for the children that others flee.

Perhaps the most disturbing effect of family violence is the way in which it teaches children that this is the way a family functions—that violence is an acceptable way to solve problems, that men should dominate and abuse women, that women should submit. Children from violent homes have a much greater chance of growing up to be abusers or victims themselves, thus perpetuating the cycle of violence over and over through the generations. According to one major research study, sons who witnessed their father's violence had a 1,000 percent higher battering rate as adults than sons who did not witness violence. When a teenage boy assaults or kills his father, the most common motive is to stop the father's battering of the mother or other children.

It is beyond dispute that many children who grow up in violent homes go on to become violent adults, both in and out of their own homes. Even those who react in the opposite manner suffer problems such as an inability to deal with conflict in a healthy manner—any confrontation makes them flee in fear. Professionals from all fields emphasize that if domestic violence is to end, families and children must unlearn old, violent patterns of resolving disputes and learn new methods. The most powerful teaching tool for children is their parents' example. "The number one priority in eliminating domestic violence is changing what children are taught in the home," says Judge Diane Dal Santo. "Children who witness violence, even though they are not abused, learn and repeat what they see at home. They start acting out when they are very young. We must teach our daughters to protect themselves and to choose nonviolent men to date, and educate our sons in peaceful ways to solve problems."

Judge Angela Jewell, former special commissioner for domestic violence cases for Bernalillo County, New Mexico, told of one afternoon when a father and son were both brought into custody for battering their wives. While the families went through the intake process, the son's wife led her small boy—about four years old—into Jewell's office through a narrow hallway. The little boy bumped his head against the wall and immediately blamed his mother. He began slapping her thigh as hard as he could. Already the message was ingrained: If you are hurt or upset, it's a woman's fault and you should hit her. Jewell believes violence is learned behavior that must be addressed as early as possible. "To prevent people from learning domestic violence it is easier if you begin to educate at an early age, rather than trying to fix it when someone is fifty years old and has been doing it for decades."

As this heartbreaking story demonstrates, most domestic violence is part of a generational cycle. Dating violence is epidemic. A boy who watches his father beat his mother often learns that abuse against women is acceptable, normal behavior, and the way to treat his girlfriend or wife. Former U.S. Surgeon General C. Everett Koop recognized this cycle that reappears through the generations, and emphasized that if the chain is to be broken, it must be broken at the childhood level.

Furthermore, children must contend with the same myths and prejudices about battering that confront their mothers. People turn away from what is still viewed by many as a personal, private matter. The problem is trivialized, treated as a "family spat." Children are told not to worry, that it will be alright, when they know darn good and well that it will not.

Society has accepted the fact that direct child abuse should be considered a serious and unacceptable social issue, but few see these "secondary" victims in the home where only the mother is battered. Definitions must change. Spousal abuse in the presence of a child is child abuse. As stated in the NCADV Voice, "If we look at nothing else except the number of children entering shelters because of domestic violence, then it seems imperative that we recognize who these children are, what they have survived, and what it is they need from us."

Children's lives are disrupted in other ways as well. Frequently, a woman escaping an abusive relationship is at an even greater risk for assault by her ex-partner after she leaves. It's no surprise abusive men often stalk and attack women who leave, and frequently terrorize children, directly or indirectly, as well. Many women flee with their children, sometimes leaving behind birth certificates, medical records, and other paperwork required for school enrollment and social services. Abusers sometimes destroy these records, too. Often a terrorized woman moves several times a year, making a consistent education almost impossible. Since school records are available to parents, abusers have sometimes used their children's records to track down the mother or kidnap the child, and mothers who fear such actions sometimes keep children out of school to try and protect the family.

Other women are virtually penniless when they run from men who have controlled all of the household finances, and ill-equipped to find employment and housing after years of isolation.

Women who seek a divorce or legal separation from their abusive husbands face special concerns in dealing with child custody arrangements. Laws and social attitudes are changing, but serious problems in custody and visitation policies remain. Abusers sometimes fight for custody of children as another means of controlling and antagonizing a woman who left them; or they abduct their children. Custody is further discussed in chapter 6. One 1991 study found that more than 50 percent of child abductions were the result of domestic violence. Not surprisingly, this type of power play with a child as pawn causes the child tremendous anxiety and, in many cases, prolonged emotional trauma. Many professionals recommend that violent men be required to attend and participate in counseling as a condition of continued contact with their children.

Additionally, abusive men often withhold child support payments to try and punish or control the mother. Children must also contend with the same stereotypes and ignorance about domestic violence that their mothers face. Both adults and other children can be vicious toward a child who doesn't "fit in" with community presumptions.

Battered women are often blamed for the trauma their children suffer from living with abusive fathers. This is both inaccurate and unfair. Battered women usually go to great lengths to try and protect their children from the violence, and strive to be good parents in spite of the circumstances that make this overwhelmingly difficult, including their own physical and psychological injuries. In many cases, when a woman becomes aware of the damage being done to her children by exposing them to violence she leaves the relationship.

Shelters and other service agencies try to serve both battered women and their children, and many do an excellent job. But it is a sad reality that there is simply not enough space in most shelters for all that need help, and many communities still have no space at all. A few shelters reportedly admit only adult victims, though most will take women and their children, and many even allow victims to bring pets.

Just one warm, caring adult to love the child and say, "What's happening to you isn't right, it isn't fair, it's not your fault, and it won't always be like this" can make a huge difference. Many shelters and social service agencies have also established support groups for children who have experienced the trauma of a violent home, and many find this type of sharing tremendously helpful. However, children are unique individuals, and it is important to keep an open mind and offer alternative forms of help. The most important factor, however, is removing the violence from the child's home.

It is estimated that up to 50 percent of all homeless women and children in America are on the run from domestic violence. Battered women and their children make up a large portion of the residents of homeless shelters. Like battered women's shelters, the existing number of homeless shelters is inadequate to serve all those who need them, so many women return to their abusers because they cannot find another place to live or their time limit has run out. In 1991, children made up 50 percent of the people living below the poverty line in America. Some social service professionals argue witnessing violence should be considered a special form of child maltreatment, requiring changes in the law and the focus of social service programs. Such changes are starting to happen, but far more reform is crucial.

ADOLESCENTS IN ABUSIVE HOMES

Adolescents from abusive homes run a much higher risk of substance abuse, suicide, or running away. The trauma continues through adulthood. Many men in prison—some estimates place the figure as high as 90 percent—were abused or witnessed abuse in the home while growing up.

Even children who break the pattern and don't grow up to be violent themselves suffer terribly. According to a Baltimore study conducted in 1992 and 1993 at the Johns Hopkins Children's Center and described in a 1993 *Washington Post* article, teenagers exposed to violence, especially in the home, are more likely than others to become depressed or hopeless. Of the two hundred randomly selected adolescents, whose median age was sixteen, nearly 60 percent reported having witnessed threats or acts of violence in their own homes—from threatening to hit to shooting or stabbing. The study found that violence witnessed in the home greatly affected their outlook on life and carried a strong association with depression and emotional distress.

In comparisons between adolescents who had witnessed violence outside and inside the home, the prevalence of depression and hopelessness was higher among those who saw violence in their homes. "It seems as though taking away the protective effect of a stable home makes teenagers less able to cope with the violence they see in the community," says Robert A. Pendergrast, an assistant professor of pediatrics who led the research. This is not surprising. A home is supposed to be a refuge, a haven from the threats of the outside world. Yet it is the second most violent institution in American society, second only to the military in times of war.

The good news is that children who escape violent homes and find healthy adult models are remarkably resilient. Often, women who divorce batterers go on to remarry kind, gentle husbands who help heal the damage done to both the woman and her children. More and more research is being conducted on such "blended" or step-families as their numbers increase. These studies reflect that in situations where continued contact with the children is allowed, the best way a mother who has left an abusive relationship and married a gentle man can balance the needs of her children, particularly sons, to maintain a relationship with the biological father, is by allowing them to sort it out for themselves, which most will do admirably. As hard as it may be, if she allows the child to love both the biological father and the stepfather, most children will take notice of the difference in the way each treats them, their mother, and other people. Long-term observation of sons of abusive men who abandoned the family, after which the mother remarried a kind man who became a stable father figure, indicate that these boys soon begin to model his appropriate behavior and eventually become as healthy as those who never witnessed abuse. The important factors seem to be a strong male role model with whom the boy is allowed to develop a positive relationship at his own pace.

Dating Violence

A chilling "new" form of domestic violence is beginning to surface, though there is every sign it has been around for years: violence that occurs during a dating relationship, otherwise referred to as "dating violence." It occurs at an alarming rate among adolescent couples, with some experts estimating that between 20 and 30 percent of teenage dating couples experience violence.

Violence between couples who are not married or living together has happened for centuries, but has only recently begun to get nationwide attention. It manifests in all the same forms as violence between spouses, with one exception: Rape and other sexual abuse is much more common, or at least more frequently reported, among dating couples.

Violence is a special problem among teenage couples. Teenage abuse victims may also have a more difficult time getting free of an abusive relationship for several reasons. Teens have less knowledge of available resources. They may find those they are familiar with, such as police and school counselors, to be unresponsive or intimidating. Unfortunately, many adults see teenage dating relationships as frivolous or naturally volatile, and do not take the risk of violence seriously.

Yet the problem is both widespread and potentially deadly. Studies indicate that at least one in ten teens will be involved in an abusive relationship and, as with other forms of domestic violence, in 95 percent of the cases it is the male who is the abuser. Pregnant teens are especially at risk, with one study finding 32 percent of the girls surveyed reporting physical or sexual abuse in the prior year. Also, both teenagers and adults who are abused tend to enter prenatal care later in the pregnancy than nonabused women.

Dating violence has been described as an epidemic among teenagers. On June 24, 1994, fourteen-year-old Rosie Vargas of Santa Ana, California, was murdered by her sixteen-year-old boyfriend. This tragedy has brought to light chilling statistics on the extreme and widespread nature of violence among teen couples.

The most common trait of this form of violence is the need to control and possess the victim just as in the violent adult relationship. An abusive boyfriend often forces his girlfriend to abandon other friends, become alienated from her family, spend all her time with him, or even, as in Rosie Vargas' case, quit school.

The abuse generally starts with intimidation and verbal abuse, including name-calling, put-downs, and exploiting insecurities that are magnified during adolescence, such as the fear that no one else will want to date the girl. It often involves the familiar control issues, such as activity control and isolation from family and friends. The abusive teen often displays the characteristic "Jekyll and Hyde" personality swings. Physical violence may follow the cyclical pattern, with tension, explosion, then promises to change. The violence is often blamed on the girl, or characterized as "no big deal." Forced sexual activity is often a feature of these relationships. And, as in adult abusive relationships, the violence often escalates when the woman asserts her independence or tries to break off the relationship.

Yet there are special factors that may make teenagers more susceptible to violent relationships than adults. As most of us recall, self-esteem is especially vulnerable during adolescence. There is probably no other time of life when self-image is so shaky, and peer acceptance is crucial to a person's sense of self-worth. People who work with teens in violent relationships repeatedly hear statements like, "I feel like nobody without him."

Additionally, teenagers simply lack life experience. They do not have the perspective of adults in making decisions. Young women tend to be susceptible to romantic notions that "true love" means an all-encompassing passion that allows for jealousy, possessiveness, and aggression as a demonstration of devotion and commitment. According to Barrie Levy, author of several books about battering and teens, "They're more apt to think that violence is what happens in a relationship. They tend to minimize or romanticize it." Levy also notes that teens tend to subscribe to more rigid gender roles and treat nonconformists harshly. Girls feel they need to have a boyfriend to have a social identity, and boys equate aggressive behavior with manliness.

Levy believes that even those with a mature perspective, who know jealousy is not love and realize their abusive boyfriends are not likely to change, still have a hard time leaving the relationship. Many are afraid to tell their parents, so they turn to friends for support. Yet their friends are likely to be in the same position or equally inexperienced in dealing with such trauma.

It is easy to see how teens from homes in which the mother is battered would have a distorted view. Yet the problem is not limited to couples from violent homes. Studies estimate that as many as two out of every five girls will be emotionally or physically abused by a boyfriend or date. Few report the abuse to parents or other adults. And the pattern starts when people are very young. According to a study conducted at the University of Illinois, fourteen-year-old girls suffer as much violence as eighteen-year-olds. The limited research that has been done on dating violence indicate the sad, but not surprising, fact that boys who beat their girlfriends are the adult batterers of the future, and girls who accept abuse as teenagers are far more likely to tolerate it as adults.

Part of the blame has to rest with social attitudes toward appropriate roles and behavior of children. Girls on grade school playgrounds often think if boys hit or shove them, it means they like them. Boys are expected to be tough; schoolyard fights are considered normal, even a necessary rite of passage, by some. Most parents still consider spanking an acceptable form of discipline. Popular fiction aimed at teens, rock and rap lyrics, movies, and music videos often mingle violence with depictions of passion and sex. One California teen, quoted in an article that appeared in *The Orange County Register* after the Vargas murder said, "Guys beating girls just seems normal. It starts when you're thirteen or fourteen. The guys brag about it."

"It drives me crazy," said Gina Philbert-Ortega, of the Southern California Coalition on Battered Women, quoted in the same article. "Adults want to dismiss it all as puppy love. But it's not. It's deadly." She describes one teenage girl she counseled. The fourteen-year-old dated a high school football star who beat her, yet she was the envy of her friends. One day he pulled a knife and nonchalantly sliced her arm for speaking to another boy—as though it was okay. Philbert-Ortega laments, "In a sense it was. Adults aren't stopping it, and girls don't know how."

Another alarming aspect of violence among teens is the prevalence of guns in the hands of increasingly younger adolescents. This is of special concern in areas plagued by gang violence. Cases in which boyfriends or ex-boyfriends use guns to frighten, injure, or kill young women and bystanders are becoming increasingly frequent.

Young women face more obstacles when they do try to use the resources available to adult victims. In many states, a minor will have a more difficult time getting a protective order, especially if she does not have an adult to support her in the process. Many shelters and counseling programs also require adult permission. Schools that do intervene often transfer the victims—reinforcing the "blame-the-victim" mentality and making the girls perceive they have done something shameful for which they are being punished.

Violence, including rape, stalking, and battering, is also on the rise on college campuses and among younger women in general. A recent Canadian government study found women between the ages of eighteen and twenty-four were twice as likely to report having been the victims of violence during the year before the study than older women.

Fortunately, more services geared toward young victims are becoming available. In 1994, the National Coalition Against Domestic Violence announced a teen dating violence resource project to collect national information for a *Teen Dating Violence Resource Manual*. The NCADV produces a video on dating violence entitled "Rough Love" and other materials especially for teen education and intervention. Many local groups, churches, and schools have also begun to establish programs to prevent and reduce violence among young couples.

One form of violence especially prevalent among young women is as misunderstood as it is common. In her book *Sexual Violence: Our War Against Rape*, Linda A. Fairstein reports that over 50 percent of rapes are assaults by men who know their victims. This statistic includes any case which involves previous, nonviolent interaction between the people involved, so it includes rapes by acquaintances, co-workers, and others as well; but there is no question that a high number of these assaults happen between dating couples.

There are two factors that make it difficult to stop this form of abuse. First, many people think it is less traumatic or serious than rape by a stranger; that it is not "real rape." In fact, it may be more damaging to a woman's long-term psychological health to be treated brutally and violated in the most intimate way possible by someone she knows and trusts. Studies of women who have endured such assaults indicate they often suffer guilt, self-blame, and social isolation, and doubt their ability to determine who can be trusted. Second, when a woman is raped by a stranger the main issue in the criminal prosecution is the identity of the rapist, the assumption being that of course she was raped, but is the accused the one who did it? A woman raped by someone she knows must face additional questions regarding whether she was raped at all. The most common defense to this type of rape is that it was consensual.

Yet those who rape girlfriends, co-workers, and friends are beginning to be convicted more often. As in any other criminal case, what is required to convict a rapist is ample evidence to prove guilt beyond a reasonable doubt. Credible testimony from the victim can be enough. However, it is essential to have as much evidence as possible. For this reason, and for the health of a victim who may have suffered greater injury than is immediately apparent, it is crucial that any rape victim seeks immediate medical attention. The information she provides will be kept confidential by the doctor unless the patient consents to its release, and many hospitals have special advocates to help and counsel all rape victims. Additionally, rape crisis hotlines and centers provide services for victims of date or acquaintance rape, as well as for those raped by strangers. Some young women, in particular, are not aware of these sources of help.

If the victim decides to prosecute—as she should—a medical report can provide powerful evidence, even if there is no serious physical injury. When sex is nonconsensual, there are physiological differences that a doctor may be able to note.

If sexual assault between dating couples is to be treated as the serious crime that it is, certain myths about rape, particularly rape by husbands or boyfriends, must be shattered. Everyone must learn what rape is and what it is not. Rape is not sex. The goal of rape is not an expression of love, desire, or affection. Rape is an act of violence. It is about control, degradation, hatred, humiliation, and terror. Victims of rape include tiny infants to the very elderly.

Rapists are not all underprivileged, unattractive, or uneducated. Highly publicized rape cases have involved doctors, judges, politicians, professors, dentists, priests, men in stable marriages. Again—it can't be overemphasized—rape is not an act of sex. Men do not rape because they cannot find a willing sex partner. They rape a woman to hurt and degrade her.

I've heard men complain that charges of date rape are "unfair" because many women play games, say no when they mean yes because they think a struggle adds to the excitement; or "nice girls" can't just consent, they have to be persuaded. I say baloney. No means no. One wise man I know, who is now married, says that in his dating days he occasionally ran across a woman who seemed to be teasing when she said no. His response? "As soon as I heard the word no, I stood up, zipped up, and headed straight for the door. It was just a matter of respecting a person, of decent behavior. And if she meant something other than no, I'd find out soon enough!" A very smart policy.

Fortunately, law enforcement, the courts, and those in the social service fields are beginning to see rape by acquaintances and partners as the serious crime it is. As Linda Fairstein explains, the goal and reward of people who work in these difficult jobs is to be able to give the victims what they least expect and most deserve: a just verdict in the courtroom and a more comfortable path navigating through the criminal justice system.

Likewise, violence between adolescents is finally being taken more seriously. Experts on dating violence generally agree that the best way to keep adults from becoming batterers and rapists is to attack the roots of the problem before and during adolescence, through education and treatment; and that parents and other authorities must snap to attention and recognize how serious the problem really is. Professionals urge that girls be taught what constitutes healthy and unhealthy dating behavior, along with some basic techniques of self-defense and safety. Boys must learn to treat their girlfriends with respect—and that no always means no. They must learn very early that power and control over women are not positive masculine traits. Besides direct education of the potential or current victims, school authorities, social service workers, and other adults need to develop programs for those involved in violent relationships that do not make the victim feel she is being punished.

A few of the leading coalitions against domestic violence have developed presentations on teen dating violence and date rape that are provided to teens in schools. These groups may also provide materials and assistance to teens for creating their own groups to work against dating violence, train teachers to present more extensive programs in the classroom, and distribute posters and brochures. Health care professionals can intervene by making victims aware of services and discussing their options and alternatives. Shelter experience can be especially appropriate for an adolescent, because she will hear the stories of older women and learn that the violence does not end if she marries the abuser, loves him more, or keeps forgiving him.

One thing that needs to be emphasized above all else: Men who are violent in dating relationships do not change with marriage—except, very often, for the worse.

SPECIAL PROGRAMS FOR CHILDREN AND ADOLESCENTS

In some areas, treatment programs are offered for the "forgotten victims." Minnesota's Domestic Abuse Project (DAP), headquartered in Minneapolis, has been a leader in this effort. It offers support groups for children ages four to five, six to eight, nine to twelve, and separate male and female groups for adolescents. The groups meet for ten weeks, with a team of male and female therapists. The program's goals are to help the children:

1. Give responsibility for the violence to the appropriate person
2. Relieve feelings of shame and isolation
3. Deal with loss or separation from the abusive parent
4. Protect themselves from violence in the home
5. Express their feelings openly and appropriately
6. Resolve conflicts nonviolently
7. Cultivate healthy sex roles
8. Develop a healthy self-image

The group's most important overall goal is to break the cycle of violence that repeats through the generations so the children can resolve their trauma and grow into healthy individuals. DAP offers manuals and training to other communities wishing to establish groups for children (see appendix).

Unfortunately, Minneapolis is the exception, rather than the rule. Children who witness violence tend to be the ignored victims, unless they are also directly abused. Those social services that do exist for children in or escaping violent families tend to focus, understandably, on short-term emergency needs like food and shelter. Given the severe trauma and ongoing psychological and social problems these children face—including a greatly increased likelihood of falling into patterns of violence themselves—greater attention to helping them is essential. Of course, not all children who witness violence in the home grow up to be abusers or have severe psychological problems. But even those who grow into exemplary adults suffer. President Bill Clinton has spoken of the anger he felt when he saw his stepfather abuse his mother.

Parents can help reassure children by explaining what is going on and acknowledging that violence is a problem, that abuse is not okay, and things need to change, but that it is not the children's fault. School personnel, teachers, counselors, psychologists, and social workers can also provide reassurance, comfort, and counseling. Many local mental health organizations offer counseling free or on a sliding fee scale according to income. More and more of the same organizations that help abused women—shelters, community programs, social service agencies, private organizations like the YWCA—are beginning to emulate Minneapolis with similar programs. Most can at least provide referrals to other services for children.

ONE WOMAN'S STORY

Author Rosemary L. Bray grew up in a home with a violent father who battered her mother. Writing in Ms., she describes the effects of this trauma on her life as an adult, wife, and mother. She describes the way her father kept the family "suspended in a state of terror," and her mother's hopeless efforts that became the single goal of her life: not to "get your father started."

Bray points out the absurdity of the fact that the most dangerous place for a woman in the United States is the very place she should feel safest, as should the forgotten victims—the children who grow up witnessing such a twisted version of the male-female relationship.

She also confirms that even children who do not witness the violence directly virtually always know ". . . the sound of every blow, the vibration of every wall as their mothers' bodies hit, the pitch of every voice raised in anger . . . those children lie crying in their beds, praying (if they have words for prayers), begging God or someone to make Mama and Daddy stop fighting, to make Daddy stop hitting, to make Mama stop crying."

Bray says that though children may forgive, they never forget, and the memories color their intimate relationships forever. She speaks of the automatic terror that made her jump away when her husband removed his belt one evening while changing clothes and folded it in the same way her father did when he was about to use his belt as a weapon. She writes of the difficulty of allowing her husband the freedom to be angry, even though he gently reminded her over and over that he was not her father, and nothing like her father.

Parenthood is a special challenge, says Bray. She is the mother of a young son, and describes how she wants, with all her heart, for the cycle of violence to end with her. Yet she expresses a fear common to children raised in violent homes, the constant worry about whether they will eventually end up like their parents. She wants her son to see parents who can become angry at one another and resolve the problem with communication and humor. Bray says she knew she would never allow a man to beat her, yet she worries about whether she has learned enough about handling her own anger. However, she says that to react toward her son with violence would have been her father's final victory—and she will not have it.

Bray also writes poignantly of the pain and loss she feels when she hears her friends describe loving relationships with gentle, protective fathers. She says, "[I] would give anything to think of my daddy the way other women do."

ONE MAN'S STORY

Andy Martinez is a man I know to be gentle, fun-loving, quick to laugh. He is a successful attorney in his early thirties, married to a social worker/therapist and is the adoring father of a young daughter. I have long been aware that he grew up in a violent home, but I could never see how profoundly his background had affected him until he agreed to share his experiences for this book.

Andy's father grew up in a large southwestern ranching family, the only one of eight children who went to college, which he accomplished on the GI bill. His mother was raised in a poorer family, more so after her father died when she was a young teenager. At a very young age she became responsible for earning money to help keep the family afloat.

Andy says his mother's first warning sign came the night before her wedding, when his father demanded she give him her paycheck. She also had a car she had shared with her sister and planned to give back to her family after the wedding, but he would not allow it, insisting she keep it for use as a family car. Soon after the marriage, he decided they would move from New Mexico to Los Angeles. "He cut her off from all her family and friends, wouldn't let her keep in touch with them. It was like a prison," Andy says.

Andy isn't sure when the physical abuse started, but believes it began early in the marriage, and continued consistently throughout. He is also uncertain when he first knew something was wrong, but believes children are aware of discord between their parents at a very young age. "My daughter is only sixteen months old, and when my wife and I were arguing the other night she picked up on the tone of our voices. She started patting me on the leg, as though she was telling me to stop."

He recalls a terrifying nightmare he had at the age of four or five, in which he dreamed he saw his mother's decapitated head rolling around the living room floor. The first time he clearly remembers seeing his father hit his mother was shortly after the family had moved back to

New Mexico, when Andy was six. He awoke to hear his mother scream-ing, felt frightened, and walked into the living room to see what was happening. His father was on the floor on top of his mother, strangling her. "She was begging him to stop, saying, 'The baby—what are you doing?' He looked up and saw me and told me to go back to my room. I did, but I knew something was very wrong. Later, my mother told me I probably saved her life that night."

Andy, like many others in abusive families, learned to recognize his father's slowly building anger. "We knew it was coming—it was like a tornado warning. The waiting was the worst part. My mother and I would be walking on eggshells. My father had all kinds of rules we had to obey. I had to have my hair combed at the dinner table, things like that. We were always living in fear, measuring our words. Little things could set him off—leaving the shampoo in the bathtub was a big deal."

A younger sister was born when Andy was eight. While the abuse con-tinued, the family dynamics had a different effect on his sister. "She never would play his game," Andy says. "She always spoke her mind and con-fronted him. And she never got hit." Andy also says his father would occasionally beat his mother in front of him, but never in front of his sister.

Andy's father would go on a severe rampage every two months or so, but the violence did not follow the classic cycle. "He usually showed no remorse. I remember a couple of times after a bad episode my parents would sit down with me and try to explain that they loved each other and these things 'just happened.' But usually we just hoped he would get it over with and be in a good mood for awhile."

Andy's father did demonstrate other typical characteristics of an abuser, however. "We never had major problems with money, but he was always miserly," Andy recalls. "He had to be in control of everyone and everything. He was always reclusive—he had no relationship with his family, no friends, no social life. He was bitter about the people he had to work with—the family was all he had. I don't doubt he was afraid of being abandoned. He and I both enjoy following politics and current events, but at home he would do the talking and my mother and I would listen."

Fortunately, Andy's mother did have a life outside the home. "She was his opposite—very outgoing, had many friends, her family was important to her." Andy grew up much like his mother. He remembers a few good times when the family seemed close, but describes them as "only a fraction of the sad times." Even his proudest childhood achievements were bittersweet. "When I was in ninth grade, I won a rotary club speech contest. There was a ceremony where all the kids who won gave their speeches and received a prize, and parents were invited to attend. My mother had to work, and my father didn't show up. I was the only one there alone."

When Andy was fourteen, he began to intervene in the beatings to try and protect his mother. Not surprisingly, his father then turned his fists against his son. "I would step in and he would go after me. Then he would stop, or at least focus his attention on me so my mother had enough time to leave." This pattern continued until his parents separated for the first time.

"My mother had tried to leave before," he recalls. "She would go to the Laundromat, or get in her car and drive to the police station and sit in the car. They knew what was going on, but didn't do anything. She went to the local shelter two or three times, but that saddened her. It was so hard for her—she was afraid, but also embarrassed." Andy says his mother felt it was important to keep the family together, and there was a stigma in the community to being divorced. "We just wanted to live a normal life," he says. "Also, my mother worried about making enough money to support us, and my father threatened that if she left, he would provide no money."

Andy's parents finally separated when he left for college, but reconciled after a couple of months. "I was really sad when my mother took him back; sad to see him back in our home." Several more separations and reconciliations followed over the next few years.

Andy spoke to his father for the last time when he was in law school and decided to get married. "I got engaged in January, but didn't tell him until April. I couldn't share this with him. When I finally went to give him the news, he just listened to me a few moments and then left the room."

The final split between Andy's parents came when his mother went to see his father to discuss plans for Andy's wedding. He was waiting for her, and grabbed her by the hair and threw a jar of urine and excrement into her face. He beat her severely, and kept her up all night, forcing her to listen to his abuse.

At this time, Andy was working as a summer law clerk. His mother asked him to prepare a restraining order to keep his father away from her and out of the home. With the assistance of one of the lawyers at the firm, he drafted the papers and helped his mother get one of the area's top family law firms to handle a divorce. "There was a moral victory of sorts in the divorce. My mother got better than a 50-50 split on the property division, and also recovered some compensation on a personal injury claim she brought for the abuse. But it was sickening to see my father lie under oath in his deposition, claiming he never hit her."

Fortunately, Andy's father agreed to leave the house and get his own apartment, and has left his mother alone for the past six or seven years.

"She's very happy now. No one will ever again tell her how to run her life. She's more assertive, and doesn't take guff from anyone. I'm proud of her. She's in her mid-fifties now, and she regrets the time she lost, but the fact that she could get out and start over after 32 years of abuse speaks volumes."

Andy reflects on the pain of his childhood with difficulty, even now. "For the first eight years, I was an only child. It was hard not having any-one—I always wondered what it would be like to have an older brother or sister. I had no close friends that I felt would understand. I thought this was a rare thing. Although we were raised Catholic, we weren't a particularly religious family, but I had no one to turn to but God. So I started praying a lot and going to church on my own. I just wanted the hitting to stop, wanted things to get better. I remember when I was in fifth grade, I tried to make a deal with God—I would stop cussing if He would make my father stop hitting my mother." He recalls many nights alone in his room, praying and hoping.

Andy sees several traits in himself he believes to be a result of grow-ing up in a violent home. "I have problems dealing with any conflict in my relationships with people. It's ironic that I became a litigator, because I can't avoid discord in my work. But I never want to address conflicts in my personal life—I just hope they'll blow over. It drives my wife crazy. That was always the bottom line at home—I didn't care about finding a solution, I just wanted the problem to go away."

Andy knew early on he would never be abusive like his father, yet he feels his upbringing has influenced the kind of women he has chosen as partners. "I've always been attracted to strong women who wouldn't allow anyone to boss them around," he says. "All the women I've loved have been very smart, tough, bright, and independent. My wife works with children who have been sexually abused, and adult incest survivors. She would never put up with being abused herself."

Andy also sees the effect of his background in his relationship with his daughter. "I was really afraid to be a parent. I want to do everything right. I want her to grow up in a peaceful home, and it's really important to me that she always sees her mother and I showing respect for one another."

He also believes it is very important for both parents to be a part of the child's life. "When my wife and I decided to have children, I was really hoping to have a son, so I could do all the things for him that my dad never did for me. I was hung up on providing what was missing in my life to a son of my own. But now I know that all children need a good father, and I can give as much to a daughter, too. Plus I'm so in love with her that I can't imagine having had any other child. We plan to have one or two more, but now I don't care if they are girls or boys."

Andy feels a void in not having had a good father to guide him in how to be a father to his own children. Yet he has always remained very close to his mother, and is grateful to have had good men, counselors, and close friends in his life to serve as role models.

"A school counselor gave me a lot of support in ninth grade. She had a really positive effect on me. My best friend's father was a strong influence, too. In high school, I made several close friends who were high achievers and showed me the importance of college," he remembers. "Sports became very important to me, too. Baseball and football gave me a chance to gain some self-confidence, and be around other people who encouraged me."

Andy continued professional counseling as an adult. "I think therapy is important for people who grew up around abuse. My therapist really helped me come to terms with the past. Yet I know the violence will always affect the way I look at things. For instance, when I heard O. J. Simpson had been charged with murder, I was really saddened. He had been a big hero of mine when I was growing up. Then I heard those 911 tapes—heard the fear in Nicole's voice—and it brought back my Mom's fear. I instantly lost all respect I'd ever had for O. J. Anyone who beats their wife is a coward and should be locked up."

Recently, Andy feels more sorrow than anger when he thinks about his father. "I saw him once, not long ago, at the legislature—I was lobbying, and he was there watching the session, as he has always liked to do. It was sad and strange—we were standing 20 feet apart, but neither of us acknowledged the other. I've done well in my life. I have a good career and a great family; I would think he would be proud, that he would want to make some attempt to know me. I can't understand why I'm not important enough to him."

Andy also feels frustration when he hears about the continuing widespread incidence of domestic violence. "We assume that if we offer help and services they will be accepted and used. This isn't necessarily true. People trying to help sometimes have no concept of what emotional wrecks the victims are, or how hard it is to pull out. These people are so damaged—many are just too screwed up to take advantage of the help that's there. But we have to try." Andy plans to volunteer for a local domestic violence hotline that provides free legal advice to the victims. He also feels personal intervention by friends who know of abuse in a home can make a big difference. "Some of the people—like coaches—who knew what was going on in my family could have helped when I was growing up, but didn't do anything. So a couple of times when I knew friends were abusing their wives and subjecting their kids to this, I told them I had first-hand knowledge of what abuse can do to a family and that they had better get help. A couple of them did. So it can be done."

Andy has become an exceptional person with a stable and rewarding life. Yet the emotional scars remain. "I've had a recurring nightmare for five or six years now, that I go home to see my mother and he's there—she has let him come back again. I've had that dream hundreds of times. I don't know if it will ever stop."

CHAPTER SIX

DOMESTIC VIOLENCE
AND THE LAW

Ironically, some of our most cherished ideals of personal liberty and individual freedom have helped create a climate in which abuse of family members has flourished. Since the Declaration of Independence, Americans have fiercely opposed government interference in private life. Limited political power and strong individual rights have been espoused as ideals since the dawn of our nation. Yet the words of the Declaration of Independence declaring "all *men* are created equal" are not without significance. Throughout the nineteenth and well into the twentieth century, all the rights belonged exclusively to men—not to women and children who were considered the chattel of males.

As recently as the 1970s, most judges followed the predominant social trend, and ultimately based their decisions on the idea that "family matters" were outside the jurisdiction of the court. They felt (as some still do) that the power of the law ended at the threshold of the home.

However, great changes have occurred over the past twenty years. During the 1980s, nearly all states enacted domestic violence reform statutes which, among other things, set procedures for obtaining a civil protection, or restraining, order. This was, in many cases, the first tool offered to victims besides filing a criminal complaint or getting a divorce.

Today, there are three basic areas of the law in which victims of domestic violence can find help. These include criminal law, civil law, and family law. Most of the laws involved are state laws, although in some instances federal law or local (city and county) law may come into play, especially in large cities. However, most of the concepts discussed in this chapter with regard to state law apply to the other laws as well.

CRIMINAL LAW AND THE CRIMINAL JUSTICE SYSTEM

Often, the first place a woman turns to stop immediate abuse is the police department. The police enforce criminal laws, and also provide referrals to available services such as shelters, medical treatment, and counseling programs.

Criminal law refers to laws against crimes such as assault, battery, and murder. These laws give police the authority to arrest a person reasonably believed to have broken the law. Then the state, through its prosecutors (district or state's attorneys), prosecutes the crime in the court system.

The goals of criminal law are deterrence (discourage the offender and others from committing the crime); rehabilitation (counseling, therapy, and education programs that teach offenders why and how to change their behavior); victim protection (in the case of domestic violence, helping the victim terminate the relationship and keep the abuser away, plus financial and psychological support); and punishment. Most sentences try to achieve all or most of these goals.

The law continues to evolve, with many new innovations and ideas being discussed and implemented. Some advocates urge strict application of the "three strikes, you're out" felony conviction laws that provide life imprisonment for anyone convicted of three felonies. Others promote a graduated penalty system, similar to that used against DUI (Driving Under the Influence of alcohol or drugs) offenders, in which each subsequent conviction brings a stiffer penalty. Efforts are also underway to invoke the same public outrage against domestic violence as has grown against DUI, another crime that kills and injures far too many innocent victims.

The Criminal Justice System

The "criminal justice system" refers to the different people and systems that work together to enforce the criminal laws. It usually includes police, prosecutors, and judges. It may also include the corrections system, which is made up of jails, prisons, probation departments, and parole boards.

The crime victim is never charged a fee in a criminal case, but under the traditional system, she must cooperate with the police by signing a report and with the prosecutor by pressing charges, appearing in court as a witness, and providing evidence of the crime. If the person accused of the crime pleads guilty or is convicted, he or she will be sentenced to various penalties, which may include paying a fine, spending time in jail or prison, serving a period of probation (supervised release with restrictions on behavior), and/or paying restitution—that is, paying the victim money to cover the damage caused by the criminal actions. In domestic violence cases, convicted abusers are also often required to obey orders to stay away from their victims, complete a program of counseling or treatment, or perform community service.

Both the criminal laws and the way in which they are enforced have been the target of serious reform efforts by advocates against domestic violence at all levels, from local groups and individuals who speak out to state legislatures and the United States Congress. Much remains to be done, but tremendous progress has been made, especially since the message is getting across that one of the best ways to put an immediate stop to a domestic assault, and to make a lasting impression on the abuser, is for the police to arrest him and take him to jail.

Domestic Violence Laws

All states now have special laws setting criminal penalties for domestic abuse. Some local jurisdictions (cities and counties) have these laws on the books as well, often to incorporate special services that are available locally, such as batterer treatment programs.

These laws are patterned after the traditional assault and battery laws, which make threatening or striking a person a crime. Most have both felony (serious crimes that can result in a prison sentence) and misdemeanor (minor crimes that bring a fine or jail sentence) classifications. They also provide for different degrees of the crime, depending on circumstances such as whether a weapon is used, the age or pregnancy of the victim, and the severity of the injuries inflicted.

Many of these laws contain special provisions to insure that the abuser can be immediately jailed for the victim's protection then swiftly brought before the court for arraignment. In this procedure, the person charged with a crime is brought to court, enters his or her plea, and is advised about alternatives. A separate hearing is usually scheduled for setting bail or denying release, but some domestic violence laws combine these proceedings. Often, a protection order (also called a "restraining order," "protective order," or "stay away order") prohibiting contact with the victim will be issued and an offender will be sent into a treatment program, with the provision that he obey the order and attend the program or return to jail.

One of the most important changes that has come about as states have modified or enacted laws specifically addressing domestic violence is the exception to the usual requirement that a police officer must witness a misdemeanor in action to make an arrest. In most states, an officer on a domestic call need only see some evidence that a crime has been committed, and a woman's injuries will suffice.

Many states now have mandatory arrest laws, which require a police officer to arrest the abuser if he or she has good reason to believe there has been a criminal domestic assault. Until recently, the usual procedure in most domestic violence cases was to try and mediate the dispute, or convince the man to calm down. However, arrest is the preferred response today. Some police departments require officers to complete an incident report even if no arrest is made, so the department can monitor the officers' response, share information with others in the system, and keep records and information about domestic abuse.

In June, 1994, the Family Violence Prevention Project of the National Council of Juvenile and Family Court Judges unveiled the Model Code on

Domestic and Family Violence, the culmination of a three-year endeavor funded by the Conrad N. Hilton Foundation. "Model laws" such as this one may be adopted in whole or in part, or declined, by each state. The council is also developing computer data bases and publications for state, community and individual use.

Laws Prohibiting Insurance Discrimination

According to an informal survey conducted in 1994 by the U.S. House Judiciary Committee, up to half of the nation's largest insurance companies have routinely used domestic violence as a factor in deciding whether to approve applicants for insurance coverage and how much to charge for premiums. Some insurers refusing coverage to victims or denying their claims have characterized abuse as a "pre-existing condition." Other companies have denied health, life, and disability insurance to victims of domestic violence on the absurd ground that abuse is a "lifestyle choice"—like smoking or skydiving. In the words of Congressman Bernard Sanders, who introduced federal legislation to prohibit such discrimination, "Domestic violence is not a choice, but a crime."

Fortunately, both the law and the insurance industry have responded to put a stop to such unfair practices. Many states have passed or introduced legislation prohibiting insurance companies from discriminating against abuse victims. As of 1996, thirteen states had already passed such laws, and bills were pending in about a dozen others. Most of these laws prohibit insurers from using domestic violence as a basis for refusing to insure an individual or from charging a higher premium because that person has been or might become a domestic violence victim. Legislation is also pending at the federal level. Congressman Sanders' Victims of Abuse Insurance Protection Act, which has been endorsed by many national advocacy groups, would prohibit discrimination against abuse victims in all lines of insurance, including health, life, property, disability, and casualty.

The National Association of Insurance Commissioners has also responded by adopting a model act prohibiting unfair discrimination against abuse victims in health benefits plans. It prohibits denial or termination of health insurance on the basis of abuse status; exclusion of coverage for losses incurred by an insured as a result of abuse; termination from group coverage of a victim who was insured in the name of her abuser, whom she has divorced or left, or who terminated her coverage; and disclosure by an insurer of any information about the insured's abuse status.

Rape and Sexual Assault

All states have laws against rape and other forms of sexual assault. Penalties for this type of abuse vary depending on the degree of the crime. Until recently, men who raped their wives could not be criminally prosecuted. This distinction was based on the ancient belief that marriage itself implied consent to any form of sexual activity at any time during the marriage. A few states still follow this ludicrous assumption.

In most states, however, these laws have been reformed as horror stories of terrifying, degrading, and truly sick sexual assaults by abusers on their wives have come to light. Now, men who rape their wives can be criminally prosecuted, although all but a few states consider marital rape a less serious crime than stranger rape. In some places, a man cannot be convicted of raping his wife unless they are living apart.

Stalking Laws

According to several credible estimates, at least half of the women who end abusive relationships are later followed, harassed, or threatened by their abusers.

"Stalking" may include following, spying upon, or harassing another person with unwanted attention, often involving telephone calls, visits, and letters. Until 1990, no state recognized stalking as a separate crime—the behavior had to cross the line to fit within one of the other recognized crimes such as trespassing, assault, or theft. Today, most states have enacted laws that give the police the power to arrest, and judges the power to punish the act of stalking itself.

Stalking is a frequent problem for women who have left a violent relationship. Dr. Lenore Walker has stated that she considers stalking a part of battering behavior. Others estimate that as many as 90 percent of the women who are eventually murdered by former husbands or boyfriends are first stalked.

Stalking laws are difficult for legislators to draft, and sometimes for police to enforce, because of the fine line between making the law broad enough to be effective against stalking behavior, without violating important individual rights of free speech, movement, privacy, and association. For example, people generally have the right to go where they please and speak to whomever the wish. But if a person persists in following, watching, and calling another who has asked to be left alone, such behavior goes beyond constitutionally protected activity and becomes a crime. The difficulty arises in trying to write a law that draws the line at the right place. Some states have had to rewrite their laws after court challenges, others are watching to see what happens as the existing laws are modified. The laws and the penalties they provide vary greatly. In California, for example, stalking may be either a felony or a misdemeanor, depending on whether a restraining order is being violated or how serious the threat or activity is.

The Police. Women are frequently advised to call 911 when attacked. This is good advice, and can save lives. But it shouldn't be the only part of the rescue plan. Depending on the community, the chances of prompt, effective, serious attention from the police range from outstanding to just about none.

Most departments now recommend or require police to arrest an abuser rather than try to mediate the dispute or make him leave for awhile to "cool down." Until recently, however, many police officers, prosecutors, and judges believed that arresting an assailant was not the most desirable alternative, and could actually make matters worse. The primary concern was to try and reduce the trauma to the family and the risk to the abuser's reputation, and perhaps his job, by avoiding the stigma associated with arrest. Furthermore, the victim was usually required to decide whether or not to press charges. Many were either intimidated or cajoled into not signing charges in the first place, or dropping them later.

These old methods remain in place in some areas, but important changes have been happening in the last ten to fifteen years as people are taking a closer look at the issue of family violence and learning that the old ways don't work. In 1980, the National Organization of Police Chiefs, a police executive research organization, studied the problem of domestic violence and issued a recommendation that police arrest batterers rather than attempt mediation. A landmark study conducted in Minneapolis in 1984 that compared three typical police responses to domestic abuse found that arrest was the most effective in stopping subsequent violence. This led to a recommendation by the U.S. Attorney General that arrest should be the standard police procedure when officers respond to domestic assault calls. Today, even states that do not have mandatory arrest laws often have departmental policies requiring arrest. A highly publicized lawsuit found that a police department that ignored a woman's pleas for help was in violation of her civil rights, and had to pay her $2.6 million dollars in 1985, helped spur widespread adoption of arrest policies.

Twenty-five states now require by law that police make an arrest when called to the scene of a violent domestic dispute in which there is "probable cause" to support criminal charges. That means enough evidence at the scene to support the reasonable conclusion that a crime has been committed. A woman's injuries will usually satisfy this requirement.

Other states have laws that require police to remain at the scene of a domestic violence call until the victim is safe, and to help her get medical treatment, shelter services, and/or a protective order. In some places, police call a shelter advocate who contacts or visits the victim. Still other officers carry written information for victims about their legal rights and social service options. Some police departments forward domestic assault reports directly to prosecutors who obtain a protection order for the victim and proceed against the criminal without her involvement.

Technology has also assisted in the battle against domestic violence. Batterers may be required to wear an electronic bracelet as a condition of a restraining order. The victim carries a beeper, which will go off if the abuser comes within one hundred yards. Although this is not widely used yet, such options are becoming increasingly available.

Better technology also allows expansion of services to victims by allowing certain procedures, which formerly had to wait until business hours, to be completed at night or on a weekend, sometimes still at the scene of the crime. For example, on-call judges, prosecutors, and advocates can work with police via fax to obtain immediate protection orders.

Cambridge, Massachusetts, and thirty other cities now have "panic buttons" that are made available to women who are especially at risk for domestic violence. Such people include women who are being stalked by a former abusive partner after leaving the relationship, those who have received threats from an abuser, those with a protection order against an abusive partner, and those whose former abuser is about to be released from jail.

The button is a small electronic device that can be carried around the home and out into the yard. It gets a message to the police more quickly than a telephone call, and the message is registered as an immediate priority. Cambridge police respond to button calls within two to three minutes.

Many states and communities have undertaken valiant efforts to improve police response to domestic violence. Such efforts include training programs to teach officers the dynamics of the abusive relationship and how to best handle family violence calls, and changes in the law so police will treat domestic violence calls as seriously as they treat calls reporting violence between strangers.

Problems sometimes arise in conjunction with mandatory arrest laws. Women may be arrested too, if they are trying to defend themselves against the batterer. In one case, a man who beat his pregnant girlfriend was arrested for aggravated assault. She threw a bottle at his truck, and was charged with assault with a deadly missile and violently resisting arrest. His bail was set at $3,000; hers was $10,000.

Mandatory arrest must also be followed by consistent prosecution. In some areas, as few as five percent of the offenders arrested are prosecuted. Furthermore, policy does not guarantee practice, and arrest rates are still not consistent in some areas, although law or policy mandates arrest. In a 1994 Associated Press news story, it was reported that a man convicted of beating a stranger in Cook County, Illinois (Chicago and vicinity), is 50 percent more likely to go to jail than if he is found guilty of beating his wife or girlfriend.

Most police officers in America have no special training in handling domestic violence, yet as many as forty percent of all calls requiring police response are domestic disturbances. Training programs such as one developed by the San Francisco Family Violence Prevention Fund are becoming widely available to teach officers both the dynamics behind the violent relationship and the practical aspects of how to handle enforcement challenges in these difficult situations.

In some areas, special domestic violence units have been established. Albuquerque, New Mexico, was one of the first U.S. cities to create a special team of police devoted exclusively to dealing with domestic violence calls. This unit, called the DART (Domestic Abuse Response Team), is composed of officers specially trained in the nature of the violent relationship, the psychology of abusers, effective communication with victims, and the steps necessary to get the abusers into court and make the charges stick. Officers not only respond to family violence calls and arrest abusers, but offer transportation for victims who need to go to a hospital or shelter, assistance with protection orders, and even on-the-spot counseling. In one case, a woman who mentioned marriage counseling after an attack was told by an officer that she didn't need marriage counseling—because she was not the problem. The officer explained that the abuser had the problem with power and control, and needed domestic violence and anger management counseling. Victims are often surprised but appreciative when they receive such advice, especially if, as with the case of this abused woman, they have not been treated well by the police on past calls.

These specially trained officers often find themselves having to educate not only victims and abusers but their fellow police officers as well. Even those in the front lines of law enforcement still ask the woman, "Why didn't you leave?" instead of asking the criminal, "Why are you beating her?"

DART officers also carry tape recorders on all calls. Because so many victims recant charges (one officer estimated the figure may be as high as 95 percent), Albuquerque has instituted a mandatory prosecution policy.

Once an abuser is arrested, charges will be filed regardless of whether or not the victim changes her mind. The district attorney can rely on the tape recording and the officer's written statement as evidence. According to former District Attorney Bob Schwartz, who instituted the policy, this mandatory prosecution also acts as a preventive measure, designed to stop the violence early before it escalates, as is often the case when abusers receive the message they are above the law and will not be punished.

An ongoing partnership between police and social services is, police officers stress, absolutely crucial. Police emphasize that they must have the tools to make the situation safe for the victim and children not just immediately, but on a long-term basis as well. This requires a coordinated commitment involving the criminal justice system, civil domestic violence commissioners, and others involved in education, services, and enforcement of the laws against family violence. Police stress that intervention needs to be strong and immediate the first time a perpetrator is caught—because that is seldom his first offense. As one member of Albuquerque's DART team remarked, "It's frustrating when you put your life on the line to save someone, then you go to work the next day and find out they're dead." Officers stress that all offenders—whether male, female, or juvenile, must be held accountable with real consequences.

This type of joint effort between police and prosecutors is essential if mandatory arrest laws are to have a meaningful effect. Dedicated police officers who follow arrest policies are understandably frustrated when perpetrators are set free and cases are never completed.

Two things seem to be necessary to assure law enforcement follows arrest rules: first, disciplinary action against officers who violate the rules and, second, training of police in the dynamics of the violent relationship so they understand why mediation doesn't work and why arrest is so important. Communities that have a coordinated program in which police, courts, and social services work and train together generally have the highest levels of arrest and overall success in lowering rates of domestic violence.

Criminal justice is changing as society finally begins to see domestic violence as a serious crime. States are also getting tougher with abusers who violate protective orders. Colorado recently passed a law that not only requires police to take an abuser into custody at the scene of the violence, but also mandates arrest for the first violation of a protection order. Subsequent violations bring mandatory jail time.

In a national crime survey conducted between 1978 and 1982, nearly half of all the incidents of domestic violence discovered had not been reported to the police. Many women do not call the police due to fear, distrust of the system, or shame, or because they do not know that domestic violence is a crime. Understandably, many fear that if they do call the police, their abusers will become more vicious. Yet the same study showed that 41 percent of the married victims who did not call the police were assaulted by their abusers again within a six-month period, while among those who did call only 15 percent were battered again within six months.

If you are given the option of whether or not to press charges so the abuser can be arrested, realize that by doing so you will be doing the best possible thing for both you and him. Some studies have shown that police arrest of batterers can cut repeat offenses in half.

If you live in an area where the police are known to respond more slowly to domestic calls, some experts suggest there is no need to state that it is your partner who is beating you when you call for help. Simply state that you are being attacked or beaten up.

Be sure the officers see your injuries and note them in the report, even if you don't think they are severe or you are not going to seek medical attention. Point out damage to property, and give them broken dishes or torn clothing as evidence if they don't ask. Be sure to tell the officers if the abuser has a history of violence, or if there is a protection order in effect. If there are witnesses such as neighbors, tell the officers their names and addresses.

It's best from both a medical and legal standpoint to get your injuries checked even if you don't think they are serious. You may be injured internally and, even if your injuries are minor, the fact that you sought medical aid for domestic abuse can be powerful evidence in later legal proceedings.

Effective police training must involve not only departmental procedures, but the rationale behind them. Officers need to understand the dynamics of the abusive home and the pressures on battered women, which may effect their willingness to be cooperative in matters such as leaving the home and pressing charges.

Prosecutors. Prosecutors are the attorneys who work for the state to put criminals behind bars. They may be called district attorneys ("DAs"), state's attorneys, city attorneys, or simply prosecutors, depending on the location. According to traditional procedures, a prosecutor could not proceed with a case against a batterer unless the victim signed a complaint against him, or pressed charges, as it was called. This was often a problem, because the victim was frequently intimidated or charmed into dropping charges. However, since domestic violence is a crime against society as well as the victim, many jurisdictions have adopted new policies that allow prosecution of the abuser without requiring the victim to press charges. These "no-drop" policies allow the prosecutor to make a strong statement to the offender and the public that domestic violence is a crime and will be treated accordingly.

In some places, prosecutors employ advocates to help victims understand and use the judicial system, to provide emotional support, and to be certain important information is exchanged between the victim and the prosecutor. Advocates help victims navigate their way through the civil and criminal court systems, coordinate with social service programs according to what each victim needs, and be sure the others in the process, like prosecutors and judges, are aware of special circumstances, such as threats and danger to victims who plan to testify.

The prosecutor usually has choices about what penalties to seek against an offender, depending on the circumstances of the individual case. Some states allow the option of sending the abuser to a treatment program, either along with some jail time or instead of incarceration. Treatment may also be a condition of probation. In most of these programs, the charges against the offender will be dropped if he successfully completes the program and obeys the court's other orders (such as staying away from the victim). If he does not finish the program, commits another crime, or violates a court order, the prosecutor can refile the charges. The programs are generally not offered to repeat offenders or those with very violent histories.

Given the increasing efforts to strengthen laws against domestic violence throughout the 1990s, most prosecutors feel that the laws on the books are now adequate, for the most part. What is needed is better application and use of these existing laws. Many areas are developing standard operating procedures for police responding to a domestic violence call, often including special tools such as Polaroid's photo kit and a checklist prepared by the prosecutor's office, so police won't overlook any important evidence and will be sure to include all appropriate charges. Also, some areas have developed special protocols for situations in which the perpetrator is a police officer. Police trainers emphasize that there should be no "professional courtesy" and that these abusers should be treated like others. The decision on what charges to file can also be crucial.

Most prosecutors believe that officers should bring felony charges where appropriate, for several reasons. In many areas, resources are limited and felonies are more likely than misdemeanors to be quickly and carefully prosecuted, investigated, and documented. The "three strikes, you're out" felony laws, which provide for life imprisonment after the third felony conviction, may be a powerful deterrent for batterers who are made aware that such laws will be strictly enforced in their jurisdiction.

What appears at first blush to be a misdemeanor battery may support felony charges upon closer examination. Everyday objects may become weapons every bit as deadly as a gun or knife in the hands of an enraged batterer. The use of an object such as a lamp, chair, or cord against a victim may constitute assault with a deadly weapon, which can raise available charges to the felony level. Also, threats or orders to a child to keep quiet about what happened—which batterers frequently make in front of police officers—amount to intimidation of a witness, and this, too, is usually a felony. Interfering with a 911 call, or any other interference with one trying to contact law enforcement about the commission or possible commission of a felony is also a felony in most states.

Judges. Judges who are committed to giving domestic violence priority as a serious crime can have a tremendous effect on both criminal justice and public attitudes. When men started murdering women—one every nine days—in Massachusetts in 1992, Governor William Weld proposed a change in the bail system. In this state, judges are allowed to consider both the traditional primary question in setting bail, namely whether or not the offender is likely to show up for trial, as well as whether or not the defendant poses a threat to any individual or the community.

Judges can make a difference in the community in several distinct ways. First, a judge who consistently holds offenders accountable by stiff, yet fair penalties, with opportunities for treatment where appropriate, sends a powerful message to other offenders and the community in general that domestic violence is serious and will not be tolerated. Second, a judge who follows through on enforcement of orders gives the victims a sense of power and security, and emphasizes the underlying message that violence will not be tolerated. Third, judges are community leaders whose opinions tend to be respected and followed. A judge can do much to influence community attitudes, both by setting an example on the bench and by actively becoming involved in domestic violence councils, education programs, and task force groups. Many training programs for judges who hear domestic violence cases are available, and some states now require them.

When the criminal justice system works as a true system, it saves lives, makes the jobs of all those participating easier and more rewarding, and increases public respect for the police, because the real consequences of their efforts are visible.

In some states, writing a bad check for twenty-five dollars is a felony, while beating a spouse nearly to death is a misdemeanor. The injuries typically suffered by a battered woman are as serious as those inflicted in 90 percent of violent felony crimes, yet, under state law, domestic assault is classified as a misdemeanor in the vast majority of cases. These laws must change. Batterers must be treated as the dangerous, violent criminals that they are, and made to answer for their crimes in the same way as other criminals. This means calling a felony a felony, with all the appropriate consequences—including life imprisonment for the third conviction in jurisdictions with the "three strikes" rule. The wisdom of such severe sanctions is supported by studies that show most batterers who are not stopped go on to abuse woman after woman.

CIVIL LAW

Civil law involves disputes between private parties. Various types of civil proceedings may be used in domestic violence cases.

Protection Orders

A civil protection order is a legally binding court order that prohibits a person who has committed an act of domestic violence from further contacting, abusing, or harassing the victim. The procedures for obtaining these orders are set up under state law. They may be issued by a state or local court, depending on the jurisdiction. They are also called restraining orders, protective orders, or stay-away orders, depending on the court that issues them. In the interest of clarity, this chapter refers to all of them as protection orders.

In addition to providing that the perpetrator must stay away from the victim, a protection order may (depending on the law of each state) divide a couple's property, require the abuser to leave the home, pay his victim's medical bills, make restitution for damage to property, and pay spousal and child support.

There are two types of protection orders. *Ex parte* orders are usually considered emergency orders that can be quickly issued to a woman on her own, without bringing her abuser into court. The victim generally files papers stating the facts of the case and providing other information, then a hearing is scheduled quickly. She appears in court, and if the judge is satisfied that there is a good reason to proceed with the order, he or she issues the order with specific rules that must not be violated. If the order is not obeyed, the abuser usually can be arrested immediately and taken to jail, as well as face additional penalties. These orders always expire after a fairly short period of time, usually thirty or sixty days. During that period, a hearing is scheduled at which both parties are ordered to appear. The court hears both sides, then decides whether or not to drop the order, extend it for another temporary period, or issue a full or permanent order—the second type. This order remains in effect much longer (up to three years in some areas) and can be renewed if the threat of violence continues. Such orders are sometimes called injunctions.

When the perpetrator appears for a hearing on a civil protection order, the proceedings are held generally on the record and under oath, with parties advised of their Fifth Amendment rights. Records of these proceedings is can be extremely helpful to prosecutors, who often admit the abuse but try to make excuses for it. When perpetrators make statements under oath in a civil hearing, prosecutors may use these statements if the victim or perpetrator recants in the criminal trial.

In most states, the judge may add various provisions besides the order to stay away. He or she may make temporary provisions to evict the batterer from the home, set child custody, and order child or spousal support. The primary goal is to keep the couple apart and prevent future harm, rather than punishing the abuser—that will be up to the criminal court.

The National Council of Juvenile and Family Court Judges recommends that civil restraining orders (protection orders) should be available to everyone, and issued *ex parte* (without requiring the other party, the abuser, to be in court) in cases where violence has happened or has been threatened. The Council believes orders should address:

1. The safety of the victims at home, school, work, and other places they could be subjected to harassment or potential violence
2. Child custody and visitation
3. Telephone threats or harassment
4. Removal of the perpetrator from the home
5. Financial support and maintenance for the victim and children
6. Weapons in the home or in the possession of the abuser
7. Physical description of the abuser
8. Expiration date
9. Instructions addressing how to modify the order
10. Service upon the abuser by a law enforcement officer, with notice and the opportunity for a speedy hearing

The order should remove the abuser from the home and allow the victim and children to remain with protection, safety plans, and support. Judges should not issue "mutual" protection orders.

Protection orders may also be issued by a criminal court as a part of the batterer's arraignment or sentencing. They are often imposed as a condition of bail or pretrial release. A divorce decree can also incorporate such an order. Prosecutors, other attorneys, victim advocates, or court office staff can provide information about the types of protection orders available in each jurisdiction.

Protection orders are important for several reasons. Obtaining such an order is often the first step a woman makes toward protecting herself, entering the network of helping agencies, and getting free of abuse. Also, police response is often quicker and immediate arrest more likely if the abuser is violating a court order. The law generally provides separate penalties for violating a protective order, in addition to the penalties a person faces for assault or stalking.

In many places, anyone found violating a protection order is sent immediately to jail. In most places he or she can be charged with civil contempt of court, and some courts allow criminal contempt charges. Others have mandatory periods of time in jail, which often increase with each new violation. Some courts order counseling and restitution for damage to the victim, as in a case where the abuser destroys a victim's property.

However, protection orders are not bulletproof. While many abusers take them seriously, many others ignore them or become more enraged. Any woman who has taken out such an order should be especially conscious of her safety. Tips on safety are listed in chapter 8.

Many women find the court system difficult and the procedure for getting a protection order intimidating. In response, many court systems have developed simplified forms, bilingual assistance, trained court employees who can help, and social or legal advocates. More progressive communities, generally in larger cities, have offices with trained personnel who do nothing but work with women seeking protection orders. Often, all that is required to set the process in motion is filling out a simple form.

For example, in Albuquerque, two domestic violence special commissioners now work with victims seeking civil protection orders. The commissioners act as an arm of the district judges, under the auspices of the state Family Violence Protection Act, primarily in family court. In other areas, court advocates or other court staff assist victims in completing forms and provide other forms of help. The roles of such individuals vary. For example, the Albuquerque commissioners are attorneys and are empowered to conduct hearings and make recommendations to judges. Others merely assist victims, the majority of whom represent themselves without a lawyer, in completing the steps required to apply for an order. According to a study published in 1997 in criminal justice literature, efforts to make civil protection orders more user friendly have worked, with more and more victims completing the process.

In others, however, loopholes and unnecessary complexity remain. Some court personnel are unable or unwilling to help women with forms and procedures. Some areas pose logistical problems such as great distances between outlying towns and the county seat, short court hours and no emergency services, and time-consuming processes that make it difficult for women who must take time off work or find baby-sitters. In other areas, systems remain complicated and require the help of an attorney. They simply aren't as "user-friendly" as they need to be if they are to fill the needs they are designed to serve. Not surprisingly, communities with coordinated systems in which all participants help and communicate have fewer problems making protective orders useful, effective tools available to all who need them.

Under the Constitution's Full Faith and Credit clause, all states must give full faith and credit to protection orders issued by courts of other states. Also, the federal Violence Against Women Act mandates that an out-of-state order of protection be "enforced as if it were the order of the enforcing State," yet problems remain. Some states still lack effective procedures to implement this federal guarantee. For example, some require that the order be filed with the court in the new state, and notice provided to the batterer—which may thwart the victim's efforts to escape and start over—and may immediately jeopardize her safety. Efforts are underway to remove the remaining glitches, but those who may need to enforce an out-of-state order would be well advised to contact a local agency soon after relocating to ensure problems won't arise later. Federal law requires that all who may have a say in enforcing a protective order—police, lawyers, judges, and court clerks—should treat an order that appears to be valid and current as though it had been issued by a court in that state.

Many states are developing statewide registries for protection orders, and work is underway to develop a system to bring all orders of protection into the National Crime Information Center, run by the FBI, so officers may verify an order's validity immediately from anywhere in the country. In the meantime, advocates urge that there should be a presumption of validity whenever an order is presented, because it probably is, and the risk of harm and police liability is far greater if a valid order is not enforced than if an invalid one is.

Another problem in some places is the tendency of judges to issue mutual orders declaring that both parties stay away from each other. Mutual protection orders are undesirable for several reasons. First, they trivialize the nature of domestic violence by suggesting both parties are to blame. Second, they are confusing to police, who often do nothing or arrest both parties—which can result in children being placed in foster care. Judges often believe that dual charges "wipe each other out." Such results discourage the victim from counting on the justice system for help.

Gaps do remain in the law, and advocates must be resourceful. For instance, in New Mexico, commissioners have no jurisdiction to issue civil protection orders against juveniles. Yet a commissioner in Albuquerque reports encountering a case involving two fourteen year olds with a one-and-a-half-year-old child! Until such shortcomings are changed through legislation, commissioners must seek the assistance of children's court or try to work informally with the parents. While they can't issue an order, they can talk to those involved about options or try to make the parents responsible. For example, a girl's parents may have an order issued against her boyfriend.

Also, enforcement of protection orders by the justice system is one of its primary weaknesses. Orders have more teeth when they are personally served upon the abuser by a uniformed police officer; when the abuser is required to report to authorities periodically (as though on probation); and when they are in effect in areas where response to reports of violation is immediate. Most jurisdictions now have mandatory arrest rules, which require an officer to arrest the violator when he or she is satisfied a violation of an order has been committed, whether or not the officer witnesses the violation. Consistent and strict punishment for violation of orders is important both to stop the abuser and to send a message to others.

Protection orders can usually be obtained in a separate civil proceeding, even if criminal charges are not filed. However, it is more effective to pursue criminal charges at the same time the victim seeks the protection order, if at all possible. A combined package that blends the traditional legal remedies with social services and other programs available in the community has the best chance of succeeding in protecting the victim, controlling the abuser, and changing both behavior and public opinion over the long run. In most areas, someone can be found to help women through the legal maze, whether it is a legal hotline, a court advocate, a shelter worker, a counselor, a legal aid clinic, or another battered woman who has been through the process.

Some have expressed concern over the lack of due process protection for the rights of the accused abuser as the law evolves to make it easier for victims of domestic violence to obtain protection orders, criminal penalties against their abusers, and other relief. Yet the traditional legal rules designed to make sure the legal process is fair to the accused remain in place. The courts recognize the special circumstances that make certain exceptions to the general rules appropriate, as they do in other types of cases. For example, in jurisdictions that allow "victimless prosecution," where the victim is not required to press charges or be directly involved in the process, other strong evidence is required before the abuser can be convicted or lose civil rights. The prosecution may use tape recordings of 911 calls, recordings by officers on the scene, photographs and physical evidence, medical records, and witness reports.

In many places, courts apply the "excited utterances" exception to the hearsay rule to allow a police officer to tell the court what the victim said at the scene. The hearsay rule says that testimony by one person about what was said to him or her by another person—"hearsay"—generally is not admissible in court. However, the court recognizes exceptions under certain circumstances that make it highly likely that the person is stating the truth. One such exception is a person who is highly agitated because of a recent traumatic experience. Thus, if an officer finds a woman who has just been assaulted and is extremely upset, her statements are considered "excited utterances." The excited utterances of a woman at the time of abuse can thus be repeated in court by an officer who was present at the scene. This is very powerful evidence.

Tort Law

Civil law also includes "tort" law. A tort is an act by one person that hurts another, either intentionally or due to unreasonably careless behavior. The law recognizes the right of the injured person to collect money "damages" from the other to compensate for his or her losses. Common torts include assault, battery, negligence, and wrongful death. As chapter 2 explains, it used to be the general rule that wives and husbands could not sue one another for tort claims. Today, nearly all states allow spouses to sue one another, at least for intentional acts such as battering. Therefore, a woman injured by a husband or partner can recover her medical costs, property damages, and compensation for emotional injury as well. Punitive damages, which courts award in cases that are especially outrageous, or in which the wrongdoer's behavior was deliberate and extreme, may be recovered in this type of lawsuit as well. In a Georgia case, a woman was awarded $10,000 in compensatory damages (to compensate her for medical costs, lost wages, and other expenses), plus $20,000 in punitive damages against her husband, who dragged her down a stairway by her feet because he thought it was "comical."

Most tort suits that are filed in domestic violence cases involve assault and battery. However, another tort, called "intentional infliction of emotional distress" is now available in most jurisdictions. This tort is defined as conduct that is "so outrageous in character, and so extreme in degree, as to go beyond all possible bounds of decency, and to be regarded as atrocious, and utterly intolerable in a civilized community." Just how outrageous the conduct must be to meet this standard varies among the courts, but much of the behavior commonly directed against battered wives, including severe psychological abuse without any physical battering, satisfies this standard. Threats, destruction of property, and stalking have also been held to amount to intentional infliction of emotional distress.

In cases where a woman is stalked or harassed by a man she has left, she may also file a tort claim for invasion of privacy. Invasion of privacy involves interfering with another person's right to be left alone if he or she wishes to be. There are several types of invasion of privacy. The one that applies the most often to abuse cases is called "intrusion upon seclusion." This may include spying on someone, reading her personal mail, or telephoning her repeatedly after she has made it clear the calls are not welcome.

Other legal claims may fit unique circumstances. For example, in one case, a battered woman took her boyfriend's car to flee his violence because hers was not running. She returned it a short time later. He accused her of stealing the car and cash from the apartment. She was arrested and charged with larceny and auto theft. He eventually dropped the charges, but harassed her and had her car towed and repaired without her permission. When she didn't pay the repair bill he sent, he sold the car. The woman hired a lawyer and sued him in a civil tort action for assault and battery, false imprisonment, malicious prosecution, intentional infliction of emotional distress, and unfair trade practices. The legal process was long and difficult, but she was eventually awarded over $75,000 in compensatory and punitive damages.

In most cases, a person has to hire a private attorney to handle a civil tort or other civil case, although, depending on the case, a person can handle his or her case "pro se" (by the person him- or herself), or with help from a legal aid or court-supported program.

Civil Rights Law

The existing laws protecting citizens against civil rights violations by the government can be useful to battered women. However, these laws only work in specific circumstances, and have many limitations. They are often very complicated, and require the help of experienced legal advisors. Yet in the right situation, these laws can be powerful tools for justice and change.

42 U.S.C. Section 1983. "Section 1983" is a federal civil rights law that gives citizens the right to sue any "person," including the states and their subdivisions (counties and municipalities), who violates their constitutional rights "under color of state law." This means that if someone employed by the government treats you in a way that is prohibited by the constitution, you may be able to sue that person and possibly the government agency that employs him or her as well.

One of the rights protected by the Constitution and enforced under Section 1983 is the right to "equal protection of the law" as guaranteed by the Fifth and Fourteenth Amendments to the United States Constitution. Equal protection requires equal application of the laws to all citizens, regardless of race, gender, or other neutral characteristics. Battered women have sued law enforcement officers and agencies that failed to treat them in the same manner as other crime victims, for violation of the right to equal protection. These cases are very hard to prove, but some amazing victories have been won.

The equal protection approach has been used by battered women to require cities and their officers to apply laws equally to violence between strangers and violence between intimate partners. In one especially disturbing case, a woman who had suffered years of brutal abuse from her husband, a police officer, showed statistics at trial demonstrating that during a certain period of time, there was an arrest rate of 31 percent in cases of stranger assault by a known perpetrator, but only a 16 percent arrest rate in cases of domestic assault. The court found that these statistics, as well as the woman's own personal history of receiving no assistance from the police department ("deliberate indifference"), were sufficient to show the type of custom or policy required for this kind of lawsuit and discrimination against domestic violence victims.

Some cases have also been brought to court for violation of the right to due process, guaranteed by the same constitutional amendments. Due process requires that officers who are aware of an individual's particular dangerous circumstances take reasonable steps to protect that person (substantive due process) or that a state that has established avenues of help, such as protection orders, follow their own rules and procedures and supply the protections they and the law say they will (procedural due process). For example, in a 1990 case, a woman who was shot by her husband after police had repeatedly failed to enforce a protection order, brought a substantive due process suit against the police department in her Pennsylvania town. The court emphasized that a special relationship had been created because the police had authority to regulate a dangerous situation, had knowledge of the situation, and had the ability to do something about it. In fact, under the state's protection order law, the order stated that it "shall" be enforced by the police, and though the woman had called them several times when her husband harassed and assaulted her between the time the order was issued and the shooting, the police department never arrested or restrained him.

Section 1983 suits are very complicated, and have several drawbacks. Only certain individuals can be sued; there are special restrictions on suing municipalities and police departments (there must be a policy, custom, or pattern of behavior, not just an isolated incident); and they involve complex matters of sovereign immunity. A 1983 suit almost always requires the assistance of an attorney well versed in civil rights law.

Yet Section 1983 can be a powerful remedy when all of the pieces fall into place. Battered women have brought several class action suits for injunctions against police departments that had non-arrest policies, would not enforce protective orders, or did not follow the state domestic violence statutes. Usually, these cases settled in exchange for reforms in police procedures. In some cases, women have collected money damage awards by proving a government agent or department deprived them of a constitutionally protected right.

Successful civil rights lawsuits can have a powerful impact on other areas of the legal system. In 1984, a woman named Tracy Thurman won a verdict of $2.6 million against the police department of Torrington, Connecticut, after they repeatedly failed to protect her from her husband's escalating brutality. The long history of abuse culminated in a severe beating in the front yard of Thurman's apartment, in which her estranged husband broke her neck as a police officer stood by, doing nothing. This lawsuit, plus a television movie made about the case, led to much greater adoption and enforcement of mandatory arrest policies.

Section 1983 seems destined to remain in a constant state of change and uncertainty. The United States Supreme Court hears many civil rights cases, and each new decision often brings a substantial alteration to the law. For this reason, it is essential to work with legal professionals actively involved in civil rights law who are aware of its constant evolution.

State Tort Claims

Traditionally, the state, like the husband, was considered practically infallible. The law would not allow a citizen to sue the state for wrongdoing, primarily because of the concept of paternalistic benevolence, but also because it was considered better for the state coffers to be used for the benefit of all citizens rather than to right a wrong committed against just one.

Some vestiges of this principle of sovereign immunity remain, but most states have enacted laws allowing citizens to sue the state for certain torts. For example, in most states, you may sue if your car is hit by a negligent driver employed by a state agency.

In the domestic violence arena, states have sometimes been sued when government employees negligently fail to protect victims, especially where there is a "special relationship" created by a protection order, or other promise of protection. Like civil rights suits, state tort actions are subject to many obstacles and barriers, but are worth considering. The same tort claims that can be brought against an individual may also be brought against the state, where immunity is waived by the state's tort claims statute.

The Family Violence Prevention and Services Act

In 1984, Congress passed this act into federal law. It does not give individuals any specific rights or remedies, but rather works to aid victims of domestic violence by providing federal funds to help states and local communities develop and support shelters, coordinate research efforts, conduct training, and continue related activities. A companion act, The Victims of Crime Act, sets aside federal money to compensate crime victims and to fund state agencies that provide assistance to victims of family violence and other crimes. In addition to allocating more money to help stop domestic violence, these acts represent the first official statement by the federal government that domestic abuse is a serious and intolerable crime.

The Violence Against Women Act of 1993. Until very recently, women had special civil rights remedies for gender crimes committed against them at work, but few to protect them at home.

A great victory in the struggle against domestic violence (and other crimes against women) recently occurred with the passage of the Crime Act of 1994. The bill includes the Violence Against Women Act, which was first introduced into Congress in 1990 and has been debated ever since. The act also established a new civil rights claim for women who are victims of crimes motivated by gender. The act says that such crimes violate a woman's civil rights, and she can sue the perpetrator who violates this law for compensatory, punitive, and other damages. This part of the act is modeled on the Civil Rights Act of 1964. One part of the act aims to deter, punish, and rehabilitate batterers in order to prevent future abuse by increasing grant funding for shelters and related programs. It also makes spouse abuse during interstate travel a federal crime, and makes it illegal for abusers to cross state lines to commit domestic violence or to violate a protection order, which must also be honored by other states when a woman travels or moves. It makes protection orders enforceable across state lines, and allows federal criminal penalties for interstate stalking. Criminal violations under the act require full restitution to the victim, in addition to other criminal penalties. Repeat offenders may be punished by a term of imprisonment up to twice the term authorized. This act also allocates money for programs to encourage the arrest of batterers; to train police officers; to help establish coordinated programs between police, prosecutors, and judges; to educate those working in the justice system about domestic violence; and various other projects to combat violence against women. Grant money and other assistance is available to states, local governments, Indian tribal governments, and in some cases, private nonprofit organizations that serve victims.

The act represents an interesting combination of traditional government remedies, including grant money for programs, changes in laws, and government recognition of citizens' own efforts to find solutions to problems—with the commitment to support what people have shown to be effective. It makes available funding for state and local educational efforts, rape prevention programs, counseling for victims, local and national hotlines, training programs for judges and police, and special units of police and prosecutors to deal with family violence. It mandates confidentiality between victims and counselors. It affords grants for shelters, youth education, rural programs, and other community programs. It requires states to show a strong commitment to arresting and prosecuting offenders in order to receive funds; and allocates grant money to help police, prosecutors, and nonprofit organizations establish the kind of coordinated community programs that have been working in communities like Duluth, Minnesota. Special protections are provided for immigrant women and children. Some believe that the most important thing about the act is not what it does, but what it says—one of the first statements by the federal government that violence in the home is a serious crime which is unacceptable.

President Clinton has committed his support to the struggle to end domestic violence, which he has called "the enemy from within." In 1996, Clinton established the first Violence Against Women office in the Justice Department to coordinate the various federal efforts in support of the Violence Against Women Act. He also assisted in achieving expansion of the Brady Bill to make it illegal for those convicted of domestic violence crimes to purchase a handgun—both to reduce the incidence of partner deaths, and to protect police officers responding to domestic violence calls.

FAMILY LAW

Although family law is a species of civil law, it is generally considered a separate, special area covering the legal relationships between family members. Family law includes divorce, legal separation, child support and custody, and support enforcement. Some special laws dealing with domestic violence may fall into this category as well. As with other civil cases, either a private attorney or the assistance of someone in a legal aid, court assistance, or advocacy program is generally (though not always) required.

Divorce

Divorce laws vary from state to state, especially with regard to issues of property division, child custody, and support. Legal separation laws generally parallel the state's divorce laws, and accomplish the same goals without legally ending the marriage.

A divorce decree provides a legal ending to a relationship, which allows a woman to get on with a fresh start. Other advantages to getting a final decree of divorce include settling matters of child custody and visitation, support, and division of property and debts.

Seeing a tangible, official end to an abusive marriage can be a great psychological boost. A divorce decree may also include an injunction that orders the former spouse to stay away. Although other types of protection orders are easier to enforce and carry more severe penalties for violation, the statement in the final decree can provide a powerful sense of closure.

One of the main disadvantages to the divorce proceeding is its tendency to drag on, and that it can be subject to manipulation by an abuser. Many favor faster divorces in cases where abuse has been involved, and some states are beginning to make special changes in their laws to speed up the process.

Generally, a woman has to hire a private attorney to handle a divorce action, although some courts, legal aid clinics, and law schools provide free representation or assistance in handling a simple procedure yourself. Naturally, the process is much easier when children are not involved. If at all possible, a woman with children should get an experienced family attorney to be sure her rights and her children's interests are protected. Some domestic violence programs have legal advocates available to refer women to attorneys who work free of charge or base their fees on sliding scales according to income. Some advocates assist with divorce petitions as another part of the process of freeing women from domestic violence. When choosing any attorney or other legal advisor, make sure he or she is well versed in local family and divorce law, and that he or she treats the issue of battering seriously.

Mediation has become increasingly popular in divorce cases as a means of encouraging couples to come to a mutually agreeable division of property and other terms of the divorce. However, most experts in domestic violence feel that mediation is not appropriate in an abusive relationship, and can even contribute to greater exploitation of the victim by the abuser.

In order to be effective, mediation must involve people of relatively equal bargaining power. In the abusive relationship, this essential assumption simply does not exist. The mediation process involves getting the divorcing couple to sit down with a mediator, usually (but not necessarily) a lawyer, psychologist, or other professional, or a team of two professional mediators. The leader may advise the couple about their legal options or make suggestions, but does not push either party to agree to any particular terms. Consequently, if one partner is bullied or intimidated by the other, she may be coerced into agreeing to terms she does not really want. The process cannot be fair if both people do not have an equal say in what goes into the agreement.

While mediation can be a wonderful tool for reaching agreements in other situations, it is best avoided when the relationship is violent. Mediation has become increasingly popular as an alternative to court in many types of cases because it relieves the overburdened court system, is less expensive, is faster, and is frequently less traumatic than a trial. Yet mediation throws the batterer into a situation he may perceive as threatening to his control over the victim, which may make him even more violent. It always forces the victim into his presence. She is often terrified, and unable to state her needs in front of someone who has brutalized her. She will be forced to listen to "his side." While a good mediator does not allow either party to become degrading or abusive toward the other, there are reports of abusers being allowed to "speak their minds" in the name of "fairness" which results, not surprisingly, in a tirade of verbal abuse and blame that the victim should not have to endure.

However, the issue of whether mediation should ever be used in formerly abusive relationships is controversial. Some experts believe it can be empowering for a former abuse victim, if the abuse has ended, both parties are in counseling, and the abuser is willing to participate in a fair manner as well as avoid outside contact with the victim, according to a current protection order.

In some areas, cases with a history of abuse are immediately screened out of mediation. But not all court systems are so enlightened. If you are forced to use mediation in a divorce, you may wish to try and get a lawyer or advocate from a battered women's program to intervene. You or your representative may be able to get a waiver from the mandatory mediation due to a history of abuse. If mediation can't be waived, a lawyer or advocate may be able to go with you, or at least talk to the mediator about the violent history of the relationship and educate him or her about the dynamics of the abusive relationship. Remember, if you do go to mediation, nothing is going to be final until you agree. If you don't agree, the case will progress to court, where the judge will decide upon a fair decree. Be sure you have a protection order in place before mediation starts, and insist on a permanent protection order as part of the settlement. Also insist the batterer agrees to a fair division of your assets and debts, and that he reimburses you for the cost of any injuries he caused.

Child Custody

One of the most controversial areas of family law in battering situations is the issue of child custody and visitation rights. Matters involving children are difficult in any divorce, and become even stickier when abuse has been involved.

As is the case for the adult victims, the effect of domestic violence on children frequently continues or gets worse after the family parts. In some jurisdictions, a temporary protection order sets out custody arrangements and provides for a penalty if they are not followed. Yet this is the exception rather than the rule. Often, a mother must wait until the hearing on the temporary order, or a divorce or separation proceeding, until any formal custody arrangements are made.

Frequently, abusers use children as pawns in the power play against the mother. Batterers use child visitation to gain access to the mother to terrorize her; they fight for custody to retaliate against the woman or to try and force a reconciliation; they abduct children; they refuse to pay child support. For one woman I spoke with, this was the greatest frustration she faced in trying to end the relationship. Although a protection order was in place and a divorce pending, no formal, enforceable visitation schedule had been established for the couple's young son. The father frequently promised to return the boy at a certain time, then would disappear with the child for several days. The mother did not believe the boy was endangered, but understandably suffered extreme anxiety when she didn't know the whereabouts of her child or when he would be back—precisely, she believed, the father's intent.

Many people argue that not enough attention is given to abuse of the mother in determining custody matters. Unbelievably, courts in Illinois and New York have ruled that a man cannot be considered an unfit parent "merely" because he has murdered the mother of his children! Courts are supposed to give first priority to the best interests of the child when deciding custody, yet family violence is frequently given little or no weight unless it is directly aimed at the child.

Activist and author Ann Jones, who has studied and written extensively on domestic violence, believes that courts ruling upon custody should truly consider the best interests of the child by including a thorough examination of the effect of what goes on between the parents upon the child. Courts should look at the history of exposure to abuse, whether or not the child is trapped between parents in conflict, use of the child as a weapon by one parent to harass the other, and whether or not safe visitation options exist.

Many states have laws that create a presumption in favor of joint custody of children whenever parents divorce. "Joint custody" does not mean a 50/50 division of the child's time between the parents, but it does mean that both parents take an active part in raising the child, sharing major decisions, and dividing the child's time according to a visitation schedule set or approved by the court. In cases where there is a legal presumption of joint custody, this is the assumption the court starts with, then it is up to the parent to convince the judge that such an arrangement would not be in the best interest of the child—the standard that is always supposed to be the bottom line.

When a peaceful marriage between two good parents ends, joint custody usually is the best choice for the child. However, when the home was violent, joint custody can create tremendous problems for both the mother and her children. Many experts, such as Dr. Lenore Walker, believe that any form of joint custody should not be allowed in violent homes. She believes, and many others agree, that sole custody should go to the woman.

Battered women also face cultural stereotypes in custody cases. They may be viewed as weak, dysfunctional, and unfit to be good parents. Women may find themselves in a Catch-22 situation. If the child was shielded from the battering, the judge may decide that the violence was not harmful to the child, so joint custody may be awarded. If the child did witness the abuse, the old blame-the-victim mentality kicks in, and the mother may be questioned as to why she "let" the child be exposed to violence.

Yet changes are happening. Most states now have laws that require the court to consider domestic violence in making custody decisions. Some legislatures have created a presumption against any award of custody (including joint custody) where there is evidence of domestic violence.

The National Council of Juvenile and Family Court Judges has recommended that each state legislature enact laws requiring the courts to consider family violence in any case relating to the family, especially child custody and visitation. For example, in 1992 Louisiana enacted a law creating a rebuttable presumption against any award of sole or joint custody of a child to a parent who had committed acts of physical, sexual, or other violence against the other parent or any of the children. In order to have visitation, the abusive parent must attend and complete a treatment program and visitation with the child must be supervised. The law also states that an injunction against family violence must be included in all divorce, separation, custody, or visitation orders where there has been family violence. The abuser must pay all court costs and expert fees related to custody or visitation in a family litigation case, plus medical and psychological treatment costs for victims.

Special care should be taken when joint or shared custody arrangements allow the children to visit the abuser's home. Children may witness the batterer abusing a new partner. Or some abusers use the children to try to control or harass the former partner—by refusing to follow schedules for returning them, by forcing them to miss counseling sessions, or by badmouthing their mother, continuing the cycle of blaming the victim. A majority of states now have laws requiring courts to consider the negative impact on the child who witnesses spousal abuse in making custody determinations.

Most judges today consider spousal abuse a serious matter that needs to be taken into consideration in custody determinations. In New Mexico, for example, exposing a child to violence by battering a spouse in the child's presence can be considered child endangerment, a crime that carries penalties of its own. In other places, it can be grounds for a claim of abuse or neglect. Some courts appoint a special person (usually a social worker or lawyer called a guardian *ad litem*) to represent the children's interests when a violent marriage ends. All jurisdictions are served by child welfare agencies that can be called in to advise the court on the child's best interests under circumstances where a child is reported to be endangered. Often judges appoint psychologists to evaluate children and parents in custody disputes and make recommendations to the court.

Of course, such laws and services can be a double-edged sword. The woman may be condemned for not leaving the relationship, instead of blaming the man who perpetuates the violence—the same old song and dance. But a good advocate, either a family law attorney, a court-appointed legal advocate, or a shelter counselor, can help a woman be sure her side of the story gets fair consideration.

It is usually illegal for one parent to take a child across state lines or otherwise defy custody or visitation orders in a way that prevents the other parent from knowing where the child is or having contact with the child. Mothers fleeing violence have been accused of child abduction. However, in the majority of states, spouse and/or child abuse is a defense to family kidnapping, child abduction, or custodial interference offenses. Most states' laws provide that when one parent believes the child is in danger of harm (including witnessing violence), he or she is usually justified in taking the child and fleeing. Even in states that do not make a specific exception for abuse to their kidnapping laws, many judges consider abuse as a general "good cause" defense to such charges.

In 1990, the United States Congress approved a resolution which calls for each state to create a presumption in its law that spouse abusers should not get custody of their children, but only supervised visitation. Many judges today are taking a stand against abusers in custody matters, often awarding sole custody to the mother, at least until the abuser completes a treatment program and demonstrates that he can obey the law, refrain from further violence, and follow court orders. Sole custody does not mean the father will have no visitation rights, nor that the decision must be permanent. Unless parental rights are terminated, a parent can always ask the court to modify a custody order when circumstances have changed. Others order supervised visitation, or require arrangements that do not include any contact between the abuser and the mother. A few communities with coordinated programs against domestic violence are coming up with truly innovative solutions, such as a community center where abusers can visit with their children in a subtly supervised setting, without having to see the mother.

For example, in Duluth, Minnesota, the local YMCA provides an area in which men with a history of abuse can visit their children in a comfortable setting with recreational facilities, yet be supervised and have no contact with the mother. In Albuquerque, New Mexico, "The Neutral Corner" provides a safe place where parents can exchange children without seeing one another, so both parents and children avoid emotional turmoil during the transfer. In any situation, the safety of the child and his or her mother must be a paramount concern in determining what is in the best interest of the child.

WELFARE REFORM

While its goals are admirable, the time limits imposed by the 1996 welfare reform laws may remove a vital safety net that allows women to leave abusive relationships. Abusers, seeking to perpetuate their control and isolation of their partners, often sabotage women's efforts to find work or complete job training programs. Many families desperately in need of a second income are kept on the welfare rolls by an abuser who prevents his wife from getting or keeping a job or studying for training classes. A comprehensive study conducted by the Washington State Institute for Public Policy found that 60 percent of women on A.F.D.C. reported that they had been abused by a partner, a statistic paralleled a similar study in Massachusetts. The new laws also include residency requirements that penalize battered women who flee to another state seeking safety.

Activists are urging states to adopt the Family Violence Option, an amendment that urges states to identify victims of family violence, refer them to counseling, and waive any requirements that unfairly penalize them. Proponents of the Family Violence Option emphasize that they do not urge that battered women on welfare be permanently exempted from work; on the contrary, jobs offer such women a vital tool for rebuilding self-esteem and staying free from abuse. However, such women often need additional time and specific services not provided by the new law if they are to escape the cycle of abuse.

Experts urge that states must address the special problems faced by victims of domestic violence if their welfare-to-work programs are to succeed. According to Martha Baker, who runs a Manhattan-based program to train women for blue-collar jobs that serves a large number of abused women, if the issue of violence is not confronted before a woman joins the work force, she will be in danger of losing her job due to not showing up or arriving injured, or because her abuser stalks her on the job.

As of early 1997, 24 of the 40 states that had submitted welfare plans had included all or part of the amendment or taken steps of their own to address domestic violence. Advocates applaud the amendment as the first time that the connection between violence and poverty has been recognized in federal law.

EVIDENCE

Evidence is crucial in any court case, civil or criminal. In some areas, the police, prosecutors, and attorneys involved are dedicated and expert in gathering evidence. In others, the indifference or incompetence is beyond belief.

Sherri Winston, who was severely beaten by her boyfriend in Miami in 1991, reported that after she went to the police station to file a report (the police refused to take her report over the telephone), she was amazed to learn two days later that a criminal charge would not be filed for lack of evidence. She asked if they had asked the neighbors about her screams, if they asked the assailant how he got scratches on his face and chest. They had not. So she went to the state's attorney's office, where she was told the case would be assigned to an investigator. The boyfriend made a statement in which he admitted the attack. Yet the prosecutor declined to file charges, supposedly because there were no witnesses, the man was "sorry," and he was concerned he might lose his job. Winston's final statement, in an article she wrote for the *Fort Lauderdale Sun-Sentinel*, sums up a common, ironic sentiment well: "Nancy Kerrigan got her knee bruised by a stranger and that was enough to warrant an FBI investigation. Good thing she didn't know the guy."

Winston's story also illustrates the importance of evidence in the criminal justice system. Unfortunately, victims often have to do a good deal of the work on their own. Yet it can be well worth the effort. The following list includes items that can be crucial in any legal case connected with domestic violence: criminal prosecution, civil suit, child custody hearing, divorce case, and others. Most of this evidence is free and you are entitled to have it by law:

1. Be certain to get a copy of any medical report prepared at the emergency room, as well as any reports on treatment you get later. Some physicians and hospitals do not give patients copies of the report, but retain it in case it is requested by a lawyer or law enforcement agency. Any medical records indicating treatment for battering injuries can be important. Make sure they list the cause of the injuries and the name of the treating physician. Whether you seek medical treatment or not, have someone take photographs of your injuries. Police, shelter workers, or someone at the hospital may be able to do this. If not, get a friend or family member to help.

2. If you receive counseling or psychological or psychiatric treatment for problems associated with abuse, be sure to get some record indicating the purpose of this treatment. Some mental health professional may be reluctant to give you your records, at least while your treatment is continuing, and there can be valid reasons for this. But you should have billing records or some type of paperwork showing when you were treated, and most counselors and doctors should be willing to provide a statement of the reason for the treatment.

3. Be sure to get a copy of the police report. Read it to be certain it is

complete and correct. If there are other things the police should know—such as prior calls you have made for domestic violence to the same or another department, or if your abuser has a record of prior abuse or other crimes—tell them. Get the names and badge numbers of the officers who are present and ask for a copy of each report that is made. Find out who is in charge, and be sure you have his or her name, telephone number, and badge number.

4. Talk to anyone who may have seen or heard the violence. If you locate any witnesses, ask them to call the officer in charge of the case and make a statement. If they seem reluctant to get involved, give their names, addresses, and/or telephone numbers—whatever information you have—to the officer in charge of your case.

5. If the officers investigating the case do not gather any physical evidence, such as torn clothing, broken dishes, or blood-stained rugs, on their own, point these things out and ask them to take them as evidence. They need to be taken from the scene by the officers and kept according to police procedures to be admitted in court as evidence, so make sure they do so immediately. Such evidence is crucial in any type of case.

Photographs taken at the scene of a domestic assault provide powerful evidence that is extremely difficult to discredit at trial. They record the terror, pain, and rage. Nothing is equal to this kind of proof. Photos are especially essential when the victim has been intimidated into refusing to testify. Judges appreciate such clear and indisputable evidence, which makes conviction of a perpetrator far easier.

Polaroid has recently implemented the Polaroid DV100 program in which it provides its Spectra Law Enforcement Kits for those responding to family violence. The program requires that community agencies or groups purchase a minimum of one hundred kits at a discounted price and provide the recipients the time to attend a hands-on training workshop on effectively collecting photographic evidence of family violence. Polaroid offers a larger discount when groups of small communities or cities get together to purchase larger quantities. In addition to initial training sessions for the law enforcement officers and health care professionals who will use the cameras, Polaroid offers free training videos and ongoing assistance. The training emphasizes not only techniques in how to best document injuries, but also teaches the importance of preserving other evidence of violence, and how to gather photographic evidence in a manner that is not threatening to the victim or the children, who may also be photographed. In turn, recipients agree to share protocols, statistics, and information on their use of the cameras.

The camera kit is specially designed for gathering the type of evidence that is most important in domestic violence cases. A special box included in the kit is used to take very close shots of wounds. Officers are encouraged to take broad photos of the scene then focus in on details such as broken dishes and toys. The kit also provides a mechanism for duplicating photos, and information on how the photos may be enlarged and put on transparencies. One particular advantage to using an instant camera is that the officer will know how the photos came out while still at the scene, and whether additional photos should be taken. Officers say that the cameras are an excellent resource, because with up to ten photos they can depict the entire crime scene. Photos of the offender when he is dirty, drunk, and enraged are also important, some say, because batterers nearly always put on a neat, charming, "choir boy" image for court appearances.

Photographs of the batterer can also provide local police patrolling the areas where the victim lives, works, and frequents with an immediate tool to enforce a restraining order against him. With the victim's approval, these photos can also be distributed to the victim's neighbors, employer, and children's school, for example.

The Los Angeles police department now places a camera in every active patrol car, and city attorney James Hahn, who believes there is no better evidence than good photos of injuries, reports a 90 percent conviction rate in cases his office handled during 1996. San Diego, which has also placed a camera in every car, likewise boasts a 90 percent conviction rate in domestic violence cases.

Polaroid has made a broad-based commitment to assisting in the battle against domestic violence. In addition to its special camera kits, the company has produced videos to train law enforcement and health care professionals in appropriate first-response procedures in assisting domestic violence victims and successfully documenting evidence of violence, as well as checklists and other printed materials to aid in identifying and documenting important facts.

Audio tapes, often carried by responding officers in a shirt pocket or belt unit, also serve several purposes. They preserve the impact of the victim's terror and pain at the scene. They provide solid evidence that is not subject to the limitations of the hearsay rule, and will remain even if the victim is intimidated into recanting her story or refusing to testify. Officers can also preserve the statements of children and other witnesses at the scene. Trained officers recommend telling medical personnel on the scene that they have a recorder turned on, to cue their comments on the victim's injuries.

Prosecutors, including San Diego City Attorney Casey Guinn, a nationally recognized leader in the field of family violence prosecution, urge police officers to bear in mind when investigating such cases that the prosecutor may have to prove the case without the participation of the victim. Thus, photos, audio tapes, and other visual evidence (such as a destroyed telephone bearing the perpetrator's fingerprints) are often crucial. Blood-stained clothing may also provide DNA evidence, which has become increasingly important in criminal prosecutions. In a domestic violence case, it may prove that the perpetrator was covered with the victim's blood, as well as disprove the type of stories batterers often concoct, such as claiming that he was the victim and the blood is his own.

Both photographs and audio tapes can be essential in providing a clear, objective picture of the scene without having to put the victim on the stand. As one police officer whose own sister was killed in a domestic violence homicide explained, policemen often become frustrated when they are repeatedly called to the same address, often only to find that the victim won't cooperate or even tries to prevent them from arresting the abuser. Yet they must realize that victims are in survival mode. The police are there momentarily, but the abuser is there for the duration. Many fear that they will be more severely battered or killed if they cooperate with law enforcement. Therefore, one goal must be to prosecute the offender as effectively as possible with as little assistance from the victim as possible.

LAWYERS

Choosing a Lawyer

As in many situations, victims of domestic abuse may need to use several different laws to gain all of the legal remedies that are available. For example, a woman often calls the police, gets a civil protection order, files for divorce, and sues her abuser for compensation for the injuries he caused her. For this reason, unless you are lucky enough to live in an area with excellent legal advocacy services, it is to your advantage to consult with an attorney if at all possible. A lawyer can advise you on the claims you have under the law, and help you pursue all of your remedies for protection and compensation. Complex actions (like a Section 1983 suit) may require expert representation, but the results can be well worth the time and expense involved. Also, many lawyers often handle good cases on a contingency basis, so you pay only the out-of-pocket costs until the case is won or settled.

If you hire a lawyer, make sure you understand fee arrangements and costs from day one, including hourly rates, retainers, extra expenses, and when and how fees will be billed. Many lawyers take credit cards or work out payment plans—a good attorney is generally flexible with methods of payment. Ask about the amount of time he or she expects to be involved in the case, and the total cost estimate. You may be able to help keep costs down by doing things such as running errands, picking up police reports, and making copies yourself.

Some unions and employment benefit packages provide prepaid legal service plans. These programs are also starting to become available to individuals. Essentially, they are a form of "legal insurance," in which members receive free or low-cost legal services through membership.

Be sure you choose a lawyer who is familiar with domestic violence and the different legal areas it can involve—civil, criminal, and family law. Don't feel awkward about changing attorneys or taking the time you need to visit with several before you choose one. You may need to spend a great deal of time working on difficult issues with this person, and you need someone you feel is trustworthy and with whom you can establish a comfortable rapport. An attorney should always be willing to answer your questions and explain matters so you understand what is going on.

Realize that lawyers are usually working on many different cases at the same time, and be aware that most of their work is done outside the courtroom. Sometimes clients are surprised when they are billed for large chunks of time associated with preparing written work and getting ready for court appearances—yet these steps are every bit as important as the more dramatic time in front of the judge. Allow him or her a reasonable time (forty-eight hours or so) to return calls, and be understanding if you have to wait a few days for an appointment if someone else's case is going to court or in a crisis mode. You will want the same priority when your case reaches the critical stage. Be considerate—don't hesitate to call anytime if you have a true emergency, but don't take advantage of your lawyer, for example, by calling him or her at home when it isn't urgent. Feel free to ask for referrals to other kinds of help—counselors, housing authorities, or vocational therapists—but don't expect the attorney to fulfill these roles or provide general advice on issues not directly related to your case.

Make a list of your questions or concerns and cover several in one call or visit (this can save you money as well, since many lawyers bill a set amount per call). Ask for help preparing your testimony if you need to testify in court. Giving testimony requires only that you tell the truth, but the experience can be intimidating. Going through what to expect can help you stay calm. It may also be helpful to have a friend or family member there when you take the stand. Don't hesitate to talk to your lawyer about any concerns you have about your case, or to bring up anything you think might be important.

Lawyers Working to Stop Domestic Violence

During the mid-1990s, the American Bar Association (ABA) took a strong stand against domestic violence under the leadership of Roberta Cooper Ramo, the ABA's first female president. Ramo crisscrossed the country during her tenure, sounding a call for an end to domestic violence through awareness, education, and action. Ramo urged that the problem is not indifference to domestic violence, but rather that our entire society has been taught to ignore it.

In 1994, then President-elect Ramo spearheaded the creation of the ABA Commission on Domestic Violence, a multidisciplinary commission composed of attorneys, doctors, educators, social workers, law enforcement officials, and national leaders. The Commission seeks to increase both public awareness of domestic violence and create awareness of concrete methods that work to eradicate it. As one of its first acts, it co-sponsored a series of regional conferences on domestic violence, along with the American Medical Association, the U.S. Department of Justice, and the Department of Health and Human Services.

Ramo emphasized that such an initiative had never happened before on a national level. She expressed particular concern about children—up to 10 million—who witness domestic violence in their homes. A separate program was held at the ABA's midyear meeting in which lawyers, judges, and psychologists stressed the importance of healing the children if domestic violence is to be stopped. To actively address this concern, the commission worked with the Walt Disney Company to develop a children's video, entitled "It's Not OK: Let's Talk About Domestic Violence," which has won national acclaim for its sensitive, practical approach toward helping professionals assist children in learning how to respond to and protect themselves from violence in their homes. The video serves dual roles by sensitizing professionals to a child's perspective on family violence, and by giving children specific information. The video is also designed to be shown to children who accompany their mothers to places such as police stations, shelters, and courts. It's mission is to tell children three key messages: Violence at home is not the child's fault; it is not right for people who love one another to be violent; and there are ways a child can try to be safe when violence occurs. It includes narratives by children who have survived life in violent homes, so the viewers know they are not alone. The video is presented in a calming tone, geared toward children ages five to eleven in language they can understand. It has also been used to train police and distributed to school counselors by the U.S. Department of Education.

The Commission has also been active in working with insurance companies to urge change in policies that discriminate against domestic violence victims, and developing programs to educate high school students about domestic violence in conjunction with sports programs. It has developed a clearinghouse of information on various domestic violence programs, developed a multidisciplinary blueprint for communities seeking to improve their response to domestic violence, sought to educate judges and those working in the various service fields, and developed a lawyer's handbook to educate lawyers on the impact of domestic violence in various legal fields. It has also worked with law schools to assist professors in incorporating domestic violence training into their curricula. Additionally, the Commission has published a manual for lawyers on how to contend with violence in their practices, entitled The Impact of Domestic Violence on Your Legal Practice.

Copies of this manual, the children's video, and other materials may be ordered by calling the ABA Services Center at (800) 285-2221.

In late 1995, New Mexico Attorney General Tom Udall convened a statewide task force on violence against women, including concerned citizens and professionals with expertise in criminal justice, victim services, education, public health, and physical and mental health care. The task force held town hall meetings throughout the state asking local participants to share information on what worked in their communities in the effort to prevent and intervene in violence against women. A multidisciplinary conference with workshops targeting various professional groups was held in 1996, and a final report with findings, goals, and recommendations was published in 1997. The concise, nine-page report contained a wealth of ideas and information, both general and targeted to specific professions.

THE DOUBLE VICTIMS: WOMEN WHO KILL THEIR ABUSERS

While the law is evolving in other areas to become more sensitive to the special circumstances of domestic violence victims, one area in particular remains in the grip of injustice. Women who kill the men who batter them frequently receive extremely harsh sentences—much longer than men who kill their wives or girlfriends. One expert who studied sentencing in domestic homicides found that the average sentence for a woman who is convicted of killing her spouse is fifteen to twenty years, while a man's average sentence is two to six years.

Several explanations for this double standard have been offered. Traditionally, society has permitted violence from men but frowned upon women who take up weapons, even in self-defense. The tired refrain, "Why didn't she just leave?" still echoes through police stations and jury rooms. But some of the worst problems are found in a judicial system that long ago fashioned a narrow definition of self-defense based on men of roughly equal size and capability fighting in the streets or bars. And this definition is not flexible enough to encompass different, yet equally compelling, circumstances.

In 1993, a documentary film entitled *Defending Our Lives* won an Academy Award for its stark profile of women who suffered brutal abuse in their homes but were offered no effective help or protection, then were sent to jail for defending their lives. When a woman kills her abuser, "Why didn't she just leave?" may be a legitimate question—but only if the justice system truly listens to her answer. A woman claiming self-defense under circumstances outside the rigid boundaries traditionally recognized should be given the opportunity to explain why she reasonably believed herself to be in imminent danger of death or serious injury. And her story should be supported by expert testimony to add credibility to her perception in the eyes of those who have never experienced the damaged, distorted world in which she lives.

Experts can also explain why a woman may reasonably believe that calling the police is futile (especially if it has proven so in the past); why her ability to leave may be thwarted by financial and social considerations; why she may fear certain death or more serious injury if she tries to leave; as well as the psychological effects of the cycle of violence, learned helplessness, and the battered woman syndrome. For example, in *People v. Reeves,* an Illinois case, an expert explained to the jury how the defendant had reasonably come to believe that her husband was capable of killing her or causing her great harm despite his lack of a weapon, based on her knowledge of his ability to inflict severe injury in the past.

The battered woman syndrome, defined by Dr. Lenore Walker and discussed in some detail in earlier chapters, holds special importance in the cases of women who kill. Women suffering from the syndrome often kill men who would not appear to outsiders to be threatening their lives. But women living with abusers over long periods often learn to pick up cues that tell them that a severe attack is on the way. Others suffer from such a distortion of perception that they see things in their world in a way completely foreign to others—but no less accurate under the circumstances.

Brenda Aris' case is fairly typical. She endured years of beatings from the man she married at seventeen. She had left her husband many times and always returned, either because he cried, begged, and promised to change, or because he threatened to track her down and kill her if she did not return. Her three daughters would cry and beg her to hurry at the supermarket, for fear that she would be beaten for taking too long with the grocery shopping. By the time ten years had passed, he was battering her almost daily and she suffered from the familiar symptoms of the battered woman syndrome. She felt worthless, saw her husband as all-powerful, and believed her life depended on her ability to placate him. Writing for *Glamour*, she said, "On the day I was arrested for killing my husband, I was black and blue from head to foot."

One night, after repeated beatings throughout the day ended with an especially brutal attack, she went to a neighbor's house to get some ice for her injuries. Seeing a gun on the top of the refrigerator, she took it, with the idea that she could use it to intimidate her husband, now drunk and passed out, and stop him from hurting her anymore when he awoke. He had threatened to kill her and she believed him. She perceived he was coming after her, so she shot him on the bed.

Despite widespread acceptance of the battered syndrome by the vast majority of professionals working in the domestic violence field, many courts do not allow expert testimony on the battered woman syndrome in the cases of women accused of murdering their abusive mates. Dr. Lenore Walker agreed to testify in Brenda Aris's trial, but the court allowed only general testimony about the syndrome—no discussion of how it applied to Aris. As a result, jurors were confused, with one later stating that because Walker did not say Aris suffered from the syndrome, the jury concluded that she did not. The appellate court found that the judge committed an error in refusing to allow Walker to offer testimony on Aris' state of mind, but found the error "harmless"—so the verdict was allowed to stand. Fortunately, California Governor Pete Wilson, responding to a growing movement for clemency for battered women, who were denied the benefit of unfettered expert testimony at trial subsequently reduced Aris' sentence and recommended parole.

In most places, the law says that a person is justified in using some form of physical force in self-defense if he or she reasonably believes that force is necessary to prevent an imminent threat of unlawful physical force against him or her. In others, there are additional requirements; for example, that retreat is impossible. A woman is usually allowed to use deadly force if she reasonably believes that her attacker is using or is about to use deadly force against her. How much force is reasonable is supposed to depend on the circumstances, including the size and strength of the attacker compared to the victim.

Things are changing, and today many women who kill their abusers in self-defense are never charged with a crime or are found innocent when the facts come before a court. However, some judges refuse to believe that self-defense can be explained in any other way than the traditional scenario, and that the "reasonable apprehension of imminent death or great bodily harm" required for the defense can never occur in a home with an unlocked door. Traditionally, the law required a battered woman who killed to satisfy three conditions for a successful claim of self-defense: first, the abuser attacked her with a deadly weapon or in a way that she reasonably interpreted as an immediate threat of death; second, she did not provoke the attack; and third, she could not retreat.

Battered women face special problems meeting these requirements because of the psychological damage inherent in most abusive relationships. A man who has repeatedly beaten a woman nearly to death in the past may put her in very reasonable fear for her life by menacing, giving subtle cues only she can recognize as a threat, or striking a single blow. Fists can be a deadly weapon, as thousands of dead victims could testify if they were still alive to do so. Yet many judges cannot see justification for using a gun against an "unarmed" person under any circumstances.

Moreover, many battered women are quite literally unable to escape, even if the door is unlocked. They may be psychologically paralyzed, or they may know that walking through the door would be tantamount to suicide. Yet some judges still refuse to admit expert testimony, arguing that it "invades the province of the jury," it is irrelevant, or it is prejudicial. Even worse, some judges have refused to allow testimony of past abuse as a "mitigating circumstance"—a factor that can help shed light on why a crime was committed and give a reason for a more lenient sentence.

Fortunately, things are changing, and as the scientific community gives increasing recognition to the battered woman syndrome, such as its endorsement by the American Psychological Association, it has become more common for testimony to be admitted. Explanation of the battered woman syndrome can support a standard claim of self-defense within the context of the abused woman's own world. It can show the reasonableness of the woman's belief that she was in imminent danger when she killed her abuser in a setting that does not look to the outside world like a confrontation. It can explain why she did not, and could not, flee the relationship.

By 1993, nine states had passed laws expressly allowing expert testimony on the syndrome. Some women who were convicted of murder or manslaughter when the testimony was not allowed have filed suit to try and obtain new trials.

Social taboos against women who kill are surprisingly powerful, even when women present evidence of the men's behavior that should warrant extreme disapproval. Many women who kill do so after their abusers endanger or sexually abuse their children. For the majority of these women, killing their partners was their first criminal act.

Yet women who plead guilty to murder often get shorter sentences than those who try to prove they acted in self-defense. There is a persistent myth, even among those in a system that sees the terrible toll taken by domestic violence, that any woman can "just leave"; that she always has a choice. Most women who kill have left, been found, and been beaten senseless. They have been told over and over that they (and often their children as well) will be beaten again or killed if they try to flee. Most have tried to use the available services and have been failed by them—by police who do nothing, courts that set abusers free, social services powerless to protect women from men determined to find them and drag them back. Women who kill their abusers do so as a last resort to save their lives or the lives of their children. These are not women with choices.

Even more puzzling is the fact that some women have been sentenced to life imprisonment for murder, even when all of the traditional elements of self-defense, and more, have been present. Consider the case of Becca Jean Hughes. After years of terror, broken bones, and skull fractures, she found herself in her husband's truck with his hands around her throat. This man had a history of extreme violence, including shooting up a house while his wife and children were inside, during his first marriage—a fact Becca was unaware of until she saw the police report at her own trial. When she told him she wanted a divorce, he tried to strangle Becca in the cab of his pickup truck. She managed to get a hold of the pistol she knew he kept under the driver's seat. She even let him see it with the hope he would stop, but he continued trying to choke her to death. Finally, she pulled the trigger.

The judge refused to allow any evidence of abuse in her trial, and the prosecutor managed to convince the jury that she had carried the gun and planned to kill him. At the end of the week-long trial, she was sentenced to life in prison without parole for premeditated murder.

Becca emphasizes that the justice system must recognize the way the battered woman syndrome robs a victim of options. "A battered woman can't leave, she can't even think for herself any more. She has no choices. I've been through it. It's not safe to leave. Divorce is a death wish! Yet the courts misunderstand or overlook the truth, and believe a battered woman can leave anytime."

When police and prosecutors do not enforce the laws against domestic violence, battered women can only protect themselves by taking justice into their own hands. Becca explains that killing an abuser in self defense is a last resort by women who must act to save their own lives. "Because no one else will. It is an unthinking act you do just to survive, The abuser's death is a repercussion of his own actions. Yet when you defend yourself, it's like you're already dead, you just haven't been buried yet. But you will be, by the abuser or by the system."

Becca believes that women who plead guilty instead of arguing self defense often get shorter sentences because they don't insist the justice system live up to the standards we have been taught to believe in. "They don't demand that the system prove itself fair, just, and honest," she says.

But there is hope on the horizon that this unspeakable tradition of injustice is finally crumbling. In 1977, after enduring twelve years of brutal abuse to herself and her children, Francine Hughes burned the home where her husband Mickey Hughes slept after exhausting himself by battering and raping his wife. Francine spent eight months in jail after being charged with first-degree murder and was held without bail, but at trial she was found not guilty by reason of temporary insanity. The case became the subject of a book, *The Burning Bed* by Faith McNulty, and a television movie of the same name which starred Farrah Fawcett. These dramatizations helped heighten public awareness of domestic violence and sparked change in both professional and general attitudes toward the terrifying world inhabited by battered women, and how it can drive them to kill.

Becca Jean Hughes and another inmate who killed her ex-husband worked with Missouri attorneys from prison to help them draft new legislation regarding battered women who kill their abusers. The legislation, passed in 1987, allows a woman charged with murder to testify about the battering she endured and to present expert testimony on the special conditions faced by battered women. A growing clemency movement has led several governors to order releases, reduced sentences, or new trials for women who were denied fair trials.

Ironically, many women who go to prison feel profound relief in a setting most of us would find horrifying. For many of these women, their lives are predictable for the first time. They find themselves in a community of mutually supportive women, with periods of time alone to think, away from the constant, exhausting threat of violence. Many receive counseling or therapy for the first time in their lives. Vocational training and education may also be available, which gives many women a sense of self-worth. Yet it is tragic that a person would have to go to prison to obtain these services. Prison is still prison, and women who are incarcerated experience the grief of losing their children, degradation, isolation, and despair.

Many victims' advocates see a paradox in working for clemency. On one hand, they feel women who kill their abusers should receive a fair defense or early release, but on the other, they don't want to advocate additional violence in a society that is already plagued by far too much. Clemency advocates emphasize that their efforts to free these women should not be interpreted as approval of a "license to kill" because each case must be considered on its own merits, with no blanket rules. And few would argue against allowing women who kill in self-defense the same right as other criminal defendants to present a full and fair defense and allowing women who were denied such rights the chance for a new, more just trial.

If domestic violence is ever to effectively end, values, laws, and attitudes that go to the very roots of our culture must be changed. While the law has at last begun to recognize that domestic violence is both a crime and a violation of civil law, such changes are remarkably recent, many only occurring over the last two decades. It takes time to implement legal evolution in a workable way, and even more time to change deeply ingrained attitudes.

CHAPTER SEVEN

WHAT WORKS TO REDUCE AND PREVENT DOMESTIC VIOLENCE?

People involved in trying to end domestic violence agree that, not only the individual abusers, but society itself needs help. Violence against women is still subtly allowed, even encouraged, some say, by various institutions that give it tacit approval. Entertainment that glamorizes the abusive treatment of women. Police that still ignore or trivialize domestic violence. Judges that release abusers without penalties.

How can these attitudes be changed? Does anything work? Duluth, Minnesota, has been a leader in both intervention efforts that serve families on an individual basis, and attempts to educate people in all walks of society with two goals: prevention of domestic violence, and improvement of programs and services seeking to end it. Duluth's education programs include seminars to train judges, prosecutors, and law enforcement officers; programs for advocates, counselors, and administrators of services for victims, abusers, and children; and presentations in high schools. Initially, the high school program was intended to be geared toward prevention, but the participants were shocked to learn how violent some of the relationships among dating teens had already become. So intervention was offered as well.

Many psychologists stress the importance of teaching children that violence is not an appropriate way of solving problems. One of the key components of such efforts must be parents who live by the same rule and set a positive example. Dr. Carolina Yahne, a psychologist and professor, believes all children should be taught nonviolence, however, it is especially important to educate children who have witnessed violence in the home. "We need to inoculate them against violence like we do against disease," she states. Dr. Yahne believes the media can play an important role in educating children and adults about the consequences of domestic violence, the effects of family discord on children, and subsequently the alternatives.

Education is also accomplished by changes in public policy and practices. When communities establish mandatory arrest and prosecution policies, a message is sent from the police and courts that domestic violence is a crime that society will not tolerate. When coupled with counseling programs for abusers, the message is that those who want to change will be given a fair opportunity. Those who do not will be treated like the criminals they are and incarcerated. Some of the most skilled and valuable counselors in these programs are formerly battered women and formerly abusive men.

Grassroots efforts to educate and capture the attention of the public continue, often in unique and creative ways. The Clothesline Project is such an effort. This nationwide project was organized with the theme of airing dirty laundry, of taking dark secrets out of the closet and into the sunlight. From 1990 to 1994, the survivors around the country set up local displays of T-shirts decorated by abuse survivors to carry their messages of anger, hope, and pain. The shirts are color-coded to indicate different forms of domestic violence. Through the project, organizers hope to heighten public awareness about crimes against women and to find some personal healing, as well as establish sisterhood with other survivors. As of the summer of 1994, more than two hundred different clotheslines bearing 20,000 shirts had been displayed across America. A national exhibit was held in the spring of 1995 in Washington, D.C. It continues to sponsor local workshops and exhibits.

Communities with the greatest success in lowering rates of domestic violence are those in which the various public and private agencies work together in a collective effort to tackle the problem. In these communities, diverse talents and services can be combined to offer those in need of help an organized system, rather than existing as piecemeal groups only vaguely aware of what else is available. Successful programs vary in their structure and scope, but all share two key elements: communication and cooperation.

Ideally, all of the entities and agencies that are involved in domestic violence issues within a given community or region should meet and interact on a regular basis to share ideas, plan strategies, develop protocols, and promote an ongoing dialog with one another and with the public. Practically, this may not always be possible. In many areas, the key participants are already spread so thin they cannot even serve all who need them. However, simple solutions have been discovered by innovative communities. One city responded to the pleas of already overworked professionals by instituting a monthly lunch program in which a task force compiled of individuals and representatives from the various groups—police, social services workers, teachers, victim advocates, medical professionals, preventionists, prosecutors—meet for lunch for an informal opportunity to tell each other what they have been doing, what they need, and how they can help others. As one shelter manager commented, "What we need is not more meetings, but more dialog." Even one or two gatherings a year, in which collaborators can compile a list of names, roles, and numbers so professionals can call each other and make referrals to service providers can make a huge difference. It is also important to consider players in the system who might not come to mind immediately because they are not in one of the traditional victim-contact roles. For example, I recently heard a criminal defense attorney comment that he, too, needs to be aware of the available resources, so he can refer the abusers he represents to qualified counselors and appropriate programs. In turn, he can make others aware of the many legal alternatives available to deal with abusers, such as electronic monitoring, work release, community service plus mandatory counseling.

As one police officer stated, "It is not fair to expect law enforcement to be district attorney, for a social worker to be a cop—we all need to do our jobs well and work together. The peculiar nature of the victim-offender relationship makes this crime different from others, combining love, terror, confusion, and other intense emotions." Everyone—especially those likely to be a victim's first contact, such as emergency room physicians, police officers, and shelter staff—need to be aware of the places available to refer the victim for various types of help. Communities can easily and inexpensively print and distribute small booklets or even business cards listing the most crucial names and numbers. For example, the Family Crisis Unit of the Albuquerque Police Department distributes a small booklet entitled, "Pocket Guide for Victims of Domestic Violence," which tells victims how and where to get help. This compact but thorough resource contains information to help victims understand and identify abuse; statistics on the prevalence of domestic violence; a summary of the effects of domestic violence on children; advice on what to do before, during, and after an attack; and concise information on how the different components of the legal system can provide help. Telephone numbers for sources of legal, social, medical, counseling, housing, and other areas of help—even education and child care—are provided.

MODEL PROGRAMS

In 1992, the National Council of Juvenile and Family Court Judges published a book entitled *Family Violence: State-of-the-Art Court Programs*, describing eighteen court-annexed programs dealing with domestic violence throughout the United States, which they considered "state-of-the-art." While no one program was perfect, the Council chose programs it believed had outstanding attributes that could be considered by all communities.

The Council also noted that some of the programs took different approaches to controversial issues surrounding the legal response to family violence, including: Whether or not a victim should be required to do certain things such as appear in court, attend counseling, or meet with the abuser in attempting to resolve such issues as child custody; whether or not batterers should be diverted out of the criminal justice system into treatment programs and, if so, when; and whether or not the court system should focus primarily on the needs of the adult victim of domestic violence or the needs of children in the family.

The Council worked with an advisory committee of national experts in the field of family violence who had a wide variety of backgrounds and perspectives. The eighteen programs selected as the best represented those who had been effective in reducing, intervening, and controlling family violence. The Council found that many of the programs attributed a large measure of their success to their ability to borrow good ideas from other programs. Some also stressed the importance of a leader within the community dedicated to the growth of the program. Others emphasized the necessity of community commitment, noting the efforts of the women who have carried on grassroots services for years. All emphasized the importance of a continuous, coordinated effort between law enforcement, prosecution, the courts, and treatment programs; as well as the involvement of more indirectly related providers such as public housing and the medical community. All found that each separate component benefitted from its regular interaction with the others. The successful programs also shared a willingness to change, and a flexibility to allow for ongoing improvement.

Although the study was published in 1992, these programs are still going strong today, following the same principles that established them as cornerstones of their communities. Several of the leading programs are described in some detail below; others are listed in the appendix. Unless otherwise stated, the views expressed in the program descriptions are those of the programs and not necessarily the policy of the Council. All have expressed a willingness to work with individuals and groups from other communities; and some publish reports, brochures, and training materials.

In another publication, *Family Violence: Improving Court Practices*, the Council pointed out that judges can also make a huge difference in both community attitudes and the effectiveness of the law. Judges must treat domestic violence as a serious crime, and not only issue strong orders but follow up to make sure batterers comply or face serious consequences, including jail time if any provision is broken. Judges who have made it clear that they mean business have found that batterers are much more likely to stay away from their victims, attend counseling and education programs, and comply with the order's other provisions. As one experienced judge pointed out, abusers are experts in control, and will be quick to detect whether their victims and the judges who sentence them mean what they say. Victims are safer and feel empowered to stand up to their abusers when the court puts its strength behind them.

Moreover, compliance reviews that make sure offenders are obeying protection orders and other court mandates take relatively little time. One judge who handles such reviews once a week for an hour and a half finds he can take on fifteen to twenty reviews per week in that time; and that time is saved in the long run by far less repeat filings. The batterer gets the message that there will be more hearings, and more penalties, until he complies.

Comprehensive Programs

The Council first described in its study what it called "comprehensive" programs. These are private, nonprofit organizations operating independent of the court system or government agencies, and funded by a variety of public and private sources. The programs provide direct services to victims, including immediate aid, court advocacy, shelter, counseling, therapy, and referrals to other sources for needs such as housing and legal assistance.

Many of these programs also provide individual and group treatment, legal assistance, intervention, outreach, detention screening, and other services for batterers. All of the comprehensive programs develop close working relationships with judges, prosecutors, and law enforcement. They provide feedback and make sure critical information is exchanged between the various people involved in individual cases. They also provide training for agency and judicial personnel, and act as conduits for information that needs to be shared by the courts and other agencies. Comprehensive programs are frequently involved in a community domestic violence task force, composed of representatives from the various court and community agencies.

Several different types of comprehensive programs the Council recognized are profiled below. Although they vary in scope and their particular approach, they share characteristics unique to comprehensive programs. Each program appreciates the importance of working to change the "big picture," and takes various steps toward improving the social and legal structure that affects its clients. These efforts include research, amending legislation, speaking, and directly working toward legal and social changes. Each program strives toward the recognition of family violence as serious criminal conduct, and tries to see that victims have the opportunity to use all the available legal remedies, without having to choose between them.

The Domestic Abuse Project (DAP)
204 West Franklin Avenue
Minneapolis, MN 55404
(612) 874-7063

Founded in 1979, DAP is one of the oldest programs against domestic violence. It serves Hennepin County, Minnesota which includes Minneapolis. DAP has two community intervention projects that work directly with prosecutors, one for felony cases and one for misdemeanors. It also has a therapy unit, which provides group, individual, couples, and family therapy services for women and children who are victims, as well as for abusive men. A unique feature of this unit is its group therapy programs for adolescents; one for boys who have been in abusive family or dating relationships, and a similar one for girls.

DAP's training program offers education and training to mental health and social service professionals and to the criminal justice system. It also gives public presentations in schools, in churches, and for community organizations. It publishes an adult treatment manual for male and female clients, publishes a children's treatment manual, and conducts training sessions and workshops tailored for different communities across the country.

DAP also has an evaluation and research program that collects follow-up data on the men's and women's therapy programs to assess their success. The program evaluates different approaches in working with abusive men, comparing education, process/self-help, and a combined approach. The children's program has also been evaluated, with published research reports available from DAP. Like most programs, DAP relies on extensive assistance from volunteers. Some work directly with victims of domestic violence, while others serve as facilitators with self-help support groups.

Minnesota police are required by law to make a written report on every incident involving a domestic assault, and officers report all arrests by telephone to DAP's twenty-four-hour crisis line. In the Minneapolis program, an advocate then calls the victim and advises her of services and legal options. The next day the advocate prepares a memo for the city attorney (the prosecutor) stating the victim's concerns and requesting a no-contact (protection) order if needed. The prosecutor brings domestic assault charges, and the victim is required to appear as a witness at the pretrial (where the man may enter a guilty plea) and the trial, if the case proceeds. The advocate assists the victim throughout this process.

The advocate also works with the prosecuting attorney in the courtroom, in staff meetings, and on a multi-agency task force that examines how the criminal prosecution and the civil protective order process can be improved. The advocate may continue to work on the case after the trial to make sure the victim's concerns about sentencing are considered by the court. He or she may also remain involved if probation is ordered and later, if the conditions of probation are violated. A similar program is provided to Hennepin County residents, with advocates working out of the county attorney's office.

One of the strengths of DAP is its funding from a wide variety of sources, including the Department of Corrections, the United Way, client fees, Hennepin County, the city of Minneapolis, private funding, and federal funds under the Family Violence Prevention and Services Act.

No program is perfect, and DAP, like others, still grapples with various problems. Not all area police are as sensitive to the victims as they should be, and funding must be sought continually. Yet DAP has proven to be one of the most impressive and effective coordinated projects in the country, and has been used as a model by many other communities.

House of Ruth, Inc.
Domestic Violence Legal Clinic
2201 Argone Drive
Baltimore, MD 21218
(301) 889-0840

The House of Ruth operates five direct service programs, including a shelter, individual and group counseling for women (including long-term group counseling for abuse survivors), a volunteer-run, twenty-four-hour hotline, a children's program for children in the shelter, and a domestic violence legal clinic. It also has an outreach program, which arranges media events, provides a speaker's bureau, and produces educational videotapes and publications for both the public and legal professionals.

One of the most unique features of the House of Ruth is its legal clinic. Staffed by four attorneys and five support professionals, it provides legal representation and advocacy, primarily for low-income victims. Based in the shelter, its main goals are to ensure the safety of its clients and to improve the laws affecting battered women. The clinic provides information, referrals, and advocacy in criminal court. Its staff directly represents women seeking protective orders, divorce, child custody, and, occasionally, in criminal defense. In especially dangerous cases, an attorney will help a woman obtain name changes, new birth certificates, and relocation. The legal clinic also helps link clients to trained *pro bono* (free) attorneys who volunteer their services.

The legal clinic has undertaken a number of unique projects in its efforts to change the law in favor of battered women. In 1990, it successfully represented Maryland's battered women in a class action suit against the Public Service Commission to obtain protection against a telephone system that allows the listener to locate the caller, posing a substantial threat to battered women and those who help them. It has worked hard to improve access to the civil system for low-income women, filed *amicus curiae* (friend of the court) briefs in cases involving such issues as expert testimony on the battered woman syndrome and evidence of violence in custody cases. These briefs educate the court about laws supporting the point of view of some person or group not directly involved in the case, and urge the judge to hand down a decision that will change or support the law in a way favorable to its goals.

One of the clinic's most impressive achievements was the Clemency Project, in which the clinic, working with the Domestic Violence Task Force, undertook various efforts to help women charged with killing or attempting to kill their abusers who were routinely denied the opportunity to present evidence on the battered woman syndrome at their trials. A class action suit was being prepared when the matter came to the attention of Maryland Governor William Donald Schaefer, so a special report was prepared for him. As a result, in February 1991, Governor Schaefer commuted the sentences of eight women incarcerated for killing or injuring their abusers. Three more women were later released, and another had her conviction overturned on appeal.

The House of Ruth is also notable for providing comprehensive services at one location. A victim can find legal assistance, shelter, counseling, parenting services, children's services, and batterer treatment all in one place. It works closely with other agencies and in 1989, worked with the city to publish *Domestic Violence Policies and Procedures*, a manual representing the cooperative efforts of each branch of the legal system to disapprove of and work to end domestic violence.

At the House of Ruth, counseling and legal activities support one another. Legal services are free to low-income clients, but the clinic believes it is beneficial to charge clients who can pay a small fee, ask them to assist with volunteer work, or ask them to help with investigation and legal work on their own cases, so they stay directly involved.

Templum/East Cleveland Domestic Violence Project
P.O. Box 5466
Cleveland, OH 44101
(216) 634-7501

Templum is another pioneer among domestic violence centers. Established in 1978, it provides shelter, counseling, outreach, community education, children's services, and legal advocacy. The East Cleveland Domestic Violence Project was established by Templum in 1986 to provide court advocacy for victims in misdemeanor domestic violence cases in the East Cleveland Municipal Court. It offers crisis intervention, hospital visitation, court accompaniment, help with temporary protection orders, individual counseling, group therapy, referrals to legal assistance, and referrals to safe housing. It also provides services for the perpetrators, including information about pending charges, court procedures, sentencing, work release, and counseling services. Its philosophy supports the criminal justice system's refusal to tolerate domestic violence, but also the belief that abusive men can end their violence and learn to be respectful partners and effective parents.

The project also facilitates coordinated efforts among the East Cleveland police, prosecutor's office, probation and parole department, judges, bailiffs, court clerks, community hospitals, social service agencies, and pastors. It is a center for information, consultation, and support for each component of the court-based intervention system. Police respond immediately to domestic violence calls. The local judge considers domestic violence a serious crime and believes the abuser is solely responsible for his conduct. A conviction often brings thirty days in jail.

The entire program is housed in the city hall, so social services and the criminal justice system share one location. While safety of victims is a priority, men are encouraged to seek help and end violence in the family.

The project works to educate the community and change attitudes about domestic violence and family life in general. People of color, mainly African Americans, comprise 99 percent of the East Cleveland jurisdiction. Participants in the project share a goal of creating a community where Black families can live free of violence and realize their potential. Working with community leaders and at the street level, its goal is to achieve a community opposed to violence and supportive of relationships based on respect and equality.

Several components of the project are rather unique. A wider variety of punishment and treatment alternatives are available for offenders than in most programs. For example, work release with electronic monitoring is an option in appropriate cases. Long-term, periodic contact with the victim provides support for her in assuring her safety and encouraging her to work toward goals such as education, while probation and parole authorities track the abuser's compliance with sentencing conditions such as desisting from violence and continuing treatment.

The judge and project coordinator are highly visible leaders in the community, and information is widely distributed. The project routinely evaluates its own effectiveness and that of the criminal justice system, and has participants complete a questionnaire when their case is closed.

The project does extraordinary work with very little money. The project coordinator, municipal court judge, and mayor of East Cleveland share the vision of creating an African-American urban community that is safe, empowering, and economically supportive of all members.

The Family Court of the Second Circuit
2145 Main Street, Suite 226
Wailuku, Maui, Hawaii 96793
(808) 244-2290

Alternatives to Violence
P.O. Box 909
Wailuku, Maui, HI 96793
(808) 242-9559

This unique family court is part of a court system with jurisdiction over all family matters, including civil restraining (protection) orders and criminal misdemeanor domestic violence cases. The court has been praised for its unusual way of offering domestic violence victims easy access to the courthouse, its ability to issue protection orders within two or three hours, and for being one of the few formal systems in the country that monitors abusers under protection orders. Much of the credit goes to an enlightened group of judges, who are willing to try new ideas and change what is not working. The Family Court works closely with Alternatives to Violence (ATV), an independent organization that offers group treatment for abusive men, programs for women, treatment for juvenile offenders, and advocacy services. The treatment programs all have very high success rates.

The process of ending domestic violence often begins at ATV. Advocates review the police report, which must be filed even if no arrest is made, and accompany the victim throughout the court process. One prosecutor works on the case, and charges are not dropped at the victim's request. Hawaii's law requires a minimum forty-eight-hour jail sentence, one-year probation, and participation in court-ordered counseling for convicted abusers.

During hearings, a secure and serious atmosphere prevails in the courtroom. All judges are trained in the dynamics of an abusive relationship. The court staff makes sure both victim and offender understand everything that happens. Usually, the victim is required to attend a twelve- or fifteen-week counseling program, and the batterer is ordered into a twenty-four-week program at ATV. A voluntary group serves men who wish to continue treatment after the mandatory period. An adolescent's group for young abusers provides a sixteen-week education program toward ending the use of violence in relationships. An anger management group is a one-day education and prevention program for adolescents involved in school or street fights. ATV also holds group sessions for children of adult clients, and the judge may order parents of children who have witnessed violence to bring their children to ATV for assessment. A domestic violence task force meets monthly with representatives from the police, prosecutor's office, shelter, family court, ATV, and the city council.

The unified family court system allows one judge to deal with all aspects of a case, civil and criminal, and to create remedies that serve the needs of all family members. Other effective features of this system include all police carrying cards about services for victims and cameras in their cars for evidence, and "Sky Bridge," a video link between the islands which is used along with fax transmissions for civil restraining order hearings.

Statewide Court Programs

The Council also looked at family violence programs serving entire states. These programs are somewhat different in that they operate inside the government system with public funds. The main advantage to such programs is that the policies and procedures for preventing and reducing family violence are set by the state legislature, and the same rules apply to all communities and citizens of the state. Also, some consistent funding is assured. However, state programs are urged to allow local communities to act independently to develop strong systems tailored to their specific needs and to locate additional sources of funding. The Council profiled the Hawaii and Connecticut systems as state-of-the-art.

Connecticut Superior Court
Family Violence Intervention Units
& Domestic Violence Projects
28 Grand Street
Hartford, CT 06106
(203) 566-8187

In 1986, Connecticut passed a law creating Family Violence Intervention Units (FVIUs). This law established these special units in the Family Division of the Conneticut Superior Court in each of the twenty-two geographical areas of the state. The legislation also established a statewide advocate program to be operated by the Connecticut Coalition Against Domestic Violence under a contract with the state. The courts also contract with private, local mental health organizations for counseling and treatment services.

In most misdemeanor cases, courts issue criminal protection orders for victims and refer first-time abusers to the six-week pretrial education program, along with supervised probation for at least three months. The law also requires arrest for family violence crimes and arraignment within twenty-four to seventy-two hours after charges are filed. Before arraignment, both victim and abuser are interviewed by a family relations counselor, who prepares a report for the judge. The report contains general information about the family, documents any prior history of abuse, and may include recommendations for services or sentencing. The victim is referred to the family violence advocate program, and offered information on a broad range of family protection and support services. She also receives information on the court process and how to protect her rights during and after the case.

At the arraignment hearing, if eligible defendants apply for referral to the pretrial education program, the prosecutor often dismisses the case with the condition that the offender successfully completes a treatment program and abides by other conditions set by the court. A protection order remains in effect, and the defendant is supervised. The victim and abuser are then referred to the FVIU, and a counselor completes interviews and prepares an in-depth, final report for the court, including an assessment of the abuser's risk to the family.

The twenty-two FVIUs employ full-time victim advocates, who provide emergency shelter, court assistance, referrals to community services, and assistance to the victim in planning for her safety. The advocates and the programs they work with also provide a twenty-four-hour hotline, a children's advocate program, and other services for children.

The Connecticut program is fortunate to be backed by state policy declaring that family violence is a crime best treated as such in conjunction with services to both victims and offenders, and backed by legislation and funding. Research is ongoing, and when the studies suggest recommendations for improvements, changes are implemented.

Another unique feature of the Connecticut system is the continual, mandatory training programs for police, judges, and service providers. Public education about domestic violence and the state's response is another effort. There is also a strong partnership between the Family Division of the Superior Court and the Connecticut Coalition Against Domestic Violence. The court staff, including counselors and advocates, is professionally trained. In its study, the Council stated, "Connecticut's public policy of reinforcing the seriousness of domestic violence issues with mandatory arrests and accelerated arraignments should be essential elements of all legislation."

Rural Programs

Rural courts and others involved in domestic violence issues in country areas face special challenges. The small-town setting in which nearly everyone knows one another makes victims embarrassed to seek help, and police and judges sometimes reluctant to hold neighbors accountable for their violence. Traditional views about families and gender roles persist in some rural areas, and isolation can be an additional problem.

Yet rural folk are known for working together to solve local problems, and community disapproval is a strong deterrent in areas with close interpersonal ties and shared values. If county sheriffs and other law enforcement agencies give priority to training officers, promptly responding to calls around the clock, providing necessary transportation to victims, and serving protection orders, excellent results can be achieved. Courts in rural areas must also make protection orders available without charge. Someone in the system, either an advocate or court employee, must also provide support to the victim. The Council found that attitude, training, and assistance for victims at the courthouse were the most fundamental elements in rural communities with effective services. Thus, each successful program listed has a strong partnership between the court and community-based programs that offer protection to victims, punishment and treatment of abusers, coordinated community work, and attention to the necessary details. Each part of this network must be well trained and serious about preventing and responding to family violence.

Tri-State Coalition Against Family Violence
P.O. Box 494
Keokuk, IA 52632
(319) 524-4445

This coalition serves both victims of domestic violence and victims of sexual assault. It provides a crisis hotline, a shelter, a crisis intervention service, community outreach, court and legal advocacy, sexual assault services, child advocacy, out-client services, a women's group, and a batterer's group.

Iowa passed a mandatory arrest law in 1986, which the coalition credits with substantially changing police attitudes and responsiveness. In most cases, assault charges are filed and police call victim advocates at the time of arrest. The advocate is given a police escort and meets police at the site of the assault, even if it means an hour's drive. Defendants are held in jail until an arraignment and hearing, which is scheduled within twenty-four hours of arrest. Courts treat all domestic violence cases as potentially lethal.

The parties have assistance at every step. All defendants have attorneys and all have advocates. The prosecutor will not drop charges. A no-contact (protection) order is usually issued as a condition of release on bond. If the batterer is convicted, this protection order will remain in effect for one to two years. Sentencing of a first-time offender usually means two to five days in jail, court costs, restitution to the coalition for service costs, participation in the sixteen-week men's group, and probation. This sentencing is supported by Iowa's state legislation.

The coalition, the courts, law enforcement, and the community see themselves as partners in a "get-tough" approach to stop domestic violence. The new law plus the partnership between the coalition and the police appears to be having a real deterrent effect, and police feel the presence of the victim's advocate is helpful to their ability to respond effectively to difficult cases. The word is out in the community that wife beating means jail. The local prosecutor has found that the policies of mandatory arrest, no-drops, and automatic requests for no contact orders have made management of family violence cases much easier for his office.

Rural neighborliness is reflected in the twenty-four-hour, "go-any-where-we-must-philosophy." The coalition's board of directors is representative of the broad community, and members are very active. Mutual evaluation and feedback between the coalition, the police, and social service agencies are given on a regular basis.

Civil Protection Order Programs

Today, all fifty states have enacted legislation providing for protection orders, which are the most available remedies for domestic violence victims. To be effective, such orders must be easily accessible, be consistently enforced, and provide detailed relief. A major weakness in many areas is monitoring compliance with these orders, and few courts have developed formal methods, such as those used to track offenders on probation. Those that do have found the use of victim advocates to be an effective method of assisting the victims and the court, screening for any ongoing violence, and making sure children in the home are safe.

Committee to Aid Abused Women
Second Judicial District Court
Protection Order Program
Washoe County Courthouse
75 Court Street, Room 103
Reno, NV 89520
(702) 328-3468

This program is noted for its streamlined procedures and dedicated judicial support. A concerned judge developed forms and procedures to make protection orders readily available. When it was deluged with applicants, the Washoe County Second Judicial District Court hired a special master (a judge with limited duties) to hear these cases full-time.

A special office for the protection order program is located in the Reno courthouse with three private interview rooms, a waiting room, a staff office, and a children's play area. Well-trained clerks and advocates assist the victim, and a bilingual advocate is available. An intake interview is conducted and detailed information is collected. The victim is given basic information about domestic violence, the court system, and community services, and views a videotape. An appointment with the special master is set, and the hearing is usually held in his or her chambers. Applications for protection orders must be heard within one day of filing, and the victim does not need an attorney. This judge is very well trained and sensitive to domestic violence issues, and generally reminds the victim that it is not her fault and that nobody deserves to be abused.

About 80 percent of the orders requested are granted. They often prohibit the abuser from any personal or telephone contact with the victim, remove him from the residence, prohibit him from going to the victim's place of work or children's school, award temporary child custody, and address other matters. When she receives the order, the victim takes it to the clerk's office for filing then to the sheriff's department. She pays a twelve-dollar fee if she can, and the sheriff's deputies serve the order on the abuser. The deputies also help the victim carry out provisions of the order such as escorting the person leaving to retrieve belongings from the home. They may assist the victim in getting custody of children, confiscating weapons or house keys, or getting an abuser out of the home. Service of a protection order by a peace officer helps convey the message that domestic violence is a crime.

The victim is usually ordered to attend the domestic violence education program. This one-session, two-hour class provides information about family violence, legal options, related issues, and community services. Each victim receives a self-help and reference manual. After a hearing at which both parties are present, generally two to four weeks later, the order may be extended for up to one year.

If the order is violated, arrest is mandatory. The abuser may be charged with violating the order or held in contempt of court, either of which can mean a fine and jail. The Committee to Aid Abused Women works under a contract with the court, and its advocates help women prepare forms, provide information about court procedures, and provide other services the victims need. The system has been praised by victims for helping them—and for working. One unique feature is gold star pins provided to victims, which help create a network in the community.

Pennsylvania Coalition Against Domestic Violence
2505 North Front Street
Harrisburg, PA 17110-1111
(717) 234-7353

The Council also praised the Pennsylvania Coalition Against Domestic Violence as one of the oldest and strongest state coalitions in the country. The coalition has been in place since 1976, when Pennsylvania passed the first domestic violence coalition in the United States. Since its beginning, the Pennsylvania Coalition Against Domestic Violence has been committed to four principle goals:

1. The development of a statewide network of direct services for the safety and welfare of victims
2. Advocacy efforts to improve the various systems and institutions directly involved with domestic violence victims
3. Community education and prevention programs
4. Providing training personnel both statewide and in different communities

The program has always focused upon a blend of services to victims and advocacy toward social change. It developed one of the first training manuals for police officers, as well as training for virtually all of the other professionals involved in the public and private systems. Today, the Pennsylvania Coalition produces a wide variety of videos, manuals, handbooks, and course curriculum materials for courts, police, family lawyers, victims, children, and the public. Its legal advocacy office assists other attorneys, advises legislators, and works with public agencies and other professionals. Pennsylvania's own laws reflect the dedication of the state toward ending domestic violence, including, among many other provisions, funding for advocacy and the requirement that domestic violence be considered in child custody cases. The first priority when committing resources is the safety of the victims.

Prosecution Programs

The Council also looked at successful prosecution-based programs. As changes in law enforcement and public attitudes have led to a dramatic increase in arrests for domestic violence, prosecutors—state, district, or county attorneys—have been faced with new challenges. Not only has the increased workload from these cases proven difficult, but the changing view of family assault as a serious crime and the lethal nature of many such cases have forced prosecutors to find new ways of responding promptly and effectively.

The Domestic Violence Unit
Office of the San Diego City Attorney
1010 Second Avenue, Suite 300
San Diego, CA 92101-4903
(619) 531-4040

The Domestic Violence Unit of the San Diego City Attorney's Office, under the guidance of Deputy City Attorney Casey G. Gwinn, has developed a strong, energetic, and well-organized system for dealing with domestic violence which has been used as a model for prosecutors across the country. The prosecutor takes full charge of each case. The victim is not required to sign a formal complaint; it will be signed by a deputy city attorney. The decision whether or not to file charges is made by the prosecutor. If there is sufficient independent evidence, charges can be filed without the victim's full involvement, though she may be subpoenaed to appear and testify at trial.

The prosecutor views all of the cases in which charges are filed as serious, violent criminal behavior. Charges are not reduced to lesser offenses. The city attorney staff notifies the victim of all hearings and outcomes, explains procedures, and tries to maintain a rapport with her throughout the prosecution of the case.

The Domestic Violence Unit has also produced a manual, *Domestic Violence Misdemeanor Prosecution Protocol,* for all its attorneys, which is an excellent resource on domestic violence dynamics, policies, requirements, and sample court forms. The unit works closely with the county attorney's office, the San Diego Domestic Violence Council, the San Diego Task Force on Domestic Violence, and many professionals who work under the guidance of the task force. Some of the accomplishments of the task force include the creation of a protocol for all law enforcement agencies, training sessions for judges and their staffs, a protocol for hospitals and physicians who treat domestic violence victims, standards for those treating batterers, advocating for funding for the Domestic Violence Unit, and helping to create a special unit in the county probation department. It also assisted in the creation of the Family Violence Project at Children's Hospital to establish a national model for intervention in cases involving both spouse and child abuse, produced a training video for law enforcement agencies, and helped reduce the 1990 domestic homicide rate in the city by 61 percent. Eighty-eight percent of the cases prosecuted are resolved with a conviction.

In all cases set for trial, the prosecutor prepares a trial brief from samples available in the training manual and on computer, which sets out the facts of the case and the applicable law that supports the prosecutor's case, as well as addresses other legal issues. This brief is a part of the thorough preparation which contributes to the high conviction rate. Sentencing following a guilty plea or conviction at trial includes jail time, a one-year treatment program, and other orders.

The Council suggested that other jurisdictions, as a starting point toward developing such a program, assign one prosecutor to specialize in domestic violence cases. This can generally be done through reallocation of staff and existing resources from non-violent misdemeanors to crimes of violence and the gradual addition of staff over time. As stated by John J. Witt, San Diego city attorney, in the Council's book, *Family Violence: State of the Art Court Programs*, "Comprehensive misdemeanor prosecution of domestic violence cases will save lives, break the generational cycle, and dramatically reduce the number of felony burglaries, assaults, rapes, kidnappings, and murders that often result if the violence is allowed to escalate. Few crimes are as central to the destruction of the American family as domestic violence. Early intervention is the only strategy that will stop the violence before it can replicate itself in the lives of the children who witness the violence."

Offender Accountability

The Council took a close look at the difficult problem of holding offenders accountable for their actions. There is substantial controversy over whether or not such programs really work, the best format for the programs, and how much time is required of the participants. Most programs work with the courts under mandatory treatment orders. Supervising a large number of cases is a difficult task for any court system. Yet a number of programs have been very successful.

The Council recommended that every sentence in a family violence case should order the offender to be involved in activities specifically designed to reduce future violence, including alcohol and drug evaluation and treatment if necessary; formal supervision and monitoring of compliance, with substantial penalties for repeat violations; diversion into treatment only after an admission of responsibility and in extraordinary cases; maximum supervision by probation departments; and specific standards for batterer's treatment and education programs.

Stipulated Order of Continuance Program
Bellevue Probation Department
P.O. Box 90012
Bellevue, WA 98009-9012
(206) 455-6956

This program, called "SOC," is the effort of four public and two private agencies which meet regularly to provide a coordinated and immediate response to domestic violence cases in the community. Each agency becomes involved right after an arrest.

The agencies involved in the program include the police department, prosecuting attorney, district court, probation department, Eastside Mental Health Agency, and Eastside Domestic Violence Program. The probation department has a unique program comprised of volunteer probation officers who are continually trained and closely supervised.

To be eligible for the SOC program, an offender must acknowledge his abusive behavior and be found amenable to supervision and treatment. The victim is also consulted for her opinion. If the batterer successfully completes the program, the complaint is dismissed; otherwise, he continues in the court system.

Washington has a mandatory arrest law where there is probable cause to believe a crime occurred. Officers also give each victim a fifty-page booklet that explains domestic violence, police procedures, security, emotional support services, and other resources. The defendant is taken to jail, booked, and if he is to be released on bail, a no-contact order is issued. If the charge is a felony or the abuser has never been arrested before on assault charges, he is not considered eligible for the SOC program. Before any abuser can be admitted, he must convince a probation officer that he understands his responsibility for the crime and really wants the treatment.

Offenders who go into the program are given the same monitoring and services as a defendant on probation. The abuser must attend individual and group therapy programs at Eastside Mental Health for at least six months. Therapy includes anger and violence counseling. Each participant is also evaluated for drug, alcohol, or mental health problems, and referred to other treatment if necessary. Defendants pay for the program on a sliding fee scale. If the abuser successfully completes the program with all required treatment and no new arrests, the complaint is dismissed after twelve months.

Two factors, in particular, make the SOC program successful: first, the high degree of cooperation by the six agencies; and, second, the immediate, coordinated response to each case. The quick response helps protect the victim and assure that the abuser will be held accountable, as well as receive the best chance to change his life.

Diversion programs are controversial, and many police and prosecutors oppose them. However, the Bellevue SOC program is strongly supported by the local criminal justice system, as well as local mental health advocates. Also, some feel that the defendants may be strongly motivated by the desire to keep a clean criminal record.

CHAPTER EIGHT

PRACTICAL INFORMATION FOR WOMEN WHO ARE ABUSED AND THOSE WHO WANT TO HELP THEM

Today, more than ever before, women who are living with domestic violence, as well as those who care about them and want to help prevent and put an end to the tragedy of family violence, have a wide array of resources available. Following is a collection of information and ideas from many different sources.

FOR THE ABUSED WOMAN

Women today who are abused or at risk for abuse have more options than ever before. Coalitions, shelters, programs, books, hotlines, advocates, and many other resources are available to nearly all women through national, state, and local services. However, before a woman can choose and locate the type of help best suited to her circumstances, some self-examination to get a clear picture of those circumstances may be required.

Are You Abused or At Risk for Abuse?

According to the Domestic Abuse Intervention Project of Duluth, Minnesota, certain behaviors of abusive men have been identified as characteristic of the early stages of abuse that often precedes physical battering. These personality traits are combined with information on the predictors of domestic violence, as identified by the National Technical Assistance Center on Family Violence and published by the National Coalition Against Domestic Violence. Women who recognize several of these traits in their partners should take a careful look at the relationship, and carefully consider getting out before it becomes violent.

1. Your partner has a history of growing up in a violent family, a setting where he learned that violence is normal behavior.
2. He has a tendency to use force or violence to try to solve problems—as indicated by behavior such as a criminal record for violence, a quick temper or tendency to overreact to minor frustrations, fighting, destructive behavior when angry, cruelty to animals.
3. He abuses alcohol or drugs.
4. He has a poor opinion of himself, often masked by trying to act tough.
5. He often exhibits jealousy, not only of other men, but also of friends and family members.
6. He exhibits hypermasculine behavior—he feels he should make all the decisions, tell you what your role as a woman and his as a man must be. He has very traditional ideas about appropriate roles and behaviors of men and women, and thinks women are second-class citizens. He expects you to follow his orders and advice and may become angry if you can't read his mind and anticipate what he wants.
7. He emotionally abuses you or other women with name-calling, put-downs, humiliation, and attempts to create guilt.
8. He isolates you by telling you who you may see or talk to, controls what you do and where you go, even what you read. He keeps tabs on your every move, and wants you with him all the time.
9. He intimidates you and makes you afraid through looks, anger, actions, a display of weapons or gestures. He destroys your property or abuses your pets. He enjoys playing with lethal weapons, and

threatens to use them against those he feels wronged him. You do what he wants you to do, and constantly work to keep him from getting angry.

10. He portrays "Jekyll and Hyde" behavior. He goes through highs and lows, as though he is two different people, and he swings from extremely kind to extremely cruel.

11. He uses coercion and threats. He tells you he will hurt you, leave you, or kill himself if you leave. If you file charges against him he makes you drop them by threatening violence or suicide. Have you changed your life so you won't make him angry?

12. He treats you roughly, and physically forces you to do things you do not want to do.

13. He often denies his actions, minimizing or making light of his own abusive behavior, refusing to take your concerns seriously, and blaming you for his behavior.

14. He economically abuses you by preventing you from getting or keeping a job, controlling all the money in the household, making you ask for money, or concealing his income.

Women in relationships where these behaviors regularly take place are already abused, even if the physical violence has not started. These signs should be taken very seriously.

Sometimes people are occasionally nasty, but generally treat their partners well, so it is not so clear as to whether the behavior is abusive or merely the less pleasant side of normal human nature. Often the way a victim feels or acts can be a clue that occasional moodiness has crossed the line into abuse. Ask yourself if you have begun to doubt yourself—do you wonder if you are crazy? Do you look at yourself and what you do in a different way? For example, if you once considered yourself a good cook, a talented singer, a competent worker, has this changed? Do you doubt your own judgment? Are you afraid of your partner? Have you stopped expressing your opinions? Do you hesitate to make decisions before asking your partner's permission? Have you stopped seeing friends, taking classes, going out when you choose? Do you spend a lot of time watching your partner's moods? One of the simplest things a woman can do to begin the process of change is to begin to say different things to herself. Reassure yourself that you do not deserve abuse, that you do not have to tolerate mistreatment. Remind yourself of your positive traits, your accomplishments, all the things you can do and have done.

We all have human imperfections. Sometimes we can benefit by working, either on our own or with the help of others, to make changes in ourselves that will improve our lives. Everyone has room to grow. But nothing gives one human being the right to use violence against another except in self-defense to stop violence. Even if you have behaved in a way toward your partner that you or he does not consider right—such as yelling, nagging, engaging in infidelity, or criticizing—that does not give him the right to hurt you. It may give him the right to get angry, to tell you to stop, to argue, or to leave you. It does not, ever, justify violence. You may have provoked his anger. But you did not provoke his violence—that is his choice, and his problem. Healthy men—the vast majority—do not hit women who make them angry. They have other ways of managing and expressing their anger. If he abuses you, it is not your fault, you did not "cause" the abuse. There is no shame in seeking assistance. And most, if not all, programs protect your privacy. The Women's Community Association of Albuquerque characterizes respect and confidentiality as mainstays of their programs.

Battery is against the law. You are not responsible for your partner's violent behavior, even though he probably tries to blame you. No one deserves abuse. You have the right to insist that you live in a peaceful home, and your children grow up in a home free from violence. Nothing justifies abuse, and if your partner is truly sorry, he needs to get help to learn alternatives to abusive behavior. As Ginny NiCarthy writes in *Getting Free: A Handbook for Women in Abusive Relationships*, you have certain fundamental rights: "The right to speak your mind. The right to privacy, choices, some free time, some money of your own, friends, work, bodily integrity, freedom from fear, treatment with respect and dignity."

Breaking Free from an Abusive Relationship

Women who are abused often feel that they have no choices. But all have at least some options, though they may be unaware alternatives exist, either because they lack the information or have been so severely abused that they are literally paralyzed. Yet women *can* escape. In the words of one survivor quoted on a public television announcement, "You can't change other people, but you can change yourself."

Following is a list of options experts in the field suggest considering. If you are an abused woman, not all of these choices may be right for you, nor all of them available. But at least some of them are worth considering, and even a small step toward taking control of your life can be the first step toward complete freedom and healing. While some women flee all at once, leaving does not have to be a snap decision, and advance planning can make separation both easier and safer.

The idea of finding another place to live, supporting yourself and your children, and changing your whole life in one fell swoop can be overwhelming, even without the added complication of living in a violent home. Add the uncertainty, psychological damage, and terror that come from constantly existing in a dangerous setting, and the situation can be almost paralyzing.

Yet there is an old saying that holds a lot of truth: Yard by yard it's hard, but inch by inch it's a cinch. You can accomplish a tremendous amount by taking small steps toward freedom so when you feel ready to leave—or when an emergency arises—you will be better prepared and it won't be such an ordeal.

The National Coalition Against Domestic Violence has prepared a list of recommendations on what a woman can do if she decides to stay for the time being, based on NiCarthy's *Getting Free*. The following list includes the recommendations of NiCarthy and the NCADV, plus ideas and suggestions from various other sources.

1. Get information. By reading this book you are taking a step toward freedom and a new life. Read others—many more are listed in the appendix. Learn about your situation and what options you have. Many of the organizations listed in the back of this book will send you free brochures and information if you write or call. Your state domestic violence coalition is a good place to start. Gather up the telephone numbers of all the people and agencies you could call

upon for help in an emergency and afterward: hotlines, the police, shelters, friends, the sheriff, family, the church, the prosecutor's office, the public library, the YWCA, the Salvation Army, state and local domestic violence coalitions, and general crisis or self-help lines.

2. Go ahead and call the local crisis line, hotline, shelter, or coalition for help and information. Even if you don't want to leave the relationship now, even if you truly believe what happened was an isolated incident that will never happen again, it is a good idea to find out what services are available in your community in case there ever is a second time. Ask about crisis accommodations for you, your children, and even your pets. Will they come pick you up in the middle of the night if necessary? Find out how long you can stay. Do they provide, or give references to, other services, such as counseling, legal assistance, court advocates? If you would have to travel to another town to reach a shelter, find out how to get there. Remember that shelters aren't only for poor people, they help women of all income levels. Also, be aware that most shelters offer support to women not living in the shelter as well. Most provide counseling, group sessions, and referrals to anyone who needs them.

3. Pack a bag with emergency supplies such as a change of clothing for yourself and your children, a toothbrush, some cash, canned and nonperishable food, and telephone numbers for friends, the local shelter, taxis, and anyone else you may need to turn to in an emergency. Try to leave it at the home of a trusted friend or family member who lives nearby. If no one you trust completely is close, you may want to consider a locker at a bus or train station or the airport.

4. Tell trustworthy, supportive friends and family members what is going on. They can be prepared if there is a crisis, offer emotional support, and help in many different ways, from simply listening to providing transportation and child care. Tell your children's teachers and school principal about your situation. If you have a protection order, give them a copy and ask them not to release the children to the abuser. Write a letter in your handwriting to someone you trust detailing what your abuser has done to you, his full name, when

incidents occurred, and sign and mail it. It may be useful later as evidence. Do be careful to confide only in those who truly care about your well-being. If anyone tells you the abuse is your fault or that you should accept abusive treatment, that person does not have your best interest at heart. Never listen to this kind of talk—it is flat out wrong.

5. Many professionals recommend self-defense training. This type of class can also help you build self-reliance and emotional strength. However, don't count on such training alone to make you safe—many women can still be overpowered by an enraged man and end up getting more seriously injured if they try to fight back. Also, most say to avoid bringing weapons into the home. Far too often, weapons, especially guns, are used against the victim or end up in the hands of children.

6. Talk to a legal advisor. Find out about restraining orders, divorce, and other legal concerns. Many communities have legal advocates, lawyer hotlines, or legal aid groups that can provide free advice and referrals to lawyers.

7. Talk to your children about what is happening—they are almost sure to know what is going on, or at least that things aren't right, even if you don't think they have ever witnessed the violence directly. Make certain they understand that the violence is not their fault.

8. Prepare a safety plan for yourself and your children. Make list of telephone numbers of people you are sure you can depend on in an emergency, preferably people you have talked to about the violence and who have offered to help. Include the phone numbers of shelters, and keep this list in your wallet. If someone you trust lives close to you, ask if you could have keys to his or her house in case of emergency. Have an extra key for your house and car made, and keep them in your wallet as well. You may also want to line up people who can loan you money in an emergency.

9. Begin thinking about what it will be like to live independently. Consider whether or not you will want to change jobs, if you are employed, or what kind of work you would seek if you are not. Look into job training programs, apprenticeships, classes in your community, public aid programs. Acquire new job skills. Learn about community

college or extension courses, teach yourself to use a computer, find out where to sell garden products, handcrafts, baked goods, or other things you know how to make. Your public library can help you get this information, as can women's self-sufficiency programs, the YWCA, local schools, and state job training and employment programs. Find out what is out there.

10. Be aware that leaving is going to be hard, stressful, and emotionally draining. Take care of your health. If you start to have doubts or fears about getting out of the relationship, keep yourself focused on why you have to go. Remember the worst of the violence. Remind yourself that women *die* by the thousands every year at the hands of men who claim to love them. Look at the statistics at the beginning of this book again.

11. Get important documents together, such as your driver's license, birth certificates for you and your children, insurance papers, passports, social security cards, wedding and baptism records, school records, investment records, documents from any public assistance program, leases, titles to your car and other property, savings account books, checkbooks, credit cards, paycheck stubs, tax returns, and medical records. If you think moving or removing these things will cause suspicion, make photocopies. Copy machines are available at public libraries, post offices, and copy shops.

12. Gather up the possessions that have special sentimental value, such as family photos, heirlooms, children's drawings, jewelry. Vengeful partners often destroy a woman's property when she leaves. Also consider pets—abusers often turn on them.

13. Don't tell anyone where you plan to go unless you trust them completely. Remember, abusers often become the most dangerous when women try to leave. Try not to leave any evidence of the changes and preparations you're making where he could find them. Have plausible excuses ready in case he does find cash you've hidden, for example. Say you were saving for a present for him, a special dinner out for the two of you, something for your child.

14. Become familiar with your monthly expenses. List what you spend for groceries, rent, medical care, child care, transportation to and

from work, insurance, and any other fixed expenses. You may need this information to complete forms for restraining orders, social assistance programs, or other purposes. It's also a good way to assess how much you will need to earn on your own.

15. Go ahead and do things on your own. Get a new job, make friends, hire a sitter, and go out now and then. Some partners won't notice the newfound behavior or will grudgingly put up with it. Some partners bully only those who are afraid of them. It may be best to make these changes during a "honeymoon phase." Do consider the risk involved, and proceed with caution.

16. Start changing your life secretly, a little at a time. Save money out of the grocery fund, garage sale proceeds, or any separate funds you may have. Even a small amount can make a big difference. Try to keep enough money with you all the time to pay for a cab to a safe place and, if you don't have a trustworthy friend nearby, enough to pay for one or more nights in a motel. Keep small change in your purse or pocket at all times for pay phones. Get a credit card in your own name, and have statements sent to your workplace or the home of a trusted friend.

17. Don't tell the abuser you're going to a daytime class or support group, but go. Join a battered woman's group—you don't have to be out of the relationship first. Get out and meet new people. Rekindle old friendships.

18. Make a list of the advantages and disadvantages of leaving and staying.

19. Learn the signs of coming violence. Work on sharpening your observation skills—Does he drink more, find petty things to complain about, want to go out everynight, sit morosely in front of the TV more than usual? Notice changes in your partner *before* he goes into a violent rage...his tone of voice, what he says, his habits, his behavior toward you and the children. Know and be as certain as you can whether these changes take place weeks or merely hours or minutes before the violence.

20. Write down these clues in his behavior. You will have a sense of the pattern and you will feel more self-confident of what you observe.

21. When you see the signs coming, or preferably before, get out. Go to a trusted friend's or relative's house—a place where there is plenty of room for you with people who care about you. Be careful not to go back too soon—he may be hanging on to the rage until you return. Stay until you can be sure the rage is spent. Use a third party to speak to your partner periodically so you can avoid being talked into returning too soon, and you'll get more reliable information.

22. Know which motel you might go to and how to get there. Travel from your house to it several times for practice so, in a time of high stress, you will be familiar with the route and the location. You may want to scout out parking that will be out of sight. It's also a good idea to consider several alternatives in case one motel is full.

23. Develop the habit of backing your car in the driveway. Leave the driver's door unlocked, but be sure to lock the other doors. Make sure your abuser doesn't block you in—in that case park on the street and make up an excuse.

24. Work out a signal system with a neighbor (preferably one who is home a lot) in case you need help, for example, a designated window shade in the down position means for him or her to call the police. Make sure the neighbor knows the signal and what to do. Some women also develop a code word to tell children, neighbors, and friends that they need to call the police and help you get out.

25. Remove from the wall or countertop any knife rack with knives in it. Get rid of the rack or put the knives in a hard-to-reach place, or give them to someone else for safekeeping. Also, put scissors, letter openers, and other sharp objects in hard-to-reach places.

26. Make a plan so you know what you can do if the phone wires are cut or if you find yourself without electricity. Keep flashlights handy and batteries fresh. Know where the closest pay phone is located and how to get there by either walking or driving. Locate the closest all-night store and other places you could go where there are people.

27. If there are guns in the house have someone teach you how to safely unload them. Keep ammunition in a separate place, or if you anticipate coming violence get rid of it. Lock it in a file drawer or put it in some out-of-the-way place. Unload any and all firearms.

28. Try not to wear scarves, long necklaces, loose clothing, or jewelry.

Clothes can be grabbed and anything around your neck can be used to strangle you.

29. Keep a good supply of gas in the car and try to have it in working order at all times. Learn to drive if you do not know how.

30. Rehearse your departure. Be sure not to tell the abuser you are leaving—to protect yourself. He will probably become more enraged and try to stop you if you do. Anticipate the violence early enough so you can slip away while he is at work, or if he does not leave the home to work, say you have to go out for a common reason, like you need to get milk, groceries, diapers, or a prescription. Offer to pick something up at the store for him. You might want to tell him you promised a neighbor you'd bring her a recipe, a book, or a scarf she asked to borrow. Have several plausible reasons for leaving at different times of the day or night.

31. If the rage builds up at night, plan to have a reason to go outside. Start to do the laundry, walk the dog, or throw out the garbage late at night. Keep things in the garage or your car that you might need inside, extra garbage bags or light bulbs, for instance. Keep coats, hats, and gloves close to each door.

32. Keep those extra keys and telephone numbers, as well as some extra cash, in your wallet purse at all times. Always know where it is and keep it within grabbing distance so you can get it on your way out.

33. Once outside the door, just keep going. Get into the car and drive away as quickly and quietly as possible. If you don't have a car, get on a bicycle, go on foot, whatever it takes.

34. Plan to take your children. They are probably terrified by the current or coming violence. They may be less frightened at getting up and being rushed away from a threatening person than finding out in the morning that you have disappeared without saying goodbye. Even if the abuser has never battered the children, you can't be sure he won't start now, especially when he discovers you have left the house.

35. Plan how you will make your escape with your children. It is more complicated than making it alone, but good preparation can make things easier. Talk with them periodically about the importance of safety. Teach older children to call a relative, a friend, or the police

when they hear *or* see violence. Teach them to go next door to a neighbor's house, business, or some place close to call the police.

36. If you have a baby, tell your partner you hear him or her crying. Take the baby out of the crib and go out a back door or window before your partner realizes what is happening. Keep extra blankets close to all doors.

37. If the events happen so fast that you have to leave without the children, arrange to go back for them as soon as possible. Either pick them up at school or return to the house with a police officer.

38. Ensure the children's physical safety. Let them know you have not abandoned them. You are also protecting your right to custody by getting them as soon as you can.

In addition to taking active steps toward ending an abusive relationship, a woman in this difficult situation needs to look within herself to begin rebuilding her sense of value as a human being, her self-image, her self-worth. Ginny NiCarthy's handbook *Getting Free* includes a series of simple exercises for women who are on this path, as well as practical ideas and advice.

Dr. Susan Forward's book, *Men Who Hate Women and the Women Who Love Them*, also contains helpful suggestions and sound advice. Among other things, Forward recommends adopting what she calls a "personal bill of rights," which includes:

1. The right to be treated with respect
2. The right not to take responsibility for anyone else's problems or bad behavior
3. The right to get angry
4. The right to say no
5. The right to make mistakes
6. The right to your own feelings, opinions, and convictions
7. The right to change your mind or decide on a different course of action
8. The right to negotiate for change
9. The right to ask for emotional support or help
10. The right to protest unfair treatment or criticism

One of the most basic rights of every human being lies at the heart of the domestic violence problem. As stated by Ann Jones, author of many books and articles on battering, "All women, like all men, have a right to live free from bodily harm."

"It does not get any better, they don't change—ask one of us. Living in fear is *not* living," says abuse survivor Jane Fraher.

Safety

As mentioned before, a woman is often in the greatest danger when she leaves a violent relationship. Many women are stalked, attacked, even killed by former intimate partners. The following safety and security recommendations can help protect you when you feel you may be at risk from someone you have left. Some are merely precautionary measures, while others can be effective if you know you are being stalked—and by whom.

Safety Plans

Safety plans have gained a great deal of attention in recent years. A simple, concrete plan—with telephone numbers, step-by-step instructions, and alternatives listed in one place—can be a life-saving tool to a victim who may not be able to locate or remember vital information in the midst of a crisis. Advocate, prosecutor and former battered woman Sara Buel often stresses the importance of a safety plan, which she describes as an action plan detailing how to stay alive, as the victim's top priority.

There are many, many forms and lists for drafting safety plans, available to those who need them. Your local shelter, police department, or domestic violence coalition may have a checklist you can use to formulate your plan. It's Not Okay Anymore, by Greg Enns and Jan Black, a book widely available at public libraries, includes detailed instructions on building a safety plan to suit your needs. Consider the tips listed throughout this chapter as you formulate your safety plan.

Residence Security

1. Be alert to any suspicious persons. Don't ignore "funny feelings." If a noise or just the atmosphere makes the hair on the back of your neck prickle, be especially cautious. Trust your intuition.
2. Ask anyone who knocks at the door to identify him- or herself before you open the door. Always ask service people, delivery workers, sales-people, charity collectors, even police for identification. Install wide-angle viewers on main entries.
3. Install a porch light at a height that makes it hard to reach. Put in other outside lighting as well. Trim and illuminate shrubbery.
4. Make sure you have dead bolts on all outside doors. If you cannot account for all the keys, get the locks changed. Have only the spare keys you absolutely need, and keep them secure. Make sure windows have sturdy locks. Put a dowel rod in all sliding glass doors and windows. Install locks on outside gates. Keep doors and windows in other rooms locked even when you are at home.
5. Keep the garage door locked at all times. If possible, get an electric door lock and opener. Always park in a secured garage if available.
6. Keep your fuse box locked. Keep flashlights and battery lanterns handy in the house and garage, with spare batteries nearby.
7. Consider installing a loud outside alarm bell that can be activated in several places inside the house.
8. Get an unlisted telephone number. Make sure your employer and all receptionists know it's unlisted and that your telephone number and address are not to be given to *anyone*. Get a caller identification box and an answering machine. With these tools, you never need to pick up the phone without knowing the caller's identity.
9. Make sure all members of your household trade information about suspicious calls or activity. If odd calls or activity continues, notify a local law enforcement agency. Ask about "panic buttons" or other special protections they may have.
10. Keep in touch with neighbors, ask them to call you if they notice suspicious vehicles or people, especially when you aren't home. Form and/or join a neighborhood watch group. Your local police department can help you set up such a group and provide training and support.

11. If there are firearms in the house, all adults should know how to use them. Store ammunition in a separate but nearby location. Be sure any guns or other weapons are stored out of the reach of children and preferably locked.

12. Report any direct threat against a member of your household to a law enforcement agency. Never dismiss a threat as just talk. Listen carefully, record it if possible, or write it down so you recall exactly what was said. If anyone else witnessed the threat, tell the police. Police officers say they would rather answer one hundred calls that turn out to be nothing than one that involves a homicide.

13. Thoroughly check out anyone employed to work in your home before you hire the person. Make sure he or she understands all security rules. Have a strict policy that the employee does not discuss family business or schedules with anyone.

14. If anything suspicious shows up, such as a box or package that you did not order or expect, do not move it. Call the police.

15. Keep fire extinguishers and smoke detectors handy in all main areas and keep them in good working order.

16. Tape emergency numbers to all telephones.

17. Get an automatic timer for your lights. Use it when you are going out for the evening, not just for extended absences.

18. Make a safe evacuation plan, make sure all household members know about it, and practice it occasionally.

19. Get a dog. A family dog is one of the least expensive and most effective alarm systems. Some breeds are considered better watchdogs, but any dog will bark at an intruder.

20. Know the whereabouts of family members at all times. Children should be accompanied to school or bus stops. Be sure children are taught basic safety rules, such as never to take rides or gifts from strangers.

21. Vary regular routes for driving and walking from time to time.

22. Keep trusted friends and neighbors informed about what's going on. Give them a photo or description of the suspected stalker and his vehicle. Be sure to tell them if you are going away on any trips. Have neighbors pick up mail and newspapers or have delivery suspended while you're gone.

23. If you live in an apartment or condominium with an on-site manager,

door attendant, or valet, give him or her a picture or description of the suspect.

24. If you are moving into a new apartment or condominium, check security features carefully and inquire about past problems. An upper floor apartment is considered safer. Insist that all windows and doors have sturdy locks.

Public housing authorities sometimes move people with orders of protection to another apartment or change their locks free of charge. For example, the Victim Service Agency in New York City employs four locksmiths who change some three hundred locks per month for crime victims, one-third of whom are battered women. New York also has a progressive human rights law that forbids landlords from discriminating against a battered woman or requiring her to divorce her abuser.

Work Security

1. If there is a receptionist, or you have a secretary, he or she should screen all calls, visitors, mail, and packages. Do not accept packages you didn't order or do not recognize.
2. Keep staff or security alerted to all suspicious people and packages that turn up somewhere they don't belong.
3. Pay attention to keys, locks, and security codes. All should be changed from time to time, especially after employee turnover.
4. Park in a secured area if possible. If you have to park in a lot, be sure there is adequate lighting. Leave the building with others if possible. If your name is on a reserved space, have it removed. Be alert to anyone watching or following you on foot or by car.
5. If there is a security director or guard on site, be sure he or she is aware of your situation and has information about the suspect.

Personal Security

1. Remove your home address from personal checks and business cards. Use your work address or get a private mailbox service (not a U.S.

Postal Service box) if necessary. Have all personal mail sent there. Make this your official address. Destroy all your discarded mail. File a change of address card with the post office listing this as your new address. Send cards with the new address to friends, creditors, and business associates, and request they remove the old address from their personal address books, files, and directories. Be careful who knows where you live.

2. Request that credit reporting agencies remove past addresses from your credit history. File a change of address with the Department of Motor Vehicles and get a driver's license with your new address. Do this for other identification or membership cards as well.

3. You can place your real estate in the name of a trust, and put your utilities and tax identification in the name of the trust. Lawyers who deal in real property matters can take care of this simple procedure for a low fee.

4. File for confidential voter status or register with a private mailing address.

5. Telephone services, such as call forwarding, caller ID, and answering services are now relatively inexpensive. Call your local service providers to find the right service for you.

6. Place residential rental agreements in another person's name. This person's name should not appear on service or delivery orders to the residence. You can use a business or other name for such purposes.

7. Notify your local law enforcement precincts about your situation. Ask for periodic police drive-bys. Some departments provide a free home security checkup.

8. Document and report any instances of harassment. Note the date and time of any telephone calls. Get statements from any witnesses. Keep mail correspondence or any notes delivered to you. If the stalker shows up, take pictures, use a video camera, and call the police every time.

9. There are support groups in some areas—look into this option. Discuss your fears and exchange ideas with people you trust.

Vehicle Security

1. Park in well-lit or secured areas. Avoid lots where doors must be left unlocked or keys surrendered; if necessary, just give the attendant or valet the ignition key. Do not allow items to be placed in or removed from the trunk except in your presence.
2. When you are parking in your residence garage, turn the light on, and lock the car and the garage doors.
3. Install a locking gas cap. The hook-locking device should be controlled from inside the vehicle.
4. Always check the back and front passenger areas before getting into your car.
5. Find a reliable service station and mechanic for service, maintenance, and repairs.
6. Keep your doors locked while you're driving.
7. Be alert for vehicles that appear to be following you. If you believe you are being followed, drive to the nearest police or fire station. Sound the horn to attract attention. If a police station isn't easily accessible, drive to a heavily populated area such as a mall. Plan ahead and know where these places are located.
8. Vary your schedule and routes.
9. Do not stop to assist stranded motorists. Drive to the nearest safe telephone and call someone to help.
10. Get a car phone. Many cellular phones can also be carried in a purse when you're out of the car. Service packages are available that can keep the monthly maintenance cost fairly low if the phone is not used often.
11. Shop at stores and shopping centers with security personnel. Ask them to escort or watch you as you go to your car. Many libraries, health clubs, and other businesses provide escorts. Find out and use their services. If your stalker tries to approach you in public, scream and run to the nearest populated area.

WHAT CAN A FRIEND OR FAMILY MEMBER DO?

Often those people who care about a woman in an abusive relationship want desperately to help her, yet feel at a loss as to just what to do. Many times the victim seems reluctant to accept help, and this can be extremely frustrating. Yet there are ways to make it easier for her to make the final decision, which can only be hers, to do something to change her life.

Above all, if she says she is being abused, believe her! Much of what she tells you may be hard to believe if you've never been in an abusive situation yourself. But women very, very rarely make these stories up. Realize that by her telling someone, she has made a tremendous step in the direction of freedom.

Offer her help whenever she needs it, day or night. Stash a bag of clothing and other emergency supplies for her. Open your home to her and her children if they need temporary shelter when fleeing violence or when their time limit at a community shelter has run out. Help her find a better job, a place to live. Give her books, pamphlets, hotline numbers, and other information on domestic violence. Provide her with a safe place to keep these things, such as at your home, the library, school, work, a church, or a counselor's office. Emphasize that it is not her fault, and that she has a right to a safe and peaceful life.

One action that does not help a battered woman is to push her or badger her to leave before she is ready. Remember, the point of departure is often the most dangerous for her and for her children. If she hides injuries or denies abuse, don't challenge her. Offer a friendly ear and an open door, but don't try to force her to talk about it or drag her out of the relationship, or you may drive her away. Respect her decisions and her sense of timing. Yet, keep in touch, even if she doesn't seem to want to maintain the friendship. Keep your presence gentle, yet visible. Avoid calling or stopping by when the abuser is likely to be there, but find a way to contact her on a regular basis, just to say hello and remind her you're there. You may be her only lifeline to the outside world.

It is essential not to be judgmental of a woman who is not ready to leave. Sometimes well-meaning friends or counselors berate a woman for staying, which only damages her self-esteem further and makes it more difficult for her to make the break. A "tough love" approach may be effective in some instances, but only within the context of building, rather than putting down, a woman's self-image. Tell her she IS strong enough to make it on her own and that you don't want to get a telephone call that tells you she has been murdered. It is her responsibility to make the decision.

Let her know that she does not have to put up with mistreatment, that you value her, that you are afraid for her safety, and how you are ready to help her. Research what is available in the community—do her homework for her. Call the shelter, hotline, and state or local domestic violence coalition. Learn about police and prosecutor policies on arrest and prosecution. Find out what programs for victims and abusers are available locally, or if none are, where the closest services are offered.

Realize that she is confused. As Ann Jones expresses, having a person beat you up and then say he loves you may be the single most confusing situation in the world. Sometimes your support will make a tremendous difference, though you may never know about it. Jones, who has interviewed hundreds of battered women, has heard many express gratitude toward such friends who made a difference, even though the woman did not feel ready to act on the help offered at the time.

Battered women need support and the reassurance that there is nothing wrong with them. Tell her she did not bring on the abuse, she did nothing to deserve it. No one does. Make her aware that she does have options. Remind her of her talents, successes, skills, and abilities. Keep letting her know what specific help you will provide—a ride, a place to stay, money. Remember that she may have been truly brainwashed. Don't expect a sudden change, though you shouldn't be surprised if she does change abruptly. If you have offered assistance, be prepared to drop everything and follow through no matter when her call for help may come.

It's also essential to remember that a woman suffering from the battered woman syndrome may say things or exhibit behavior that seems crazy or senseless. These actions are survival techniques that have their own logic and purpose in the context of a life filled with violence and terror. Try not to judge and, remember, once she is free, the bizarre behavior stops and her old self usually returns.

Also be aware that for some battered women, the most difficult step is not leaving but staying away. Offer her whatever support you can to help her remain free from her abuser. Simple friendship can make all the difference. For one woman, the crucial factor was the kindness of a gentle man who befriended her while she and her children were staying at a shelter, wondering whether to return home. He told the woman she was worthwhile, pretty, a good person—exactly the opposite of the things she had been hearing for years from her abuser.

WHAT HELPS ABUSIVE MEN CHANGE?

Men's groups seek to prevent the recurrence of violence in the relationships of the the men who have come to the group as batterers, and many also work to stop new violence before it starts through education and changing community attitudes.

This can be difficult work in a society in which many men are taught over and over that violence is an acceptable, manly response to anger. Most children receive little or no training in how to have successful relationships or deal with anger in healthy ways. Boys are taught they must "act like a man," which means being tough, dominating, and in control. They are expected to fight to solve problems. Many men's groups discuss these roles and expectations, and the effect they have on men. The group setting allows the participants to see that they are not alone, that other men have suffered from similar fear, confusion, and lack of comfort in intimate relationships. While the men are always required to take responsibility for their actions, they are also recognized as human beings who have the potential to change if they are committed to doing so. They are helped to heal and learn how to have healthy relationships based on equality and respect. Some of the leading men's programs in the country are listed in the appendix.

Men who admit that they are responsible for abusing their partners, who realize that they did something wrong and want to change, have the best chance of successfully turning their lives around. Most batterer's programs are open to any man who wants to enroll. Most are either free or charge on a sliding fee scale, according to income. Private therapy is also available in most communities, and free or low-cost counseling is offered by many churches, community mental health organizations, and other sources. State domestic violence coalitions and local organizations can provide referrals.

The earlier a man gets treatment, the better chance he has of changing his behavior. Sometimes an older brother, trusted friend, or other male the abuser looks up to can convince him he has a problem. If some-one you know or care about is abusive to his wife, try to talk to him and urge him to get help, or discuss the problem with someone else you think might be able to get through to him.

Domestic violence is not a "natural" behavior. It is a learned behav-ior that takes years of training—most often years spent in a violent home where the father controls other family members through intimida-tion and abuse. Not surprisingly, it takes time to unlearn such ingrained behavior and to replace it with positive relationship skills. According to EMERGE, a leading Boston-based men's program, success—defined as the total elimination of violence—is most likely for those men who complete at least an eight-month counseling program.

Batterer programs are expanding and improving as more is learned about why the batterer behaves as he does and what works to change this behavior. Many programs today cover subjects such as developing better communication and coping skills to prevent the cycle of violence from starting up again, building self-esteem, stress management, setting boundaries, anger management, and parenting skills.

San Diego County has one of the most effective batterer treatment programs. There, prosecutors enforce a mandatory treatment program, which requires at least six months of treatment (up to two years) taught by certified, trained counselors. Over the two years that followed the activation of this program, the female homicide rate was cut in half.

Men who aren't willing to seek help on their own must suffer the consequences. If they get treatment, it is often by court order. Abusers are manipulative by nature, and quickly learn whether or not they can get by with their behavior without suffering any real punishment. The most successful programs combine at least a taste of jail, some individual therapy, and group counseling that covers education about the abusive relationship, behavior modification training, anger management, and separate treatment for substance abuse, if necessary. Above all, the abuser must be held responsible and admit that the abuse is his fault, not his partner's, if he is to make any meaningful changes. Sometimes, helping to see that an abuser is arrested can be the kindest act you can do for him, as well as for his victims.

WHAT CAN CITIZENS AND COMMUNITIES DO?

One of the most unique features of the movement to end domestic violence is that it came about almost entirely due to the efforts of the victims themselves. Beginning in the early 1970s, women who had lived with the tragedy of abuse, and others who cared about their efforts, decided to do something about the problem. They were fed up with the lack of response from the criminal justice system, the scarcity or nonexistence of social services, and the prevailing social attitudes that ranged from apathetic to accepting violence in the home. So they began to organize shelters, support groups, and safe houses; pressure legislature and law enforcement for changes in law and policy; and spread the word that domestic violence is a serious social problem, not a "private family matter."

The changes made by these dedicated individuals have been phenomenal. Many of the programs started at the grassroots level now receive support from government agencies. Yet the plague of domestic violence continues, especially in areas where few or no programs have been established at the local level to attack the problem. Community involvement and support is crucial. Virtually all shelters, community associations, hotlines, advocacy programs, and counseling groups depend on volunteers.

Volunteers need not have any special skills or education. You may be surprised at the variety of talents and services shelters and community groups are in need of. For example, the Women's Community Association in Albuquerque, New Mexico, puts out a brochure listing some of the most common volunteer jobs: crisis phone workers, intake and caseworker assistants, child care workers, children's activities coordinators, field trip chaperones, receptionists and clerical workers, gardeners, maintenance personnel, painters, plumbers, drivers, public speakers, computer operators, and electricians. Donations of money, household goods, food, and housekeeping supplies are also needed. Everyone willing to volunteer can provide something a local program needs.

Those who work with victims need to remember to keep sight of her perspective. For example, many are in desperate need of simple, practical matters that are essential if they are to take the initiative to change their lives. Instructions on how to replace lost or destroyed identification, where to park to go to the courthouse, and the availability of child care during counseling sessions can make all the difference for a person so close to despair that she may give up if she cannot cope with the details incidental to getting the help she needs. As one police officer stated, "An uninformed victim is at greater risk for further crime."

Don't be afraid to "get involved." If you hear your neighbors screaming and furniture breaking, call the police. True, you may be wrong, but respect for your neighbors' privacy is not as important as their lives, which could very well be at stake.

Over and over, victims tell chilling stories of being stalked in public and begging for help from strangers who did nothing—often because the abuser offered a pat explanation or told them they didn't need to get involved. The obvious moral of this story is that anyone witnessing violence or hearing a plea to call the police should do so—immediately! I have heard police officers state that they would much rather respond to one hundred false alarms than to one homicide.

People can make a difference in other ways, as well. Lobbying and political advocacy are always needed at the local, state, and national levels. Big Brother/Big Sister and similar programs can provide nonviolent role models for children from abusive homes. Opportunities abound both to support existing programs and start new ones.

The same kind of grassroots efforts that began the first wave of awareness about domestic violence are still vitally important. Fortunately, it's much easier to get involved today due to the efforts of those who not only pioneered the movement, but took steps to see that it would keep its momentum. Individuals and groups working to fight domestic violence have an enormous amount of information available, and numerous sources of assistance, including the national and state coalitions. The names, addresses, and telephone numbers of these organizations are listed in the appendix.

These groups vary with regard to the materials they make available and the services they provide, but all can supply basic information and referrals to other groups that handle specialized needs. The National Coalition Against Domestic Violence provides a free information package and membership for a low annual fee, which includes a newsletter.

Mike Jackson and David Garvin of the Domestic Violence Institute of Michigan developed a "Community Accountability Wheel" to illustrate the appropriate community response to domestic violence. The gist of the wheel is to demonstrate that community opinion must strongly state that battering is unacceptable, thereby leading all off our social institutions to hold the batterer accountable by applying appropriate consequences. The wheel calls for consistent, coordinated efforts toward education, outreach, and sanctions against batterers from the media, social service providers, government, employers, the justice system, men, clergy, and the education system. Additional information is available from The Domestic Violence Institute of Michigan, P.O. Box 130107, Ann Arbor, MI 48113-0107, (313) 769-6334.

Find out what goes on in your community. Work with others or on your own to support those people who are helping to bring public pressure onto those who are still stuck in the Dark Ages. If you or someone you know has been treated unfairly, the local police refuse to make an arrest, the prosecutor won't follow through, or judges refuse to enforce the law, go to the local news media.

Call (800) 777-1960 to get a community action kit that includes information on how to help someone who is being abused, and what you can do to help reduce and prevent domestic violence in your community. Check the blue government pages, white pages, and yellow pages of your telephone directory for hotlines, shelters, and victim services. This information is often posted on community, hospital, government office, YWCA, Salvation Army, and clinic bulletin boards. A call to these agencies can be a way to learn about services available in your community. You can share this information with others who need it, and find out what goods and services are lacking in your community—perhaps things you can help locate or provide.

Working directly with victims through local programs does not usually require any extensive training. Many programs require several nights plus one weekend, or something similar. And involvement from men, as well as women, is essential. While men may not be directly involved in working with victims, due to the victims' recent trauma with male violence, there is ample room and a great need for male volunteers in virtually every other area of the campaign against domestic violence. "We need to engage the help of the good men—the vast majority—to help make the world safer," says civil rights attorney Randi McGuinn.

Students can sometimes earn class credit hours through such work.

The Duluth Domestic Abuse Intervention Project has a national training program that provides seminars and training materials for shelter advocates, police officers, prosecutors, probation officers, judges, counselors, group facilitators, human service providers, and Native American service providers. Duluth, Minnesota, has been widely recognized as a leader in confronting the problem of domestic assault in a coordinated effort by the police, courts, and service providers in both the public and private sector.

The national training program holds week-long training institutes several times a year for representatives from communities interested in developing a coordinated response to domestic assault cases. The institutes include seminars, observation of the programs in action, and training. The program also offers on-site training in the community. Consultation is also available for both new and established programs.

Specialized, shorter seminars are offered in Duluth for people already working with, or interested in learning how to work with, women's or men's groups. These programs may also include a session on cultural issues for communities with large populations of African Americans, Latinos, and Native Americans. Short seminars are also given for law enforcement officers, administrators, and trainers, and prosecutors, lawyers, and legal advocates. A special seminar is also available for people working to end violence in the Native American community, conducted by the Intertribal Council to End Violence in Families.

The project also maintains a speaker's bureau so programs and associations wishing to set up conferences in their communities may be provided with speakers associated with the project, who offer training and expertise on a broad range of issues. A broad variety of materials are available from the project, including videos, manuals, books, articles, and educational curriculums. Included are manuals for those wishing to organize various types of community support groups. A free brochure detailing the project and its many offerings is available on request. See the appendix for the project's address and telephone number.

Lawyers can help the effort to end domestic violence in several ways. When important cases on domestic violence come before the higher courts, with the potential to "set precedent" (create a legally binding decision that lower courts will be required, or may choose, to follow), lawyers can write *amicus curiae* or "friend of the court" briefs. These briefs argue that the court should decide in a certain way based on both the law and public policy. Psychologists, sociologists, and other professionals often work with the attorneys preparing such briefs so that statistics and scientific findings may be added to the other facts the court will consider.

Lawyers, paralegals, and others in the legal profession are also needed as volunteers to perform *pro bono* (free) legal services. There are opportunities for lawyers to work directly with clients through programs that provide legal aid to low-income persons. Some of the leading coordinated programs described in chapter 7 use volunteer attorneys to help both victims and those charged with abuse make use of the legal system. Other communities have programs offering free advice, such as the New Mexico State Bar Association's statewide, toll-free domestic violence legal hotline. This service allows victims to receive free, anonymous advice on legal issues associated with domestic violence, such as protection orders, divorce, alimony, child support and custody, criminal procedures, even bankruptcy. Volunteers are given training and a manual that contains information on social services such as shelters, support groups, emergency rooms, and counseling. Volunteer lawyers receive credit toward required continuing legal education, and are asked only to take at least one four-hour shift a month—a good way for those who don't have time to help out on an entire case. And this type of project—funded by local, state, and national attorney's organizations—is relatively inexpensive to establish and administer. Similar efforts have been made by other professionals, including psychologists and physicians. There is both ample room and dire need for anyone who wants to help make a difference.

STARTING OVER

In the words of Dr. Lenore Walker, "Better behavior exists between people." Even if an alarmingly high percentage of people inflict or encounter abuse at some point in their lives, the vast majority never do, or escape before becoming trapped. Most men are kind and fully capable of loving, caring for, and respecting women. Even if 15 million American men are abusive, that leaves about 110 million who are not. Most men want to share a loving and harmonious relationship with an equal partner.

Dr. Walker has found that, contrary to what many women fear, once a battered woman gets free of the abusive relationship, she is unlikely to become involved in another relationship with an abuser. Women do not become addicted to violent relationships. Once they are free, most can lead satisfying lives and form good relationships with gentle, nonviolent men. Ginny NiCarthy's book, *Getting Free: A Handbook for Women in Abusive Relationships*, includes a very good section on rebuilding a new life after escaping an abusive relationship.

THERE IS HOPE

Domestic violence is a worldwide tragedy of staggering proportions. Countless families have been, and continue to be, devastated by its ravages. Yet there is a great deal of reason to be hopeful. People everywhere are standing up to say, "Battering is not right, it is not acceptable, and it is not a private family matter." Legislators, judges, police, and prosecutors are giving an official voice to society's disapproval. Social workers, teachers, medical professionals, and mental health experts are speaking out against the horrible damage caused by family abuse. The same grassroots organizers who first brought to light the widespread devastation wrought by such violence, many survivors of violence themselves, continue their dedicated work to protect victims, punish and/or treat abusers, and prevent the destruction of more families and individuals.

Perhaps the most heartening fact is that all of these people, along with others who care, are coming together to combine their talents and coordinate their efforts to try and end domestic violence—and progress *is* being made. Not fast enough, as the frustrating statistics show, but change is happening. Not only change in available services to victims, in law enforcement, and in alternatives for people caught in the cycle of violence, but change in public attitudes. Finally, fewer people are asking, "Why doesn't she just leave?" and instead more want to know, "How do we stop this?" I believe that we are discovering small answers, and that if we keep asking this question, the final answer will someday come.

RESOURCES AND SUGGESTED READINGS

Ackerman, Robert J., and Susan E. Pickering. *Abused No More: Recovery for Women from Abusive or Co-Dependent Relationships*. Blue Ridge Summit, PA: Human Services Institute/TAB Books, 1989.

Allen, Robert L., and Paul Kivel. "Men Helping Men." *Ms.*, Vol. V, No. 2 (September/October 1994): 50-53.

American Medical Association Council on Scientific Affairs. "Adolescents as Victims of Family Violence. *JAMA*, Vol. 270, No. 15 (October 20, 1993): 1850-1855.

Ammerman, Robert T., and Michel Hersen. *Assessment of Family Violence: A Clinical and Legal Sourcebook*. New York: John Wiley and Sons, 1992.

Andrews, James DeWitt, and Thomas M. Cooley, eds. *William Blackstone, Commentaries on the Laws of England*. Chicago: Callahan, 1981.

Aris, Brenda. "Battered Women Who Kill: The Law Still Denies Us a Fair Hearing." *Glamour* (April 1994): 160.

Barnett, Ola W., and Alyce D. LaViolette. *It Could Happen to Anyone: Why Battered Women Stay*. Newbury Park, CA: Sage Publications, 1993.

Becker-Greenfield, Judi. "Reflections from the Rural Task Force." In *Our Vision: Newsletter of Virginians Against Domestic Violence*. Fall 1993.

Benedict, Helen. *Recovery: How to Survive Sexual Assault for Women, Men, Teenagers, Their Friends and Families*. Garden City, NY: Doubleday, 1985.

Bernfield, Lynne. *When You Can You Will: Why You Can't Always Do What You Want to Do and What to Do About It*. Los Angeles: Lowell House, 1992.

Biden, Joseph J. "Violence Against Women: The Congressional Response." *American Psychologist* 48 (1993): 1059-1061.

Blinder, Martin. *Lovers, Killers, Husbands and Wives*. New York: St. Martin's Press, 1985.

Boulder County Safehouse. Guidebook for Parents, bk. 1, *We Can't Play at My House: Children and Domestic Violence*. (Boulder, CO: 1989).

Boulder County Safehouse. Handbook for Teachers, bk. 2, *We Can't Play at My House: Children and Domestic Violence*. (Boulder, CO: 1990).

Boulder County Safehouse. Handbook for Health Care Providers, bk. 3, *We Can't Play at My House: Children and Domestic Violence*. (Boulder, CO: 1993).

Bowker, Lee H. *Ending the Violence: A Guidebook Based on the Experience of 1,000 Battered Wives*. Holmes Beach, FL: Learning Publications, Inc., 1986.

Bray, Rosemary L. "Remember the Children." *Ms.*, Vol. V, No. 2 (September/October 1994): 38-41.

Brinegar, Jerry. *Breaking Free*. Minneapolis: CompCare Publishing, 1992.

Brookoff, Daniel; Kimberly K. O'Brien; Charles S. Cook; Terry Thompson; and Charles Williams. "Characteristics of Participants in Domestic Violence." *JAMA*, Vol. 277, No. 17 (May 7, 1997): 1369.

Browne, Angela. *When Battered Women Kill*. New York: Collier MacMillan, 1987.

Capellaro, Catherine. "Help for Battered Immigrant Women." *The Progressive*, 1997.

Cassell, Carol. *Tender Bargaining: Negotiating an Equal Partnership with the Man You Love*. Los Angeles: Lowell House, 1993.

CBS News, "Sunday Morning." No. 796, Livingston, New Jersey: Burrell's Information Services, June 26, 1994.

Clark, Marcia, with Teresa Carpenter. *Without a Doubt.* New York: Penguin Viking, 1997.

Colburn, Don. "Study Ties Domestic Violence to Teen Depression." *The Washington Post* 1993

Continuing Legal Education of New Mexico, Inc. *Women: An Endangered Species?* Albuquerque, New Mexico: Women's Bar Association/CLE of New Mexico, Inc., 1994.

Conway, Janelle. "Airing Dirty Laundry." *Albuquerque Journal* (June 10, 1994): C-1.

Conway, Janelle. "Wounded Women Seeking Justice." *Albuquerque Journal: Sage Magazine,* (September 1994): 10-12.

Davidson, Terry. *Conjugal Crime.* New York: Hawthorne Books, 1978.

Davis, Diane. *Something Is Wrong at My House: A Book About Parents' Fighting.* Seattle, WA: Parenting Press, 1984.

deBecker, Gavin. "Security Recommendations." Albuquerque, New Mexico: Gavin deBecker, Inc./CLE of New Mexico, Inc., 1992.

D.G. "What's Love Got to Do with It?" Ms., Vol. V, No. 2 (September/October 1994): 34-37.

Del Tufo, Angela. *Domestic Violence for Beginners.* New York: Writers and Readers Publishing, 1995.

Digirolami, Karla M. "Myths and Misconceptions About Domestic Violence." *Pace Law Review,* Vol. 16:41, 1995.

Dougherty, Steve, Kristina Johnson, and Lorenzo Benet. "Bye Bye Love." *People* (July 18, 1994): 48-53.

Driscoll, Lisa. "Domestic Violence Hotline Counters Victims' Isolation." *New Mexico Bar Bulletin,* Vol. 33, No. 32 August 11, 1994.

Dunkin, Tish. "The Myth of the Violent Femme." *Mademoiselle,* April 1994.

Dutton, Donald G. *The Batterer: A Psychological Profile.* New York: Basic Books, 1995.

Editors. "Domestic Violence: Setting the Record Straight." Ms., Vol. V, No. 2 (September/October 1994): 33.

Edleson, Jeffery L., and Richard M. Tolman. *Intervention for Men Who Batter: An Ecological Approach.* Newbury Park, CA: Sage Publications, 1992.

Engel, Beverly. *Encouragements for the Emotionally Abused Woman.* Los Angeles: Lowell House, 1993.

Enns, Greg and Jan Black. *It's Not Okay Anymore: Your Personal Guide to Ending Abuse, Taking Charge and Loving Yourself.* Oakland, CA: New Harbinger Publications, 1997.
An excellent, easy-to-use, step-by-step workbook for victims to use before, during, and after the process of breaking free of an abusive relationship. Included are survivor's stories, with a photo accompanied by the date she decided that violence would no longer be a part of her life; detailed forms for compiling alternative safety plans; and tips for rebuilding self-esteem and taking care of yourself. A coaching system guides the reader through the process of living abuse-free. The book also features a "cycle of personal responsibility" created by survivors. This cycle illustrates a step-by-step pattern of behavior that moves the victim away from abuse and into personal safety and success. Key to the cycle is the first step—turning away from fear.

Facts on File. Vol. 52 No. 2713 (November 19, 1992): 874.

Fairstein, Linda A. *Sexual Violence: Our War Against Rape.* New York: William Morrow & Co., 1993.

Fedders, Charlotte, and Laura Elliott. *Shattered Dreams.* New York: Harper & Row, 1987.

Ferrato, Donna, with Ann Jones. *Living with the Enemy.* New York: Aperture Foundation, Inc., 1991.

Fleming, Jennifer Baker. *Stopping Wife Abuse.* New York: Anchor Books/Doubleday, 1979.

Flitcraft, Anne M.D. "Learning From the Paradoxes of Domestic Violence." *JAMA,* Vol. 277, No. 17 (May 7, 1997): 1400.

Forward, Susan, and Joan Torres. *Men Who Hate Women and the Women Who Love Them.* New York: Bantam, 1986.

Fraher, Jane. "There Are Ways That We All Can Counter Domestic Abuse." Letters to Editor, *Daily Pantagraph,* Bloomington, IL, August 1994.

Gardiner, Jeff. "Why Did I Take It?" *Mademoiselle,* (April 1994): 153.

Gelles, Richard J., and Donileen R. Loeske. *Current Controversies on Family Violence.* Newbury Park, CA: Sage Publications, 1993.

Gelles, Richard J., and Claire Pedrick Cornell. *Intimate Violence in Families* (2nd. Ed.). Newbury Park, CA: Sage Publications, 1990.

Gelles, Richard J., Regina Lackner and Glenn D. Wolfner. "Men Who Batter: The Risk Markers." *Violence Update,* Vol. 4, No. 12 (August 1994):1.

Gelles, Richard J., *Family Violence.* Newbury Park, CA: Sage Publications, 2nd Edition, 1987

Gelles, Richard J., *The Violent Home: A Study of Physical Aggression Between Husbands and Wives.* Newbury Park, CA: Sage Publications, 1970.

Golden, Kristen. "Behind Closed Doors." *Ms.,* (March/April 1997): 61.

Goldberg, Stephanie and Patricia Gallagher. "Basking in a Year's Triumphs." *ABA Journal* (October, 1996): 112.

Gondolph, Edward W. *Men Who Batter: An Integrated Approach for Stopping Wife Abuse.* Holmes Beach, FL: Learning Publications, 1985.

Gonnerman, Jennifer. "Welfare's Domestic Violence: The Rules Ending Welfare as We Know It Will Trap Women in Abusive Situations." *The Nation,* Vol. 264, No. 9 (March 10, 1997): 21.

Goodman, Ellen. *Turning Points.* New York: Fawcett, 1980.

Gray, George C. "Women: An Endangered Species." *The New Mexico Verdict,* Vol. 1, No. 2 (June 1994): 6.

Hancock, LynNell. "Why Batterers So Often Go Free." *Newsweek,* Vol. 126, No. 16 (October 16, 1995): 61.

Hart, Barbara. "Children of Domestic Violence: Risks & Remedies." *Protective Services Quarterly,* Winter 1993.

Harvey, Mildred G., and Nan H. Troiano. "Trauma During Pregnancy." *NAACOG's Clinical Issues,* Vol. 3, No. 3 (1992): 521-529.

Helton, Anne Stewart. *Protocol of Care for the Battered Woman: Prevention of Battering During Pregnancy.* White Plains, NY: March of Dimes Foundation, 1987.

Hensley, Alice. "Justice for My Mother." *NCADV VOICE,* Winter 1994: 1-2.

Hilton, N. Zoe. *Legal Responses to Wife Assault: Current Trends and Evaluation.* Newbury Park, CA: Sage Publications, 1993.

Hirshman, Linda. "Making Safety a Civil Right." *Ms.*, Vol. V, No. 2 (September/ October 1994): 44-47.

Horsburgh, Beverly. "Jewish Law and Jewish Battered Women." *NCADV Voice,* Winter, 1994: 9-12.

Horton, Anne L., and Judith A. Williamson. *Abuse and Religion: When Praying Isn't Enough.* Lexington, MA: Lexington Books, 1988.

Hunsberger, Brett. "A Girl, A Boy and a Gun." *AlbuquerqueTribune*, July 7, 1993.

Ingrassia, Michelle, and Melinda Beck. "Patterns of Abuse." *Newsweek* (July 4, 1994): 26-33.

"Insurance Discrimination Against Victims of Domestic Violence." *Clearinghouse Review* (Special Issue 1996): 206.

Jaffee, Peter G., David A. Wolfe, and Susan Kaye Wilson. *Children of Battered Women.* Newbury Park, CA: Sage Publications, 1990.

Jensen, Rita Henley. "A Day in Court." *Ms.*, Vol. V, No. 2 (September/October 1994): 48-49.

Jones, Ann. *Next Time, She'll Be Dead: Battering and How to Stop It.* Boston: Beacon Press, 1994.

Jones, Ann. "Putting the Focus on the Batterer." *Pace Law Review*, Vol. 16:33 (1995).

Jones, Ann. "Still Going On Out There: Women Beaten Senseless By Men." *Cosmopolitan* (September 1994): 228-231.

Jones, Ann, and Susan Schechter. *When Love Goes Wrong: What to Do When You Can't Do Anything Right.* New York: HarperCollins, 1993.

Jones, Ann, and Gloria Jacobs. "Where Do We Go From Here?" *Ms.*, Vol. V, No. 2 (September/October 1994): 56-63.

Jones, Ann. *Women Who Kill.* New York: Holt, Rinehart & Winston, 1980.

Kaye, Alice. "The Four Words That Saved My Life." *Redbook* (April 1997): 75.

Keeva, Steven. "Striking Our at Domestic Abuse." *ABA Journal* (April, 1995): 115.

Kiley, John Cantwell. *Self-Rescue*. Los Angeles: Lowell House, 1993.

Kinports, Kit, and Karla Fischer. "Orders of Protection in Domestic Violence Cases: An Empirical Assessment of the Impact of the Reform Statutes." *Texas Journal of Women and the Law*, Vol. 2 (1993): 163.

Krantzler, Mel. *Learning to Love Again*. New York: Bantam Books, 1979.

Krause, Gregor. "Stalking: The Crime of the Nineties." *Albuquerque Monthly* (January 1993): 26.

Kreps, Bonnie. *Loving Without Losing Yourself*. Los Angeles: Lowell House, 1992.

Kuhle, Shirley J. "Domestic Violence in Rural America: Problems and Possible Solutions." *The Nebraska Police Officer* (January 1981): 44.

Langly, Robert, and Richard C. Levy. *Wife Beating: The Silent Crisis*. New York: E. P. Dutton, 1977.

Levinson, David. *Family Violence in Cross-Cultural Perspective*. Newbury Park, CA: Sage Publications, 1989.

Levy, Barrie. *Dating Violence: Young Women in Danger*. Seattle: The Seal Press, 1991.

Levy, Barrie. *In Love and Danger: A Teen's Guide to Breaking Free of Abusive Relationships*. Seattle: The Seal Press, 1993.

Lewin, Tamar. "New Laws Address Old Problem: The Terror of a Stalker's Threats." *New York Times* (February 8, 1993): A12.

Lutz, Victoria L., and Cara M. Bonomolo. "How New York Should Implement the Federal Full Faith and Credit Guarantee for Out-of-state Orders of Protection." *Pace Law Review*, 16:9 (1995).

"Malik Yoba Urges Male Radio Listeners in Los Angeles Not to Abuse Females." *Jet*, Vol. 92, No. 4 (June 16, 1997): 34

Marano, Hara Estroff. "Inside the Heart of Marital Violence." *Psychology Today*, Vol. 26, No. 6 (November/December 1993): 49.

Marano, Hara Estroff. "Why They Stay: A Saga of Spousal Abuse." *Psychology Today* (May/June 1996): 56.

Martin, Del. *Battered Wives*. San Francisco: Volcano Press, 1981; New York: Pocket Books, 1983.

Martin, Sue, Mary McNeill, and K. Kaufmann. *Domestic Violence: A Training Curriculum for Law Enforcement*. San Francisco: Family Violence Project, District Attorney's Office, 1988.

Marwick, Charles. "Health and Justice Professionals Set Goals to Lessen Domestic Violence." *JAMA*, Vol. 271, No. 15 (April 20, 1994): 1147-1148.

McAfee, Robert E. "Breaking the Cycle, Controlling the Costs: Physicians' Role in the Fight Against Family Violence." *North Carolina Medical Journal*, Special Edition, September 1994.

McDermott, Judith, and Francis Wells Burck. *Children of Domestic Violence (A Guide for Moms)*. Spring Valley, NY: Rockland Family Shelter, 1990. Available from the Company of Women (see appendix).

McGinnis, Alan Loy. *The Friendship Factor: How to Get Closer to the People You Care For*. Minneapolis: Augsburg, 1979.

McNulty, Faith. *The Burning Bed*. New York: Bantam Books, 1981.

McShane, Claudette. *Warning! Dating May be Hazardous to your Health!* Racine, WI: Mother Courage Press, 1988.

"Meeting the Needs of Older Battered Women." *Aging* (Spring, 1996): 98.

Murphy, Patricia A. *Making the Connections: Women, Work & Abuse*. Winter Park, FL: GR Press, 1993.

Murphy, Patricia A. *The Making the Connections Workbook: A Career and Life Planning Guide for Women Abuse Survivors*. Winter Park, FL: GR Press, 1995.

National Center on Women and Family Law. *Assisting Rural Battered Women*. Item no. 51. New York: 1994.

National Center on Women and Family Law. *Domestic Violence as a Statutory Defense to Custodial Interference or Kidnapping*. Item No. 126. New York: 1991, 1992.

National Center on Women and Family Law. *Resources on Legal Representation of Battered Women*, Item no. 59. New York: 1992, 1993.

National Clearinghouse for the Defense of Battered Women. *Double-Time* (newsletter).

National Coalition Against Domestic Violence. *National Directory of Domestic Violence Programs*. 1994. Updated every two years.

National Coalition Against Domestic Violence: *The Voice*. Special Edition: Mediation, Winter 1988.

National Coalition Against Domestic Violence, Battered/Formerly Battered Women's Task Force. *A Current Analysis of the Battered Women's Movement*. Denver, CO: NCADV, 1992.

National Council of Juvenile and Family Court Judges. *Family Violence: Improving Court Programs*. Reno, Nevada: The Council, 1990.

National Council of Juvenile & Family Court Judges. *Family Violence: State-of-the-Art Court Programs*. Reno, Nevada: The Council, 1992.

National Council of Juvenile and Family Court Judges. *The Model Code on Domestic and Family Violence*. Reno, Nevada: 1994.

National Institute of Justice, *User Guide to NCJRS Products and Services*.

Newell, Brenda. *NCADV Voice, Special Edition on Children's Civil Rights*. Winter 1993.

NiCarthy, Ginny. *Getting Free: A Handbook for Women in Abusive Relationships*. Seattle: The Seal Press, 1982.

NiCarthy, Ginny. *Getting Free: You Can End the Abuse and Take Back Your Life*. Seattle: The Seal Press, 1986. May be ordered from the Company of Women (see appendix).

NiCarthy, Ginny. *The Ones Who Got Away*. Seattle: The Seal Press, 1987. Also available from the Company of Women (see appendix).

NiCarthy, Ginny, and Sue Davidson. *You Can Be Free: An Easy-to-Read Handbook for Abused Women*. Seattle: The Seal Press, 1989.

NiCarthy, Ginny, Karen Merriam, and Sandra Coffman. *Talking It Out: A Guide to Groups for Abused Women*. Seattle: The Seal Press, 1986.

Noel, Nancy L., and Marylou Yam. "Domestic Violence: The Pregnant Battered Woman." *Women's Health*, Vol. 27, No 4 (December 1992): 871-883.

Norwood, Robin. *Women Who Love Too Much*. Los Angeles: Jeremy P. Tarcher, Inc., 1985.

Note: "Developments in the Law: Legal Responses to Domestic Violence." *Harvard Law Review*, Vol. 106, No. 7 (1993): 1498-1620.

Parker, Barbara. "Abuse of Adolescents: What Can We Learn from Pregnant Teenagers?" *AWHONN's Clinical Issues*, Vol. 4, No. 3 (1993): 363-370.

Pascal, Harold. *Secret Scandal*. Canfield, OH: Alpha House, 1977.

Paymer, Michael. *Violent No More: Helping Men End Domestic Abuse*. Alameda, CA: Hunter House, 1996.

Phillips, Deborah, with Robert Judd. *How to Fall Out of Love*. New York: Fawcett, 1978.

Pizzey, Erin. *Scream Quietly or the Neighbors Will Hear*. New York: Penguin Books, 1984.

Pratap, Natasha. "If You Are in Crisis: Resources." *Ms.*, Vol. V, No. 2 (September/October 1994): 64.

Ralston, Jeannie. "He's Going to Kill Me." *Glamour* (September 1994) 264.

Ramo, Roberta Cooper. "Ending the Violence." *ABA Journal* (February, 1996): 6.

Randall, Teri. "Domestic Violence Hotline's Demise: What's Next?" and "While National Domestic Violence Hotline's Down, Other Resources Can Assist Physicians, Patients." *JAMA*, Vol. 269, No. 10 (March 10, 1993): 1224-1225.

R.A.P.P. Relationship and Abuse Prevention Project. *A Domestic Violence Education and Prevention Curriculum for High School Students*. San Rafael, CA: Marin Abused Women's Services, 1986.

Reed, Susan. "The Kindest Cut." *People Weekly*, Vol.45, No.16 (April 22, 1996): 67.

Reske, Henry J. "License to Kill?" *ABA Journal* (April 1993): 37.

Richardson, Scott. "Battling the System in Domestic Violence Cases." *The Pantagraph* (June 11, 1995): A2.

Roberts, Jenny. "Domestic Violence Training for Rural Law Enforcement: A Case Study." *Response*, Vol. 12, No. 3 (1989).

Robson, Elizabeth, and Gwenyth Edwards. *Getting Help: A Woman's Guide to Therapy*. New York: E. P. Dutton, 1980.

Rodriguez, Rachel. "Forgotten Pain: Migrant Farmworker Women and Domestic Violence." *Violence Update* (June 1994): 9.

Roy, Maria. *Children in the Crossfire*. Deerfield Beach, FL: Health Communications, 1988.

Russell, Diana E. *Rape in Marriage*. New York: MacMillan, 1982.

Salber, Patricia R., M.D., and Ellen Taliaferro, M.D. *The Physician's Guide to Domestic Violence*.

Schaef, Anne Wilson. *Co-Dependence: Misunderstood, Mistreated*. San Francisco: Harper & Row, 1986.

Schecter, Susan. *Women and Male Violence*. Boston: South End Press, 1983.

Schoichet, Barbara. *The New Single Woman: Discovering a Life of Her Own*. Los Angeles: Lowell House, 1994.

Schuerman, Sue Ellen. "Establishing a Tort Duty for Police Failure to Respond to Domestic Violence." *Arizona Law Review*, 34 (1992): 355-374.

Seidman, Carrie. "What Works." *Albuquerque Journal: Sage Magazine*, (September 1994): 13-14.

Shepard, Melanie. "The Effect of Battering on the Employment Status of Women." *Women and Social Work*, May 1988.

Skolnick, Andrew A. "NMA Seeks Prescription to End Violence." *JAMA*, Vol. 270, No. 11 (September 15, 1993): 1284.

Smolowe, Jill. "Sleeping with the Enemy." *Time* (July 4, 1994): 18-25.

Statman, Jan Berliner. *The Battered Woman's Survival Guide: Breaking the Cycle*. Dallas: Taylor Publishing Company, 1990. Highly recommended.

Stein, Robert A. "Changing Attitudes About Abuse." *ABA Journal* (October, 1996): 106.

Steinmetz, Suzanne, and Murray Straus, Ed. *Violence in the Family*. New York: Dodd & Mead, 1977.

Stewart, Gail B. *The Other America: Battered Women*. San Diego: Lucent Books, 1997.

Stordeur, Richard A., and Richard Stille. *Ending Men's Violence Against Their Partners: One Road to Peace*. Newbury Park, CA: Sage Publications, 1989.

Straus, Murray, Richard Gelles, and Suzanne Steinmetz. *Behind Closed Doors: Violence in the American Family*. New York: Anchor Books, 1977; Newbury Park, CA: Sage Publications, 1988.

Switzer, M'Liss, and Katherine Hale. *Called to Account: The Story of One Family's Struggle to Say No to Abuse*. Seattle: The Seal Press, 1987.

Tapp, Anne; H. David Banks; Francine Garland Stark; Rus Ervin Funk; Eris Adams; David Houseal. "Special Edition: Men's Role in the Battered Women's Movement." *NCADV Voice*, Fall 1992.

Titus, Karen. "When Physicians Ask, Women Tell About Domestic Abuse and Violence." *JAMA*, Vol. 275, No. 24 (June 26, 1996): 1863.

Tomkins, Alan J., Michael Steinman, Mary K. Kenning, Somaia Mohamed, and Jan Afrank. "Children Who Witness Woman Battering." *Law & Policy*, Vol. 14, Nos. 2 & 3 (April/July 1992): 169-181.

Turner, Tina, with Kurt Loder. *I, Tina*. New York: Morrow, 1986.

Ungar, Alan B. *Financial Confidence for the Suddenly Single: A Woman's Guide*. Los Angeles: Lowell House, 1992.

"Violence Report Finds Double Standard" (AP) *Daily Pantagraph*, August 1994.

Walker, Lenore, *The Battered Wife Syndrome*. New York: Springer, 1984.

Walker, Lenore. *The Battered Woman*. New York: Harper & Row, 1982.

Walker, Lenore. *Terrifying Love: Why Battered Women Kill and How Society Responds*. New York: Harper & Row, 1989.

Watson, Rita E. *Decision Making for Women*. Los Angeles: Lowell House, 1994.

Weston, Bonnie "To Many Teens, 'Guys Beating Girls Just Seems, Well Normal." *The Orange County Register*, July 3,1994.

Winston, Sherri. "Five Minutes in Hell: Battered Woman Fights Back." *Albuquerque Journal* (July 10, 1994): C2.

Woodhouse, Violet and Victoria Felton-Collins. *Divorce & Money: How to Make the Best Financial Decisions During Divorce*. Berkeley, CA: Nolo Press, 1993.

Wsititz, Janet Geringer. *Struggle for Intimacy*. Pompano Beach, FL: Health Communications, 1985.

Zorza, Joan. "Woman Battering: A Major Cause of Homelessness." *Clearinghouse Review*, Special Issue, 1991.

Readings on Battered Women of Color

Agtuca, Jacqueline R. A Community Secret: For the Filipina in an Abusive Relationship. Seattle: Seal Press, 1992, 1994.

Allen, Paula Gunn. "Violence and the American Indian Woman." Working Together, April 1985.

Bachman, Ronet. Death and Violence on the Reservation: Homicide, Family Violence, and Suicide in American Indian Populations. New York: Auburn House, 1992.

Hampton, Robert L. Black Family Violence: Current Research and Theory. Lexington, MA: Lexington Books, 1991.

Lai, Tracy A. "Asian Women: Resisting the Violence." Working Together, February 1985.

White, Evelyn C. Chain Chain Change: For Black Women Dealing with Physical and Emotional Abuse. Seattle: The Seal Press, 1985. Highly recommended for Black women in abusive relationships and those working to help them.

White, Evelyn C. Chain Chain Change: For Black Women in Abusive Relationships. Seattle: The Seal Press, 1985,1995. Revised and expanded second edition

Zambrano, Myrna M. Mejor Sola Que Mal Acompanada: Para la Mujer Golpeada/ For the Latina in an Abusive Relationship. Seattle: The Seal Press, 1985. Bilingual Spanish-English book addressing domestic violence from a Latina perspective, emphasizing alternatives for Latina battered women (including undocumented women) and offering information for those working with them. May be ordered from the Company of Women (see appendix).

Zambrano, Myrna M. ¡No Mas!: Guía Para la Mujer Golpeada. Seattle: The Seal Press, 1994. Written in Spanish. This book provides a broad range of information for Latina women in abusive relationships.

Violence in Gay and Lesbian Relationships

Hammond, Nancy. "Lesbian Victims of Relationship Violence." Women and Therapy: 8 (1989): 89-105.

Island, David, and Patrick Letellier. Men Who Beat Men Who Love Them: Battered Gay Men and Domestic Violence. New York: Harrington Park Press, 1991.

Journal of Gay and Lesbian Social Services: First Edition, Same-Sex Domestic Violence. Hawthorne Press, 1994.

Kanuha, Valli. "Compounding the Triple Jeopardy: Battering in Lesbian of Color Relationships." *Women and Therapy:* 9 (1990): 169-184.

Lobel, Kerry (Ed.). *Naming the Violence: Speaking Out About Lesbian Battering*. Seattle: The Seal Press, 1986.

Obejas, Achy. "Women Who Batter Women." *Ms.*, Vol. V, No. 2 (September/ October 1994): 53.

Renzetti, Claire. *Violent Betrayal: Partner Abuse in Lesbian Relationships*. Newbury Park, CA: Sage Publications, 1992.

Robson, Ruthann. *Lesbian (Out)Law: Survival Under the Rule of Law*. Ithaca, NY: Firebrand Books, 1992.

APPENDIX

National Organizations

National Domestic Violence Hotline
1-800-799-SAFE (7233)
1-800-787-3224 (TDD)
The national hotline is staffed 24 hours a day by trained counselors who can provide crisis assistance and information about shelters, legal assistance, health care, and counseling. During its first eight days in operation, the hotline received over 10,000 calls.

National Coalition Against Domestic Violence (NCADV)
National Office
P.O. Box 18749
Denver, CO 80218-0749
(303) 839-1852
(303) 831-9251 Fax

NCADV Membership/Public Policy Office
P.O. Box 34103
Washington, DC 20043-4103
(703) 765-0339
(202) 628-4899 Fax

The NCADV serves as an information and referral center for victims of abuse, shelters, service programs, and others assisting battered women and their children. It helps other agencies develop programs; publishes information packets, service directories, and a newsletter, The Voice; helps acquire funding for shelters and other services; promotes community awareness and education about domestic violence; sponsors conferences and regional training seminars for advocates; and supports task forces for subgroups within the battered women's movement. Those interested in becoming members should contact the Washington, DC office. Five categories of membership are available for individuals, organizations, and youth.

Battered Women's Justice Project
4032 Chicago Avenue South
Minneapolis, MN 55407
(612) 824-8768
(612) 824-8965 Fax

This organization studies abused women in the criminal justice system, and provides information to attorneys, and advocates for battered women or others working with them.

Domestic Abuse Project (DAP)
204 West Franklin Avenue
Minneapolis, MN 55404
(612) 874-7063

DAP publishes treatment manuals, research reports, and other materials. It also conducts tailored training sessions and workshops for professionals involved in mental health, social services, and criminal justice, as well as education for the general public, across the country. DAP is especially active in working with children from violent homes, and publishes reports and manuals on children's treatment.

The Family Violence
Prevention Fund
383 Rhode Island Street, Suite 304
San Francisco, CA 94103-5133
(415) 252-8900
(415) 252-8991 Fax
1-800-313-1310

This group runs public education programs, provides direct services to victims, and develops public policy and training programs for policymakers and health care providers. It also addresses the legal rights of battered immigrant and refugee women. It includes the Health Resource Center on Domestic Violence.

National Council on Child Abuse
and Family Violence
1155 Connecticut Avenue NW,
Suite 300
Washington, DC 20036
(202) 429-6695
1-800-222-2000

Provides information and referrals on spouse, child, and elder abuse through this toll-free helpline operated 8:00 A.M. to 5:00 P.M. Monday through Friday, Pacific Standard Time. Also gives assistance and information for community-based programs, and publishes brochures, periodicals, and a newsletter.

National Victim Center
309 West 7th Street, Suite 705
Fort Worth, TX 76102
1-800-FYI-CALL

The National Victim Center provides research, education, training, advocacy, and resources for those working for the victims of all types of crime. Its INFOLINK line (above) provides information and referrals to victims of crime and people who work with them. While INFOLINK is not a crisis line and does not provide counseling, its volunteers and staff give callers information and referrals to victim assistance agencies in the callers' areas. Resource packages on domestic violence, stalking, and other topics are available free of charge by calling INFOLINK.

National Battered Women's Law Project
275 Seventh Avenue, Suite 1206
New York, NY 10001
(212) 741-9480
(212) 741-6438 Fax

This project serves as a clearinghouse for information for attorneys, advocates, and others. It publishes a wide range of information packets for those offering legal assistance to battered women. The publications address specific issues affecting domestic violence victims, such as child custody, litigation strategies, case law, the special needs of rural women, and many others. It also disseminates law, cases, model briefs, statistics, protocol, and studies.

National Clearinghouse for the Defense of Battered Women
125 South 9th Street, Suite 302
Philadelphia, PA 19107
(215) 351-0010
(215) 351-0779
1-800-903-0111 ext. 3

This organization provides information and resource materials to attorneys, advocates, and expert witnesses who assist battered women charged with crimes, as well as the women themselves, particularly those who kill in self-defense. It publishes the newsletter, Double-Time, and coordinates a national network of people working with women in prison.

National Institute of Justice/NCJRS
Box 6000
Rockville, MD 20850
1-800-851-3420
(301) 251-5500 in Maryland and Washington, DC

The National Institute of Justice is the principal criminal justice research agency of the U.S. Department of Justice. It develops research and collects information about crime, its causes, and its control; trains practitioners; and distributes information. Its clearinghouse is the largest network of criminal justice information in the world, and maintains a document data base, electronic bulletin board, specialized data bases, publications, and a reference and referral service. A user's guide is available upon request.

Duluth Domestic Abuse Intervention Project
National Training Project
206 West Fourth Street
Duluth, MN 55806
(218) 722-2781
(218) 722-1545 Fax

This organization publishes and distributes a wide variety of training materials including books, curricula, research reports, training manuals, and videotapes. It also conducts training seminars for people involved in social programs to assist victims of domestic violence and those in the criminal justice system. It provides specialized training materials for those working with Native American families. The project is especially active in helping other communities establish or improve their own programs. A free brochure describing these publications and services is available by writing or calling.

National Resource Center on
Domestic Violence
6400 Flank Drive, Suite 1300
Harrisburg, PA 17112
1-800-537-2238
(717) 545-9456 Fax

This center furnishes information and
resources to advocates, policymakers,
and the media.

National Clearinghouse on Marital
and Date Rape
2325 Oak Street
Berkeley, CA 94708
(510) 524-1582

This business provides rape prevention education through speakers,
publications, and consultation by
telephone or in person. It produces
charts and packets that answer the
most common questions and provide
information on marital and date rape.

Law Students for Pro Bono
1666 Connecticut Avenue NW,
Suite 424
Washington, DC 20009
(202) 462-0120

This group provides information on
free services from law students, and
assists law students interested in starting pro bono programs at their
schools.

ABA IOLTA Clearinghouse
541 N. Fairbanks Court
Chicago, IL 60611-3314
(312) 988-5748

This office of the American Bar
Association coordinates the programs
in most states which collect funds
from Interest on Lawyers Trust
Account (IOLTA). The money from
these programs is distributed to legal

service providers who provide free
legal services to low-income persons.

Center for Women's Policy Studies
2000 P Street NW, Suite 508
Washington, DC 20036
(202) 872-1770

This organization focuses on combat-
ting gender-motivated hate crimes
and studies the efficacy of civil rights
remedies. Its National Program on
Girls and Violence collects information from girls and teenagers
throughout America on the violence
in their lives, and studies increasing
youth violence. A fact sheet on girls
and violence is available now, with
more data to be published as studies
continue.

National Coalition
for Low-Income Housing
1012 14th Street NW, Suite 1200
Washington, DC 20005
(202) 662-1530

Resource Center on Child Custody
and Protection
National Council of Juvenile and
Family Court Judges
Family Violence Project
P.O. Box 8970
Reno, NV 89507
1-800-527-3223
(702) 784-6012
(702) 784-6060 Fax

The center, operated by The National
Council of Juvenile and Family Court
Judges, provides general information,
consultation, and training related to
child protection and custody issues. It
cannot provide legal assistance in
individual cases. Call for a publication list.

Health Resource Center on Domestic Violence
Family Violence Prevention Fund
383 Rhode Island Street, Suite 304
San Francisco, CA 94103-5133
1-800-313-1310

This organization is dedicated to strengthening the health care response to domestic violence. It provides information packets, publications, and technical assistance for those wishing to set up programs and protocols.

Center for the Prevention of Sexual and Domestic Violence
936 North 34th Street, Suite 200
Seattle, WA 98103
(206) 634-1903
(206) 634-0115 Fax

This center provides educational materials for religious organizations and institutions to use in preparing curricula for clergy and Sunday school classes. It also trains clergy and lay leaders in issues of child abuse, clergy sexual misconduct, and domestic violence. It is not a direct service agency, but sometimes provides referrals.

National Organization for Women (NOW)
1000 16th Street NW, Suite 700
Washington, DC 20036
(202) 328-5160

NOW maintains a task force on domestic violence and is active in a broad range of issues important to women.

NOW Legal Defense and Education Fund
99 Hudson Street, 12th Floor
New York, NY 10013
(212) 925-6635

This sister organization to NOW focuses on litigation and education in the areas of gender discrimination and related issues. It sponsors a Family Law Project and publishes various materials, including a state-by-state guide to womens' legal rights.

Domestic Violence Project of the American Academy of Facial Plastic and Reconstructive Surgery (AAFPRS)
1110 Vermont Avenue NW, Suite 220
Washington, DC 20005
1-800-842-4546

In 1994, the educational and research foundation for AAFPRS, in cooperation with the NCADV, embarked on a campaign to provide free facial and reconstructive plastic surgery to victims of domestic violence. For information, call the toll-free number above or contact Rita Smith at the NCADV, (202) 638-6388.

Domestic Abuse Awareness Inc.
P.O. Box 1837
Old Chelsea Station
New York, NY 10013-1837
(212) 367-7004

This visual resource center on domestic violence provides traveling photo exhibitions, featuring the work of renowned photographer Donna Ferrato, who founded the organization in 1991, as well as photo archives, slide shows, and books to assist organizations working to end domestic violence.

American Bar Association
Commission on Domestic Violence
740 15th Street NW
9th Floor
Washington, DC 20005-1022
(202) 662-1737 or 662-1744
(202) 662-1594 Fax
Service Center (to order materials):
1-800-285-2221
e-mail: abacdv@abanet.org
http://www.abanet.org/domviol/home.html

The Nicole Brown Simpson
Charitable Foundation
15 Monarch Bay Plaza, Box 380
Monarch Beach, CA 92629
(714) 443-4200
(714) 443-4171 Fax
http://www.nbscf.org/core.html

This foundation, founded by Nicole Brown Simpson's sister Denise Brown, raises money to fund shelters and educational programs which help women and children who have become victims of domestic violence. It also produces an on-line newsletter and other information about domestic violence at its Internet website.

National Resource Center on
Domestic Violence
c/o Pennsylvania Coalition Against
Domestic Violence
6400 Frank Drive, Suite 1300
Harrisburg, PA 17122
1-800-537-2238
Fax (717) 545-9546

National Network to End Domestic
Violence
c/o Texas Council on Domestic
Violence
8701 North Mopac Expressway, Suite 450
Austin, TX 78759
(512) 794-1133
(512) 794-1199 Fax

Battered Women's Justice Project
c/o PCADV—Legal Office
524 McKnight Street
Reading, PA 19601
(610) 373-5697
(610)373-6403 Fax

National Network to End Domestic
Violence
701 Pennsylvania Avenue NW, Suite 900
Washington, DC 20004
1-800-903-0111 Extension 3
(202) 434-7405
(202) 434-7400 Fax

Legal Aid for Abused Women
(LAAW)
3524 S. Utah Street
Arlington, VA 22206
(703) 820-8393
(703) 820-7968 Fax
http://ourworld.compuserve.com/homepages/laaw

LAAW provides legal aid to men and women trying to remove themselves from an abusive situation.

Women's Initiative of the AARP
601 E. Street NW
Washington, DC 20049
(202) 434-2400.

The U.S. Government Violence Against Women Act Grant Office provides funding to qualified local domestic violence programs. For information, call (202) 307-6026.

Polaroid DV 100 Program

For information on how local organizations or agencies can participate, call 1-800-811-5764, ext. 163. Polaroid also prints and distributes manuals, videos, and other training materials designed to assist police, prosecutors, and others learn more about domestic violence and how to respond to it in their communities. Information may be obtained by calling the number above.

Project Protect
1-800-507-2560

Family Service America
11700 West Lake Park Drive
Milwaukee, WI 53224
(414) 359-1040

State Coalitions

Alabama Coalition Against Domestic Violence
P.O. Box 4762
Montgomery, AL 36101
(334) 832-4803

Alaska Network on Domestic Violence and Sexual Assault
130 Seward, Suite 501
Juneau, AK 99801
(907) 586-3650

Arizona Coalition Against Domestic Violence
100 W. Camelback Street, Suite 109
Phoenix, AZ 85103
(602) 279-2900
1-800-782-6400 (crisis line)

Arkansas Coalition Against Domestic Violence
#1 Sheriff Lane, Suite C
Little Rock, AR 72114
(501) 812-0571

California Alliance Against Domestic Violence
619 13th Street, Suite I
Modesto, CA 95354
(209) 524-1888

Northern California Coalition for Battered Women & Children
1717 5th Avenue
San Rafael, CA 94901
(415) 457-2464

Southern California Coalition for Battered Women
P.O. Box 5036
Santa Monica, CA 90409
(310) 655-6098
(310) 658-8717 Fax

Colorado Domestic Violence Coalition
P.O. Box 18902
Denver, CO 80219
(303) 831-9632

Connecticut Coalition Against
Domestic Violence
135 Broad Street
Hartford, CT 06105
(860) 524-5890
1-800-281-1481

Delaware Coalition Against
Domestic Violence
P.O. Box 847
Wilmington, DE 19899
(302) 658-2958

DC Coalition Against Domestic
Violence
P.O. Box 76069
Washington, DC 20013
(202) 783-5332

Florida Coalition Against Domestic
Violence
1535, C-5 Killearn Center Boulevard
Tallahassee, FL 32308
(904) 668-6862
1-800-500-1119 (toll free)

Georgia Advocates for Battered
Women and Children
250 Georgia Avenue SE, Suite 308
Atlanta, GA 30312
(404) 524-3847
1-800-643-1212

Hawaii State Coalition Against
Domestic Violence
98-939 Moanalua Road
Aiea, HI 96701-5012

Idaho Coalition Against Domestic
Violence
200 North Fourth Street, Suite 10-K
Boise, ID 83702
(208) 384-0419

Illinois Coalition Against Domestic
Violence
730 East Vine Street, Suite 109
Springfield, IL 62703
(217) 789-2830

Friends of Battered Women and
Their Children
Chicago, IL
(773) 274-5232
1-800-603-HELP (hotline)

Indiana Coalition Against Domestic
Violence
2511 E. 46th Street, Suite N3
Indianapolis, IN 46202
(317) 593-3908
1-800-332-7385 (toll free)

Iowa Coalition Against Domestic
Violence
1540 High Street, Suite 100
Des Moines, IA 50309-3123
(515) 244-8028
1-800-942-0333 (hotline)

Kansas Coalition Against Sexual and
Domestic Violence
820 S.E. Quincy, Suite 416
Topeka, KS 66612
(913) 232-9784

Kentucky Domestic Violence
Association
P.O. Box 356
Frankfort, NY 40602
(502) 875-4132

Louisiana Coalition Against
Domestic Violence
P.O. Box 3053
Hammond, LA 70404-3053
(504) 542-4446

Maine Coalition for Family Crisis
Services
128 Main Street
Bangor, ME 04401
(207) 941-1194

Maryland Network Against Domestic
Violence
11501 Georgia Avenue, Suite 403
Silver Spring, MD 20902-1955
(301) 942-0900
1-800-MD-HELPS (toll free)

Massachusetts Coalition of Battered
Women's Service Groups
14 Beacon Street, Suite 507
Boston, MA 02108
(617) 248-0922

Michigan Coalition Against
Domestic Violence
913 W. Holmes, Suite 211
Lansing, MI 48910
(517) 887-9334
E-mail: mcadv@pilot.msu.edu
http://pilot.msu.edu/user/mcadv

Minnesota Coalition for Battered
Women
450 North Syndicate Street, Suite 122
St. Paul, MN 55104
(573) 646-6177
1-800-646-0994 (toll free)

Mississippi State Coalition Against
Domestic Violence
P.O. Box 4703
Jackson, MS 39296-4703
(601) 981-9196
1-800-898-3234

Missouri Coalition Against Domestic
Violence
331 Madison Street
Jefferson City, MO 65101
(314) 634-4161

Montana Coalition Against Domestic
Violence
P.O. Box 633
Helena, MT 59624
(406) 443-7794
http://www.initco.net/~mcadv/

Nebraska Domestic Violence and
Sexual Assault Coalition
315 South 9th, Suite 18
Lincoln, NE 68508-2253
(402) 476-6256
1-800-876-6238 (toll free)

Nevada Network Against Domestic
Violence
2100 Capurro Way, Suite E
Sparks, NV 89431
(702) 358-1171
1-800-500-1556 (toll free)

New Hampshire Coalition Against
Domestic Violence and Sexual
Violence
P.O. Box 353
Concord, NH 03302-0353
(603) 224-8893
1-800-852-3388 (multi-issue state
hotline)

New Jersey Coalition for Battered
Women
2620 Whitehorse/Hamilton Square
Road
Trenton, NJ 08690
(609) 584-8107
1-800-572-7233 (state hotline)
1-800-224-0211 (battered lesbian crisis line)

New Mexico State Coalition Against
Domestic Violence
P.O. Box 25266
Albuquerque, NM 87125
(505) 246-9240
1-800-209-DVLH (legal helpline)
1-800-773-3645 (crisis line)
http://www.nmcadv.org/dv/

New York State Coalition Against
Domestic Violence
Women's Building, 79 Central
Avenue
Albany, NY 12206
(518) 432-4864
1-800-942-6906 (English hotline)
1-800-942-6908 (Spanish hotline)

North Carolina Coalitions Against
Domestic Violence
P.O. Box 51875
Durham, NC 27717
(919) 956-9124

North Dakota Council on Abused
Women's Services
418 E. Rosser Avenue, Suite 320
Bismarck, ND 58501
(701) 255-6240
1-800-472-2911 (state hotline)

Ohio Domestic Violence Network
4041 North High Street, Suite 101
Columbus, OH 43214
(614) 784-0023
1-800-934-9840 (toll free)

Oklahoma Coalition on Domestic
Violence and Sexual Assault
2200 Classen Boulevard, Suite 610
Oklahoma City, OK 73801
(405) 557-1210
1-800-522-9054 (toll free)

Oregon Coalition Against Domestic
and Sexual Violence
520 N.W. Davis Street, Suite 310
Portland, OR 97204
(503) 223-7411
1-800-622-3782 (crisis line)

Pennsylvania Coalition Against
Domestic Violence/National
Resource Center on Domestic
Violence
6400 Flank Drive, Suite 1300
Harrisburg, PA 17112-2778
(717) 545-6400
1-800-932-4632 (state hotline)

Rhode Island Coalition Against
Domestic Violence
422 Post Road, Suite 104
Warwick, RI 02888
(401) 467-9940
1-800-494-8100 (toll free)

South Carolina Coalition Against
Domestic Violence and Sexual
Assault
P.O. Box 7776
Columbia, SC 29202-7776
(803) 750-1222
1-800-260-9293 (toll free)

South Dakota Coalition Against
Domestic Violence and Sexual
Assault
P.O. Box 141
Pierre, SD 57401
(605) 945-0869
1-800-572-9196 (toll free)

Tennessee Task Force Against
Domestic Violence
P.O. Box 120972
Nashville, TN 37212-0972
(615) 386-9406
1-800-350-6767 (toll free)

Texas Council on Family Violence
8701 North Mopac Expressway,
Suite 450
Austin, TX 78759
(512) 794-1133
1-800-252-5400 (hotline)

Utah Domestic Violence Advisory
Council
120 N. 200 West
Salt Lake City, UT 84145
(801) 538-4100
1-800-897-LINK (toll free)

Vermont Network Against Domestic
Violence and Sexual Assault
P.O. Box 405
Montpelier, VT 05601
(802) 223-1302

Virginians Against Domestic
Violence
2850 Sandy Bay Road, Suite 101
Williamsburg, VA 23185
(804) 221-0990
1-800-838-VADV (toll free)

Washington State Coalition Against
Domestic Violence
2101 4th Avenue E, Suite 103
Olympia, WA 98506
(360) 352-4029
1-800-562-6025 (toll free)

West Virginia Coalition Against
Domestic Violence
P.O. Box 85
181B Main Street
Sutton, WV 26601-0085
(304) 765-2250
1-800-352-6513 (crisis line)

Wisconsin Coalition Against
Domestic Violence
1400 E. Washington, Suite 232
Madison, WI 53703
(608) 255-0539

Wyoming Coalition Against
Domestic Violence and Sexual
Assault
341 East E Street, Suite 135A
Pinedale, WY 82601
(307) 367-4296
1-800-990-3877

Puerto Rico:
Comision para los Asuntos de la
Mujer
Calle San Francisco 151-153
Viejo San Juan,
San Juan, Puerto Rico 00901
(809) 722-2907
(809) 722-2977

U.S. Virgin Islands:
Women's Resource Center
8 Kongens Gade
St. Thomas, U.S.V.I. 00802
(809) 776-3699

Women's Coalition of St. Croix
P.O. Box 2734
Christiansted
St. Croix, U.S.V.I. 00822
(809) 773-9272

Local Programs

Local domestic violence shelters, programs, hotlines, and other services can be found in your local telephone directory. Look in the blue or white pages under "Domestic Abuse Information and Treatment Centers," "Social Service Organiz-ations," "Human Service Organizations," "Shelters," "Women's Organizations," or "Family Services." They can help and advise you on locating emergency and permanent housing, and provide information on your legal rights, welfare or public aid application, counseling, support groups, and services for children. Some have brochures that address issues of concern and list other local resources and services. Most of these programs offer their help free of charge or on a sliding fee scale, according to income. Your state coalition (see above) can also refer you to sources of information and help in your community.

Internet Websites

Many of the organizations listed in this section have websites that contain a wealth of information, including links to other sites of interest. These website are listed with the information provided on each organization, above. A few of the many, many other websites dealing with domestic violence and related issues are listed below. Bear in mind that website locations change frequently, and new ones appear every day.

National Domestic Violence Hotline Resources List
http://www.feminist.org/911/crisis.html

Family Violence Awareness Page
http://www.famvi.com/

Family Violence Prevention Fund
http://www.igc.apc.org/fund/index.html

Domestic Violence Resources Page
http://www.igc.apc.org/woman/activist/domestic.html

U.S. Justice Department Violence Against Women Office
http://www.usdoj.gov/vawo/

The Clothesline Project
http://www.cybergrrl.com/planet/dv/orgs/cp.html

Other Sources of Information, Referrals, and Help

Black Battered Women's Project
Minnesota Institute on Black
Chemical Abuse
2616 Nicollet Avenue South
Minneapolis, MN 55408

Boulder County Safehouse
P.O. Box 4157
Boulder, CO 80306
(303) 449-8623

The Safehouse publishes a series of books on children and domestic violence, including books especially for parents, teachers, and health care providers. The books are inexpensive and are available in English and Spanish.

The Company of Women
102 Main Street, P.O. Box 742
Nyack, NY 10960-0742
(914) 353-0940
(800) 937-1193

This mail-order catalog business specializes in products of interest to women, many produced by women-owned businesses. Information on domestic violence and sources of help are included in the catalog as well. The Company of Women is a subsidiary of the Rockland Family Shelter in Spring Valley, New York, which serves victims and survivors of domestic violence and sexual assault as well as homeless women and children. Profits from the catalog go to support its programs and services. It also provides a community action kit for those wishing to end domestic violence in their own community, which may be obtained by calling (800) 777-1960.

Women of Nations
P.O. Box 4637
St. Paul, MN 55104
(612) 222-5830

Provides information on American Indian women against domestic violence.

American College of Obstetricians and Gynecologists
409 12th Street
Washington, D.C. 20024
(202) 638-5577
Publishes *The Abused Woman* for patients.

Special Resources for Immigrant and Refugee Women
Immigrant Assistance Line
(415) 554-2444 (English and Spanish)
(415) 554-2454 (Cantonese, Mandarin, and Vietnamese)

Military Family Clearinghouse
4015 Wilson Boulevard, Suite 903
Arlington, VA 22203-5190
(703) 696-5860
(800) 336-4592

Provides information on military support centers.

National Lawyer's Guild
National Immigration Project
14 Beacon Street, Suite 560
Boston, MA 02108
(617) 227-9727

This group of lawyers, law students, and legal workers educates and organizes for progressive immigration law; defends civil liberties of foreign born people, and distributes publications.

Family Violence Prevention Fund
383 Rhode Island Street, Suite 304
San Francisco, CA 94103-5133
(800) 313-1310

Produces a brochure on the rights of immigrant and refugee women in violent homes, which is available in Spanish, Chinese, Tagalog, and Korean. Also produces a manual with more in-depth coverage entitled *Domestic Violence in Immigrant and Refugee Communities: Asserting the Rights of Battered Women.*

American Immigration Lawyers Association
1400 Eye Street NW, Suite 1200
Washington, D.C. 20005
(202) 371-9377

This association is composed of lawyers specializing in immigration and nationality law. It can provide referrals to such lawyers in local areas.

National Immigration Project
(617) 227-9727

Help for Battered Gays and Lesbians
Lesbian Battering Intervention Project
Minnesota Coalition for Battered Women
1619 Dayton Avenue, Suite 303
St. Paul, MN 55104
(612) 646-6177

National Gay and Lesbian Domestic Violence Victim's Network
3506 S. Ouray Circle
Aurora, CO 80013
(303) 266-3477

Provides support for victims and publishes a handbook on same sex-domestic violence issues.

Family Violence Councils

The councils listed below are coordinating groups that were recognized as notable by the National Council of Juvenile and Family Court Judges in their 1992 publication, *Family Violence: State-of-the-Art Court Programs.* Such councils have been described as "a remarkable agent for change within a community." Each council may be contacted for information on how it was created, how it has been maintained, and the goals it has accomplished.

Multnomah County Family Violence Council
c/o Multnomah County Legal Aid Service
1020 Board of Trade Building
310 SW Fourth Avenue
Portland, OR 97204
(503) 226-7991

Santa Clara County Domestic Violence Council
c/o Board of Supervisors
Attn: Clerk of the Board
70 West Hedding
San Jose, CA 95110
(408) 299-4321

San Diego County Family Violence Council
Domestic Violence Unit
Office of City Attorney
1010 Second Avenue, Suite 300
San Diego, CA 92101-4903
(619) 533-3000

Human Services Roundtable
King County
1220 Smith Tower
Seattle, WA 98104
(206) 623-7134

Baltimore City Violence
Coordinating Council
500 E. Baltimore Street
3rd Floor Domestic Violence
Baltimore, MD 21202
(410) 396-3133

Project Safeguard
1207 Pennsylvania Street
Denver, CO 80203
(303) 863-7233

Hawaii Family Court
First Circuit
777 Punch Bowl Street
Honolulu, HI 96813
(808) 548-6369

Alternatives to Violence: East Hawaii
P.O. Box 10448
Hilo, HI 96721-7798
(808) 969-7798

Protection Order Advocacy Program
Victim Assistance Unit
King County Prosecuting Attorney
E223 King County Courthouse
Seattle, WA 98104
(206) 296-9547

San Francisco District Attorney's
Domestic Violence Programs
850 Bryant Street, 3rd Floor
San Francisco, CA 94103
(415) 552-7550
(415) 553-9743

Family Violence Prevention Fund
Building One, Suite 200
1001 Potrero Avenue
San Francisco, CA 94110
(415) 821-4553

Prosecutor's Victim Assistance
Program
Municipal Courts Building
1101 Locust Street
Kansas City, MO 64106
(816) 274-1517

Project Assist
Legal Aid of Western Missouri
1005 Grand Avenue, Suite 600
Kansas City, MO 64106
(816) 474-6750

Quincy District Court Domestic
Violence Prevention Program
Quincy Division District Court
Department
One Dennis F. Ryan Parkway
Quincy, MA 02169
(617) 471-1650

Domestic Abuse Intervention Project
(DAIP)
206 West Fourth Street, Room 201
Duluth, MN 55806
(218) 722-2781

Men's Programs

These programs have been recognized as successful in working with batterers on changing their abusive behavior. Many provide information, publications, and assistance to other organizations or communities seeking to establish batterer's programs.

Oakland Men's Project
440 Grand Avenue, Suite 320
Oakland, CA 94610
(510) 835-2433

Abusive Men Exploring New Directions (AMEND)
777 Grant Street, Suite 600
Denver, CO 80203
(303) 832-6363

Provides training programs, conventions, and publications for others.

Domestic Abuse Intervention Project (DAIP)
206 West Fourth Street
Duluth, MN 55806
(218) 722-4134

EMERGE: A Men's Counseling Service on Domestic Violence
18 Hurley Street, Suite 100
Cambridge, MA 02141
(617) 547-9870

Serves as a model for similar groups, provides technical assistance and training for human services and law enforcement professionals, and distributes publications and information.
Men Overcoming Violence (MOVE)

54 Mint Street, Suite 300
San Francisco, CA 94103
(415) 777-4496

Batterers Anonymous (BA)
8485 Tamarind, Suite D
Fontana, CA 92335
(714) 355-1100

BA's publications include an annual national directory, a handbook, and a self-help manual for batterers.

National Organization for Changing Men
RAVEN
7314 Manchester, 2nd Floor
St. Louis, MO 63143
(314) 645-2075

INDEX